D1757523

University of Edinburgh

30150 025267011

Theatre Censorship in Britain

Also by Helen Freshwater

THEATRE & AUDIENCE

Theatre Censorship in Britain

Silencing, Censure and Suppression

Helen Freshwater

First published 2009 by
PALGRAVE MACMILLAN

Palgrave Macmillan in the UK is an imprint of Macmillan Publishers Limited, registered in England, company number 785998, of Houndmills, Basingstoke, Hampshire RG21 6XS.

Palgrave Macmillan in the US is a division of St Martin's Press LLC, 175 Fifth Avenue, New York, NY 10010.

Palgrave Macmillan is the global academic imprint of the above companies and has companies and representatives throughout the world.

Palgrave® and Macmillan® are registered trademarks in the United States, the United Kingdom, Europe and other countries.

ISBN-13: 978–0–230–22378–3 hardback
ISBN-10: 0–230–22378–8 hardback

This book is printed on paper suitable for recycling and made from fully managed and sustained forest sources. Logging, pulping and manufacturing processes are expected to conform to the environmental regulations of the country of origin.

A catalogue record for this book is available from the British Library.

A catalog record for this book is available from the Library of Congress.

10   9   8   7   6   5   4   3   2   1
18   17   16   15   14   13   12   11   10   09

Printed and bound in Great Britain by
CPI Antony Rowe, Chippenham and Eastbourne

Contents

List of Figures

Acknowledgements

I would like to express my thanks to the many teachers, colleagues, students and friends who have supported me during the several lives of this project. I owe a particular debt for advice, support and inspiration to Olga Taxidou, Lee Spinks, Randall Stevenson, Cairns Craig, Sarah Carpenter, Ken Millard, and James Loxley at Edinburgh University; Jo Robinson, Janette Dillon, James Moran and Julie Sanders at the University of Nottingham; and Sally Ledger, Rebecca Beasley, Aoife Monks, Tom Healy and Rob Swain at Birkbeck College. Thanks too, for constructive commentary and close reading at a range of stages, go to Baz Kershaw, Freddie Rokem, Matthew Reason, Beate Muller, Maggie Gale, James Knapp, John Miles, Dafydd James, Lu Kemp and Paul Dillon. Elaine Aston provided hugely helpful feedback in the later stages of this project, and the comments from the anonymous reader at Palgrave made this a much better book. The support of my editor at Palgrave, Paula Kennedy, has also been invaluable.

I am grateful to the Arts and Humanities Research Council for funding a period of research leave, and to the University of Nottingham for granting a period of study leave. Thanks are also due to helpful staff at the British Library Manuscript Room; the Taylor Institute, at Oxford University; the Gabrielle Enthoven Collection, at the Theatre Museum; the Mander and Mitchenson Collection; and the University libraries in Edinburgh, Glasgow, Nottingham and Birkbeck. Particular thanks go to Kathryn Johnson, curator of the Lord Chamberlain's Plays and Correspondence Archive at the British Library, who did everything she could to help me locate material, and to Michael Wilson who offered helpful advice on the London Grand Guignol.

Teaching and public presentation have played an important role in the development of this book. Particular thanks go to the students at Nottingham University whose engagement with the issue of censorship taught me a lot about how to present this material. Thanks to audience members who asked questions and proffered information at the University of Utrecht, the University of Amsterdam, the University of Mainz, the University of Sussex, the University of Manchester, the University of Newcastle, South Bank University, the University of Birmingham, Roehampton University, Queen Mary and Royal Holloway (both University of London). A version of Chapter one was published as 'Sex, Violence and Censorship: London's Grand Guignol and the negotiation of the limit' in *Theatre Research International* 32.3 (2007); and a version of Chapter 3 appeared as 'Suppressed Desire: dramatic inscriptions of lesbianism in 1930s Britain' in *New Theatre Quarterly* XVII.4 (2001). Thanks to Cambridge University Press for permission to reproduce this material.

The author and publishers also wish to thank the following for permission to reproduce copyright material:

A&C Black for extracts from Philip Osment, ed., *Gay Sweatshop: Four Plays and a Company* (London: Methuen Drama, 1989); John McGrath, *The Bone Won't Break: On Theatre and Hope in Hard Times* (London: Methuen Drama, 1990); Jill Davis, ed., *Lesbian Plays* (London: Methuen, 1987); and Howard Brenton, *The Romans in Britain* (London: Methuen, 1982).

Gurpreet Kaur Bhatti for permission to reprint extracts from *Behzti (Dishonour)* (London: Oberon Books, 2004).

Casarotto Ramsay & Associates for extracts of *The Romans in Britain* (London: Methuen, 1982) in the USA (The Romans in Britain, © 1980, 1981 by Howard Brenton. All rights whatsoever in this play are strictly reserved and application for performance, etc. must be made before rehearsal to Casarotto Ramsay & Associates, Ltd., 7–12 Noel Street, London W1F 8GQ. No performance may be given unless a licence has been obtained).

Country Life for Ian Stewart, 'The Curse of Empire', *Country Life*, 13 November 1980.

Daily Telegraph for extracts from W.A. Darlington, 'Marriage or a Career: Old Conflict in a New Play', *The Daily Telegraph*, 2 June 1935; John Barber, 'Rape of the Senses', *The Daily Telegraph*, 18 October 1980; 'Peter Hall Defends Sex Scene in Romans Play', *The Daily Telegraph*, 30 June 1981; Dominic Cavendish, 'Less Nudity, Fewer Dogs', *The Daily Telegraph*, 6 February 2006; and a cartoon published in the *The Daily Telegraph* on 20 October 1980.

Donald Cooper for the photograph of *Soldiers*, © Donald Cooper/Photostage.

David Edgar for extracts from his letter to *The Guardian*, 28 January 1988.

The Galton Institute for extracts from Marie Stopes's *Married Love* (London: Victor Gollancz, 1995).

The Getty Research Institute for extracts from *Censorship and Silencing: Practices of Cultural Regulation*, ed. by Robert C. Post (Los Angeles: Getty Research Institute for the History of Art and the Humanities, 1998).

The Guardian for extracts from Jonathan Miller, 'Censorship', *The Guardian*, 16 October 1967; Maev Kennedy, 'News Team Repels Invaders', *The Guardian*, 24 May 1988; Stephen Bates, 'Ministers in Culture Clash as Drama Upsets Blunkett', *The Guardian*, 24 March 1998; Tania Branigan, 'Tale of Rape at the Temple Sparks Riot at Theatre', *The Guardian*, 20 December 2004; Philip Toynbee, 'Playing with History', *The Observer*, 1 December 1968; Anushka Asthana, 'Art vs Religion: Tempest of Rage Shakes Sikh Temple', *The Observer*, 26 December 2004; and Merrily Harpur's cartoon which appeared in *The Guardian*, 4 July 1981.

John Hunt and Outrage! for the photographs of demonstrations which took place in London on 3 July 1999.

Sarita Malik for extracts from her letter to *The Guardian*, 18 January 2005.

Malachi O'Docherty for extracts from Malachi O'Docherty, 'The Arts Council are Wrong', *Fortnight*, September 1999, Issue 380.

Mike Wilson for the images from the Hand and Wilson Collection.

The National Theatre for *The Romans in Britain* poster image designed and illustrated by Richard Bird for the National Theatre.

Punch for the Haselden cartoon which was published in *Punch* on 21 November 1923.

Sunny Hundal and Asiansinmedia for extracts from Sunny Hundal, 'The Violent Reaction to Behzti is Despicable and Hypocritical', 20 December 2004, and Sunny Hundal, 'Sikh Leaders are Not Without Blame for Behzti Controversy', 4 January 2005.

Salman Rushdie for extracts from Salman Rushdie, 'Coming After Us', in *Free Expression is No Offence*, ed. by Lisa Appignanesi (London: Penguin, 2005), pp. 21–26.

Gurharpal Singh for an extract from his 'Sikhs are the Real Losers from Behzti', *The Guardian*, 24 December 2004.

Theatre Record and Ian Shuttleworth for extracts from Ian Shuttleworth, 'Prompt Corner', *Theatre Record*, 2004, Issue xxiv, p. 1659.

Verso for extracts from Susan Buck-Morss, *Thinking Past Terror* (London and New York: Verso, 2003).

Every effort has been made to trace rights holders, but if any have been inadvertently overlooked the publishers would be pleased to make the necessary arrangements at the first opportunity.

Special thanks go to my Mum and Dad, Jean and Alan Freshwater, for their unconditional love and support. Finally, my love and thanks to Mark Ridsdill Smith for seeing this project through to completion with me.

This project was supported by:

Arts & Humanities
Research Council

Each year the AHRC provides funding from the Government to support research and postgraduate study in the arts and humanities, from archaeology and English literature to design and dance.

The quality and range of research supported not only provides social and cultural benefits but also contributes to the economic success of the UK. For further information on the AHRC, please see our website www.ahrc.ac.uk.

Introduction

When I first became interested in the silencing, censure and suppression of performance in the late 1990s, I found that many of the people I spoke to about my research assumed that censorship was not a problem for contemporary theatre makers. In 2001, when I started teaching the subject at University, my students insisted that artists and writers were no longer troubled by censorship and that images available on the Internet showed that 'anything goes'. None of the theatre practitioners I knew at the time believed that censorship was likely to have a significant impact upon their work, or upon the decisions taken by theatre companies in the future.[1] Instead, I found that theatre censorship was usually viewed as a historical curiosity, through which we could look back on past sexual and social sensitivities with amused detachment.

Today it is hard to imagine these certainties. Censorship of the arts has become a hot topic, and theatre practitioners regularly reflect publicly upon the constraints and limitations placed on their work.[2] This shift can be traced back to the final months of 2004, when a series of controversies over the artistic representation of religious icons, customs and communities received extensive coverage in the British press. This reportage ranged from serious in-depth investigation of the murder of the Dutch journalist and film-maker Theo van Gogh by a Muslim extremist, front page coverage of the violent demonstrations over Birmingham Repertory Theatre's production of Gurpreet Kaur Bhatti's play *Behzti* and tabloid ridicule of the lone religious protestor whose physical attack upon Madame Tussaud's nativity scene succeeded in wrecking the waxwork figures of Victoria and David Beckham, posed as Mary and Joseph.[3] The media interest continued in 2005, as the BBC received a record number of complaints about the broadcast of Stewart Lee and Richard Thomas's *Jerry Springer: the opera*, whilst their producers

1

were harassed following the publication of their home addresses and phone numbers on the website of the group leading the campaign against the broadcast.[4] It was also reported that the playwright Gary Mitchell, whose plays focus upon violence in the Protestant working-class community in Belfast, was forced into hiding after death threats and attacks on his home by paramilitaries.[5]

Details of decisions made by directors, programmers and curators also began to make the news in 2005. The Tate Britain gallery withdrew a work by John Latham entitled 'God is Great' (which presented copies of the Bible, the Talmud and the Qur'an embedded in a six foot sheet of glass); and the director of the Bristol Old Vic's production of Christopher Marlowe's *Tamberlaine* removed pejorative references to Muhammad and altered a scene which includes the burning of the Qur'an.[6] 2006 saw the board of trustees at Hull Truck Theatre require the removal of references to Muhammad from Richard Bean's play, *Up on Roof*; the withdrawal of a production of Mozart's *Idomeneo* by Berlin's Deutsche Oper – which included a scene which portrayed the severed heads of Jesus, Buddha and Muhammad – following a warning from the police about threats to the production; and the closure of a London exhibition of the work of the Indian painter MF Husain after anonymous death threats and a campaign of protest by the 'Hindu Human Rights' group.[7] These decisions were often cited as evidence that a new culture of intimidation was encouraging self-censorship.

In the UK, concerns over the censorious pressures being brought to bear upon the art world were heightened by growing unease over the steadily lengthening list of new legislation designed to ensure national security and tackle terrorism. The powers to detain foreign nationals indefinitely without charge, to extradite suspects to the United States without *prima facie* evidence and to place terrorist suspects under house arrest through the use of 'control orders' were fiercely criticised as attacks upon civil liberties.[8] There was also opposition to the loss of privacy inherent in the broadening of surveillance powers and infor- mation gathering, and the government's continuing commitment to the introduction of Identity Cards and a National Identity Register database.[9] It has also been claimed that some of these new laws, includ- ing the 2005 Serious Organised Crime and Police Act (which made unlicensed demonstrations within one kilometre of Parliament illegal) and the criminalisation of 'glorification' of terrorism in the 2006 Terrorism Act, have been used to silence public debate at a moment when many wished to protest about the invasion and ongoing occu- pation of Afghanistan and Iraq.[10] Indeed, the government's apparent commitment to curtailing dissent was illustrated by events at the Labour party conference in 2005, when an eighty-two-year-old delegate was dragged from the venue by stewards for shouting 'nonsense' during a speech by the foreign secretary, Jack Straw.[11]

Debates over civil liberties and freedom of expression were focused by the campaign against the government's Racial and Religious Hatred Bill, which made slow progress through Parliament in 2005 and 2006. These plans to extend the existing law against racial hatred to cover religious hatred encountered strong opposition in the House of Lords and in the press from a coalition of writers, comedians, lawyers and academics, who argued that this extension of the law would undermine freedom to satirise and critique religion. Shortly after the Bill went for royal assent in January 2006, the hypothetical questions rehearsed in the debate over its merits were given practical application as British newspaper editors considered whether to publish the cartoons of the prophet Muhammad which first appeared in the Danish Jyllands-Posten newspaper in September 2005. The publication of the images in newspapers across Europe in the Spring of 2006 led to widespread protests, with death threats being made against the artists and publishers; a consumer boycott of Danish goods across the Islamic world; attacks upon Danish embassies in Syria, Iran and Lebanon; and deaths in riots in Nigeria, Libya, Pakistan and Afghanistan.[12]

These controversies over censorship have opened up difficult and important questions: how might we best balance commitment to the principle of freedom of artistic expression with respect for religious belief and sacred imagery? Should there be limits to freedom of speech in the interests of public safety? Who might we trust to delineate and police these limits? The discussion and debate they provoked in the British press also revealed that certain attitudes and assumptions were broadly shared. Many commentators cautioned that long-standing liberal commitments to freedom of expression were in danger of being compromised, proceeding from the position that the right to freedom of expression requires robust defence.[13] The response of novelist Salman Rushdie (whose experience of Ayatollah Khomeini's fatwa has made him a regular contributor to debates over freedom of expression) was typical. He insisted that events such as the murder of Theo van Gogh were 'warnings that the secular principles that underlie any humanist democracy need to be defended and reinforced'.[14]

These responses indicate how deeply ingrained the antipathy towards censorship is in the Western liberal tradition. This attitude is so pervasive that some critics have observed that it has become all but impossible to discuss censorship in positive terms. Frederick Schauer comments that 'to praise an act of censorship is to verge on committing a linguistic mistake' whilst Timothy Murray goes so far as to describe this an 'anti-censorial prejudice'.[15] Evidence of this prejudice is not hard to find. It is at work in the widespread rejection of the title of censor, as those who find themselves given the label are quick to try to disassociate themselves from the term, arguing that it is being cynically or inappropriately applied, or proposing that they are simply attempting to protect the vulnerable or to defend reputations, morality or the rights of minorities. Similarly, institutions which perform an overtly censorious role in the West are careful to describe themselves as licensing authorities or classificatory bodies: in the UK we have a British Board of Film *Classification*, not Film Censorship. The label 'censor' is applied, it is almost never claimed.

These prejudices are also easy to detect in the study of censorship, as the retrospective inspection of instances of censorship is usually produced by those who deplore social coercion, exclusion and oppression. Consequently, these analyses are predisposed towards critique and condemnation, rather than defence or justification. This is very evident amongst publications dedicated to the analysis of censorship in twentieth-century British theatre. Richard Findlater's *Banned*, Nicholas de Jongh's *Politics, Prudery and Perversions: The Censoring of the English Stage, 1900–1968* and Steve Nicholson's multi-volume *The Censorship of British Drama 1900–1968* are up front about their allegiances. De Jongh declares his 'hostile' attitude to censorship in the short acknowledgements which preface his book, and Nicholson's first volume, which provides invaluable insights into the complexities of the subject, explicitly positions its author on one side of the ideological divide in its dedication to 'those who corresponded, and especially argued, with the Lords Chamberlain'.[16]

Of course, this book is not a prejudice-free zone. In fact it was initially conceived as a critique which would condemn the agents of censorious oppression. But my decision to engage with the detail of eight case studies – which illustrate the wide variety of censorship that has controlled and conditioned the realisation of theatre in twentieth and twenty-first century Britain – has resulted in an awareness of the complexities of the subject. The exploration of these case studies has involved encounters with evidence of constitutive forms of censorship, and the realisation that the censored may at times be complicit in the system of censorship, together with a growing recognition that some censored material may be difficult to defend. This experience has tempered my own brand of anti-censorial prejudice, bringing me closer to an understanding of why people wish to censor, as well as an appreciation of how they do so.

This process was aided by insights provided by Nicholas Harrison's work, *Circles of Censorship*, a history of French literary censorship which provides an eloquent critique of anti-censorial prejudice. Harrison traces unquestioning valorisations of free speech back to the psychoanalytic commitment to uncovering repressed material in the psyche, commenting:

> Psychoanalysis [...] aims to uncover that which has been censored, and the idea that that which is censored is more important, more *fundamental*, than the social conventions which marginalise, distort, and hide it, is both a starting hypothesis and a conclusion of this process.[17]

Harrison infers that the psychoanalytic procedures of *'tout dire'* are supposed to overturn mundane truths and expose their superficiality. According to this logic, saying what the censor has declared unsayable is intrinsically beneficial and liberatory. But Harrison challenges the notion that there is any such inherent value in *'tout dire'*. He argues that censorship has no fundamental relation to truth; that censored material neither possesses an essential or transcendent value nor shares a universal quality. He maintains that we should cease presenting cultural confrontations over censorship as a matter of ongoing conflict between the forces of oppression and the forces of liberation, as he uses a reading of the politics of pornography to disassociate censored material from subversion.

Unsurprisingly, polemical accounts of contemporary censorship tend not to engage with these issues, preferring instead to illustrate arguments about the threat to civil liberties or freedom of expression with a cursory list of examples of censorship which cannot begin to address the complexities of each case and the differences between them. The interests of polemic are well served by ignoring the complexities and contradictions present both in the artwork at the centre of a controversy, and in censorship itself. It is, after all, much simpler to champion the unfettered dissemination of a controversial art work if you insist that it has great artistic value, and much more straightforward to reject calls to censor if you have not engaged with the beliefs which underlie such demands. It is also much easier to invoke the right to freedom of expression if you temporarily forget that you, yourself, believe that there should be limits to this freedom.

This convenient amnesia is frequently found in debates over censorship. Despite widespread antipathy towards censorship, it is actually very difficult to find an advocate of absolute freedom of expression in all circumstances. Though many are ready to insist on the overriding importance of freedom of speech, citing the authority of John Milton's *Areopagitica*, John Stuart Mill's *On Liberty*, or Article 19 of the 1948 Universal Declaration of Human Rights, these statements often come with caveats. Those who begin by championing free speech often find themselves modifying their position with an acknowledgement that this right should be used 'responsibly', that the vulnerable and the young require protection from certain material, that rights can conflict with each other and that sometimes we have to choose between them.[18]

Given the difficulties of maintaining a commitment to absolute freedom of speech, this rhetorical manoeuvre is performed with unsurprising regularity. Supporting the right to freedom of expression in all circumstances entails accepting the dissemination of statements or images which are widely judged to be abusive, bigoted, offensive or simply false. When faced with beliefs and images which we find unacceptable – child pornography, holocaust denial, hate speech – most of us are quick to draw up a set of criteria which will allow us to set aside material which we do not consider to be protected by the right to free expression. In practice, almost everyone ends up drawing the line somewhere. In the case of the government's controversial Racial and Religious Hatred Bill, campaigners were quick to acknowledge the need for a ban upon incitement to racial hatred and based their attack on the bill upon the perceived difference between race and religion. This argument is set out in a speech made to the House of Lords by one of the leading figures in the campaign against the Bill, comedian Rowan Atkinson: 'it is clear to most people that race and religion are fundamentally different concepts, requiring completely different treatment under the law. To criticize people for their race is manifestly irrational but to criticize their religion – that is a right.'[19] Even Ronald Dworkin, a London-based law expert who is unusual in his unqualified support for freedom of expression, has been known to acknowledge that occasionally self-censorship may not be such a bad thing. Writing on the Danish cartoons controversy, he accepted that the British media's decision not to republish was the right one. Weighing up the likely outcomes of publication in Britain – 'more people killed and more property destroyed' – he noted 'the public does not have a right to read or see whatever it wants no matter what the cost.'[20]

Dworkin's judgement that the likely material and human cost of republication legitimises the decision not to publish rests upon a distinction between words and actions which commonly grounds explanations and justifications of limitations to freedom of expression. This distinction is the basis of legislation against direct incitements to violence or abuse which silences and marginalises. Oliver Wendell Holmes's judgement on the limitations of the First Amendment in the 1919 *Schenck v. United States* Supreme Court case, which describes a situation in which speech is likely to cause confusion, chaos and injury, finds itself frequently cited as an authority on this division:

> The most stringent protection of free speech would not protect a man in falsely shouting fire in a theatre and causing a panic. It does not even protect a man from an injunction against uttering words that may have all the effect of force. The question in every case is whether the words used are used in such circumstances and are of such a nature as to create a clear and present danger that they will bring about the substantive evils that Congress has a right to prevent.[21]

The image Holmes conjures up has proved to be powerfully evocative. It now circulates in debate as a free-floating, bowdlerised one-liner (which usually makes reference to a 'crowded theatre'), cut adrift of its original context.[22] But the question of whether words and images presented within the theatre's conventionally fictional framework can be considered 'fighting words' or hate speech remains a fraught one.

The distinction between words and deeds received comprehensive analysis in an area of linguistics that is now regularly referenced in Performance Studies. J.L. Austin's attempts to clarify the linguistic category of the performative – where 'the issuing of the utterance is the performing of an action' – infamously excluded theatrical instances of the performative from analysis:

> A performative utterance will, for example, be *in a peculiar way* hollow or void if said by an actor on stage, or if introduced in a poem, or spoken in soliloquy [...] Language in such circumstances is in special ways – intelligibly – used not seriously, but in ways *parasitic* upon its normal use – ways which fall under the doctrine of *etiolations* of language. All of this we are *excluding* from consideration.[23]

The fact that Austin does not feel the need to justify his casual statement that theatre does not possess the power of the performative – that it is 'hollow or void' – is instructive: his verdict is representative of a deeply ingrained cultural prejudice.[24] Nonetheless, Austin's assertion that the theatre is fundamentally ineffective or 'non-serious' is surprising. Censorious responses to the theatre are usually the product of anxiety over its potential effect, rather than its impotence. As we shall see, Holmes's decision to illustrate his argument with an image of fright and confusion spreading throughout a credulous theatre audience as a result of a fictitious, misleading performance feeds into deep-seated anxieties about the kinds of communication that may be possible when a group of people gather together to watch a performance. But before we can begin to explore these anxieties, we need to step back. First, we need to get a grip on what censorship actually is.

Part of the difficulty of defining censorship is the way in which those who apply the term usually assume that it is self-evident that the behaviour, decision or action they are describing belongs to this category. As Janelle Reinelt observes, the term is often employed as 'a common-sense catchword'; and its indiscriminate use may elide the differences between particular actions and events.[25] The definition of censorship was also stretched – and perhaps strained – during the twentieth century by a wide range of critical theory which proposed that our psyches, identities, languages and structures of power are dependent upon processes of exclusion and repression.

Central to this shift was the development of psychoanalytic thought, inaugurated by Sigmund Freud, whose speculative description of the division of the psyche suggested that the shadowy and mysterious area of the subconscious functions as an internal censorship mechanism, suppressing problematic and distressing areas of thought, memory and experience. Following Freud, Jacques Lacan's theories encouraged consideration of the way in which identity is formed through language and linguistic structures, as it comes to reflect a symbolic order which is dependent upon margins, limits, borders and boundaries. Our entry into language, which Lacan describes as the transition from the 'Imaginary' to the 'Symbolic' phase, constitutes the entry into a cultural order that forms the infant's identity.

The work of philosopher Michel Foucault also had a major impact upon our understanding of censorship. *The Archaeology of Knowledge* and *The Order of Things* provide analysis of the forms of discourse which structure our knowledge of the world, whilst his radical reformulation of the concept of power encourages us to think of it as being something which is pervasive – spreading throughout society – rather than being held by a single institution or authority.[26] *Discipline and Punish: The Birth of the Prison* interrogates the development of systems of correction and social control during the eighteenth and nineteenth centuries and provides analysis of disciplinary codes which were introduced to measure, supervise and correct the 'abnormal'. It also contains a now standard description of the architectural principles of philosopher Jeremy Bentham's Panopticon: a prison designed so that the inmates never know whether or not they are being watched.[27] Within this structure, internal codes of control displace external methods of punishment and surveillance. As Foucault observes (in typically androcentric style):

> he who is subjected to a field of visibility and who knows it, assumes responsibility for the constraints of power; he makes them play spontaneously upon himself; he inscribes in himself the power relation in which he simultaneously plays both roles; he becomes the principle of his own subjection.[28]

The Panopticon provides Foucault with a blue-print for analysis of the operation of other disciplinary regimes: education, medicine and the law. Within the Panoptic society we come to police our own behaviour, having internalised the institutional values of these regimes so thoroughly that we may no longer realise that they originate from an external source.

There are now a plethora of critical theories which inform analysis of censorship. Jacques Derrida's theories, which demonstrated that the categories central to Western systems of thought depend for their coherence upon the qualities that they ostensibly exclude, have had a profound impact upon our understanding of the function of binary categories, whilst Louis Althusser's theory of interpellation and description of the work of Ideological State Apparatuses also feed into an appreciation of constitutive forms of censorship.[29] By the end of the twentieth century, the combined influence of these and other theories had produced a profound alteration in the understanding of the operation of censorship. Analyses of censorship now regularly address implicit as well as explicit forms of cultural control and covert proscriptions as well as overt prohibitions. Annette Kuhn's conclusions to her valuable analysis of the censorship of sexuality in early twentieth-century film are representative of this shift, as she avers:

> censorship is not reducible to a circumscribed and predefined set of institutions and institutional activities, but is produced within an array of constantly shifting discourses, practices, and apparatuses. It cannot, therefore, be regarded as either fixed or monolithic. [It...] is an ongoing process embodying complex and often contradictory relations of power.[30]

The cumulative effect of the work of Freud, Derrida, Lacan and Foucault is also reflected in the work of theorist Judith Butler, whose engagement with the theory of the performative speech act, and the question of when and how words become actions, has led her to fruitful and provocative analysis of the form and function of censorship. Butler's essay 'Ruled Out: Vocabularies of the Censor' aims to unsettle the 'conventional' model of censorship, which assumes that it is imposed upon an individual by an external body (the state, an institution or another individual); that it takes place after the act of expression; and that this act of expression is 'free', or uncensored, before the intervention occurred.

Butler sets out an alternative approach which inverts the traditional temporal relationship between censorship and speech, so that 'censorship produces speech.' She acknowledges that this formulation of power may seem counter-intuitive and clarifies her position:

> By 'productive', I do not mean positive or beneficial, but rather, power as formative and constitutive, that is, not conceived exclusively as an external exertion of control or the deprivation of liberties. According to this view, censorship is not merely restrictive and privative, active in depriving subjects of the freedom to express themselves in certain ways, but it is also formative of subjects and the legitimate boundaries of speech.[31]

Still, as Butler acknowledges, there are problems with this expansion of the category of censorship.

Some critics have argued that a broad definition renders the term meaningless, whilst others suggest that wide application of the term may overwhelm or trivialise its significance, as critical censure or the removal of subsidy come to be equated with the human rights abuses brought to our attention by organisations such as Amnesty International.[32] Robert Post, for example, proposes that the adoption of this inclusive definition of censorship effectively flattens out the differences between 'hard' and 'soft' forms of control and may draw attention away from 'strong' repressive measures.[33] It is important to acknowledge that by interpreting censorship as a constitutive, productive power, there is a danger that we diminish the term's power to invoke protest and outrage. And it is easy to understand the desire to reserve the term 'censorship' for instances of intervention which are blatantly oppressive: the banning or burning of books; the imprisonment, torture, or murder of writers, journalists, artists and politicians; death threats or physical attacks.

I have, however, decided to work with a broad definition of censorship in this book. Following Butler, I think of examples of censorship on a continuum, with the brutal extremes of incarceration or murder at one end and the constitutive operation of self-censorship at the other. Their connection is thus established, without negating their differences.[34] In consequence, this book includes examples of a wide range of interventions and silencings. The case studies I cover explore both legislative and economic modes of control and examine the internalisation of the censorious impulse. They identify its presence in authorial self-censorship; the decisions of theatre boards; the selection processes of corporate sponsors; the representations of the media; and the actions of public pressure groups, as well as the autocratic judgements of the Lord Chamberlain. In part, my decision to adopt this inclusive approach is informed by the use of the term by those on the receiving end of acts of critical exclusion, authoritarian intervention and institutional interference. Where they had an opportunity to express their opinions, the playwrights, performers and producers involved in the events I discuss were adamant that they had experienced censorship. From Marie Stopes's publication of *A Banned Play and a Preface on Censorship* in 1926 to Pam Brighton's denunciation of Northern Ireland's Arts Council following their withdrawal of funding from the play *Forced Upon Us* in 1999, the term 'censorship' is used without reservation.[35] The language which such artists employ as they discuss the treatment of their work makes it clear that they believe that they have experienced egregious and excessive intervention. To suggest that they did not do so because their experience does not correspond to a predefined category would represent an untenable re-inscription of the original act of exclusion. The case studies presented in this book also demonstrate the difficulty of classifying particular forms of censorship and separating them out from one another.

It is hard to imagine a better example of the complexity of censorship than the British state-sponsored system of theatrical licensing. Without close inspection, it appears that this extraordinarily long-lived system conforms very neatly to the conventional model of censorship which associates censorious intervention with the activities of a discrete institution. The system of censorship was established in 1737 when the Lord Chamberlain, an official of the royal household, was invested with the power to approve the establishment of theatres and control the dissemination of the actor's art. Until this ancient system was bought to an end by the Theatres Act on 26 September 1968, every play destined for the public stage was required to be licensed before performance by the Lord Chamberlain under the auspices of the 1843 Theatres Act, which threatened fines and the loss of the theatre's licence as penalties.[36] Existing publications in the field thus focus primarily upon the actions of the Lord Chamberlain and predominantly upon the pre-1968 period.

The Lord Chamberlain, however, was neither an independent adjudicator nor the representative of a monolithic authority. Technically, he wielded absolute power over the theatre, though the behind-the-scenes records held in the Lord Chamberlain's Plays and Correspondence Archive at the British Library reflect the different constituencies that sustained this censorship system. This extraordinary archive includes a file for almost every play submitted for licensing during the twentieth century, and consequently the total number of files has been estimated at approximately 45,000. These files demonstrate that the operation of the system was nowhere near as consistent, calculated or effective as some commentary on the field implies.[37] The reports, letters, memoranda and notes collected in this archive show that although the Lord Chamberlain's decisions were final, they were also highly unpredictable and likely to be generated by any number of different considerations.

Eight different Lord Chamberlains sat in office during the years 1900–1968, each bringing their own personal prejudices and preferences to the job, as did the Lord Chamberlain's staff (who included examiners who read the plays and Comptrollers and deputy Comptrollers who dealt with difficult cases). The Lord Chamberlain also drew on his connections beyond his office at St James's Palace in order to gauge opinion on controversial plays. These contacts were often within government: the files include missives between the Lord Chamberlain and the Foreign Office, the Home Office and the War Office. He also approached Church leaders, foreign embassies and the monarch for instruction on his decisions and took advice from an Advisory Board.[38] The correspondence that records these exchanges of opinion reveals the rationale behind each decision to sanction or suppress instances of theatre and also demonstrates that there was often disagreement, and sometimes dissent, between these many different figures. The establishment had no party line.

Despite the felicitous tendency to horde paper at St James's Palace, assessment of the day-to-day workings of the office reveals that the system generally proceeded on an *ad hoc* basis and that the judgements it produced could sometimes appear arbitrary. In retrospect, the system appears extraordinarily inconsistent; plays written before 1737 were technically 'immune', as were performances given at music-halls and private theatre clubs.[39] Unsurprisingly, the lack of a clear code of practice produced some curious anomalies, and in 1909 complaints concerning the 'unsportsmanlike' character of theatrical censorship provoked an investigation. The Parliamentary Joint Select Committee on Censorship concluded that a play could be cut or banned completely if it was considered:

a) to be indecent
b) to contain offensive personalities
c) to represent upon the stage in an invidious manner a living person or any person within fifty years of his death
d) to do violence to the sentiment of religious reverence
e) to be calculated to conduce crime or vice
f) to be calculated to impair friendly relations with any foreign power
g) to be calculated to cause a breach of the peace.[40]

The Lord Chamberlain and his examiners were, however, not obliged to adhere to these guidelines. And even where they wished to make reference to them they were free to use their discretion in their interpretation. This flexibility was to prove extremely useful, as they often appeared to object to the form rather than the content of theatre.

The files also indicate that the system was dependent upon public acquiescence, the theatre industry's compliance and the active support of the governmental establishment. The Lord Chamberlain was sustained and supported by a wide network of theatre owners, managers, producers, board members, reviewers and even playwrights. His licensing function took its place within a much larger framework of authority, censure and constraint. Accordingly, the first four chapters of this book discuss plays which were either banned, altered or censured by the Lord Chamberlain and his staff before the removal of his licensing function in 1968, but they move this discussion beyond preoccupation with the figure of the Lord Chamberlain. Chapter 1 examines the reception of the horror sketches produced at the short-lived, but infamous London Grand Guignol, and demonstrates that anxiety over the extremes of this new genre was voiced by the press and some of the performers, as well as the Lord Chamberlain's examiners. This chapter also illuminates the connections between censorious, critical and academic definitions of value: the Lord Chamberlain's staff condemned the London Grand Guignol for meaningless and excessive use of violence; the contemporary media dismissed it as a commercial exercise; and its reputation as popular, 'low' entertainment has been blamed for its relative obscurity in theatre history.

Chapter 2 investigates the suppression of a series of sex education plays written by Marie Stopes in the 1920s. This chapter reveals that Stopes and the Lord Chamberlain's examiners shared similar concerns when it came to the representation and regulation of the female reproductive body, as they reiterate the terms of ancient anti-theatrical prejudices, contrasting the physical to the verbal, the corporeal to the linguistic and the stage to the page. Chapter 3 examines the changing attitudes of the Lord Chamberlain's examiners towards the dramatisation of lesbianism in six different plays in the early 1930s, and explores what Butler refers to as the 'acts of self-reproach, conscience and melancholia that work in tandem with processes of social regulation'.[41] Chapter 4 chronicles Kenneth Tynan's efforts to bring Rolf Hochhuth's iconoclastic and controversial play *Soldiers* to the London stage and reveals the full extent of the theatre industry's collusion with the Lord Chamberlain. In this instance, the arts dignitaries who graced the National Theatre Board, and the managers of London's theatre owning monopolies did their best to dismiss Hochhuth's imaginative rewriting of the Churchill legend, whilst the press also voiced concern about the propriety of the play.

The final four chapters demonstrate that a wide variety of institutions and individuals have sought to silence and censure the theatre during the forty years since the removal of the Lord Chamberlain's responsibilities for licensing. Chapter 5's reassessment of Mary Whitehouse's infamous attack on Howard Brenton's historical epic *The Romans in Britain* also foregrounds the power of the media and the influence wielded by public pressure groups, whilst Chapter 6 explores the effects of Section 28 of the 1988 British Local Government Act. The penultimate chapter focuses upon the reaction of business sponsors to Diane Dubois's play, *Myra and Me*, and Owen O'Neill's comic monologue, *Off My Face*, in 1998, and also investigates the decision of the Arts Council of Northern Ireland to remove funding from *Forced Upon Us*, a community drama produced by the theatre company Dubbeljoint, in 1999. The final chapter covers the violent protests that led to the Birmingham Rep's decision to close their production of Gurpreet Kaur Bhatti's play *Behzti* in December 2004.

This emphasis upon analysis of the broader structures of reception does not, I hope, downplay the historical reality of cuts, curtailments, silencing and suppression. A symptomatic reading of the history of British theatre – which is alert to the gaps, omissions and aporia created by various types of censorship – exposes much material that has previously been ignored, elided or dismissed as unworthy of academic attention. Yet this book also explores the possibility that constitutive forms of censorship shaped productions that did reach the stage. It presents evidence of complicitous, interdependent relationships between censor and censored and highlights the beliefs about theatre that are articulated in debates over censorship, demonstrating that the agents of censorship may well have stifled and subdued British theatre but that their interventions have been realised through the complex interaction of valorisation and legitimisation, coercion and collusion. Extending the field of enquiry into the twenty-first century allows me to demonstrate that the Lord Chamberlain functioned as part of a larger network of censorious forces – and to show that much of this network remains in place today.

As a result, the majority of the examples of censorship presented in this book occupy the middle ground in Butler's censorious continuum. This represents both a challenge and an opportunity. Butler discusses the dangers inherent in the examination to this middle ground, as she cautions that our approach to examples of censorship which contain both implicit and explicit forms of censorship tends to be confused. She argues that, all too often, 'social forms of censorship come *to appear* and *to operate* as constitutive and inalterable conditions of speech' and urges us to consider the possibility that some forms of censorship would perhaps prove less fixed than we believe them to be, should we choose to challenge them.[42] By exploring the complexities of theatrical censorship, I hope to encourage just such a process of re-evaluation, thus helping us to distinguish between those forms of censorship which are contingent and alterable, and those which are not.

1
London's Grand Guignol: Sex, Violence and the Negotiation of the Limit

Despite scholarly efforts to unsettle simplistic equations between stimulus and response, or image and influence, the belief that there is a straightforward, causal connection between exposure to the portrayal of violence and its subsequent perpetration is still commonplace, and frequently employed to justify censorious intervention. Many journalists are happy to play on the fear that exposure to violent imagery stimulates our basest emotions, animalistic lusts and depraved desires; ultimately encouraging impressionable youngsters to imitate the actions of bloodthirsty or sex-crazed protagonists. Media discussion of new artistic genres, from the pulp fiction of the 1950s to the latest gruesome development in horror films, focuses upon the deleterious psychological effects of violent imagery.[1] News coverage of the murders of children or students by their peers, such as the murder of James Bulger in 1993 or the killings at Columbine High School in 1999 and Virginia Tech in 2007, is frequently framed by discussion of the harmful influence of violent computer games or films.[2]

This belief in the connection between exposure to violent imagery and anti-social behaviour is not, however, the exclusive preserve of reactionary tabloid columnists. The British Board of Film Classification's decision to withhold a licence from *Manhunt 2*, a new computer game, in 2007 indicates that the concern about the link between the depiction of violent action and visceral response can still lead directly to decisive acts of censorship.[3] And, as Jon McKenzie points out in *Perform or Else*, many theatre practitioners and scholars remain deeply attached to the notion that the transgressive energies of performance can effect profound change and transformation amongst those who participate in it.[4]

This chapter, however, concentrates on fears about theatre's negative effects and, specifically, upon anxieties about the visceral impact of staged scenes of violence. It explores the response to the horror sketches presented at the London Grand Guignol, which until very recently has been little more than a footnote in theatre history, despite the notoriety it enjoyed between its opening night at the Little Theatre in September 1920 and its closure in June 1922.[5] Analysis of the response to this short-lived venture provides important insights into the operation of censorship and troubles the reductive rhetoric that often surrounds the discussion of censorship. It shows that censorious attitudes were not exclusive to the Lord Chamberlain and his staff, as concerns over the extremes of this new theatrical form were expressed by the press and even, eventually, by the performers themselves. Assessment of the response to the London Grand Guignol also reveals connections between censorious, critical and academic definitions of value, as the notion of 'gratuitous' violence is used by examiners, critics and scholars alike.

The venue's publicity indicates that its producer, José Levy, was happy to highlight the literally sensational pleasures of the genre, providing a useful reminder that performance may occasionally exploit, or even trade upon, the admonition of its excesses. Further to this, Foucault's essay on the work of philosopher Georges Bataille, 'A Preface to Transgression', encourages reflection upon the nature of the London Grand Guignol's appeal through its suggestion of the interdependence of transgression and taboo, as it observes:

> The limit and transgression depend on each other for whatever density of being they possess: a limit could not exist if it were absolutely uncrossable, and, reciprocally, transgression would be pointless if it merely crossed a limit composed of illusions and shadows.[6]

Bataille's theory and fiction is also employed here in order to assess the audience's scopophilic – and often very physical – responses to Grand Guignol, as well as the ocularcentric preoccupations of the genre. Finally, examination of Levy's negotiations with St James's Palace delivers a clearer understanding of the limitations of the British text-based licensing system, as well as raising questions about whether the textual remnants of the form can provide an adequate basis for any account of the effects of Grand Guignol.

Figure 1.1   Aubrey Hammond's front cover for *The Grand Guignol Annual Review*, 1921.

Utility and excess: the evaluation of staged violence

The opening of the London Grand Guignol was greeted with scepticism in the British press. Previous tours of the French Grand Guignol to London and New York had not been successful, and the reviewer at *The Stage* predicted that manager Levy would encounter insurmountable problems with the project, observing that the London and Parisian stages were:

not only miles, but moral temperaments apart, and what the one may swallow with avidity the gorge of the other may rise at. Nor, on the other hand, is it much to the purpose to talk about creating a restricted but sufficient public in England for the real Grand Guignol play so long as our drama is controlled at St James's Palace. Mr Levy, then, must make his bricks with as many or as few straws as may be allowed him. At the best, he may give us but partly Anglicised Grand Guignol; the Gallic cock must lose many of his best and gaudiest feathers in crossing the Channel.[7]

Levy, however, had the good fortune to employ the considerable acting talents of Sybil Thorndike, her brother, Russell Thorndike, and her husband, Lewis Casson, and the London Grand Guignol became a sensation, attracting sell-out audiences and copious coverage in the press. Nonetheless, as *The Stage* had anticipated, the 'gaudiest feathers' of the 'Gallic cock' – exhibitions of sustained and explicit violence – were greeted with unequivocal disapprobation at St James's Palace. The Lord Chamberlain took the unusual step of banning four plays (*Euthanasia, Dr Goudron's System, Blind Man's Buff* and *Coals of Fire*) completely for their inclusion of scenes of murder and mutilation.

The reports and memoranda covering Levy's planned productions preserved in the Lord Chamberlain's correspondence files reveal the rationale behind the censorship's response. They are peppered with the adjectives 'horrible', 'disgusting' and 'revolting', indicating that the Lord Chamberlain's staff took particular exception to the form because they considered it a meaningless exercise in gratuitous violence. Examiner George Street objected to *The Old Women* (written by Christopher Holland) because it was 'purposeless' and refused to recommend a licence for *Blind Man's Buff* (adapted from the French version by Charles Hellem and Pol d'Estoc) on the same grounds: 'I see no reason why this loathsome nightmare should be inflicted on the public. It has no excuse. It is devised with some ingenuity, of course, but apart from that its only appeal is to brutish or degraded natures.'[8] The Advisory Board unanimously rejected the play for the same reasons. Board member Lord Buckmaster commented: 'its senseless cruel horror has no redeeming feature.'[9] These objections suggest that horror could have a place upon the stage provided that it had a 'purpose', or an 'excuse': it seems that terror could be tolerated by the Lord Chamberlain and his examiners as long as it could be justified as educational or improving. Grand Guignol, however, did away with the predictable moral structure of melodrama. Its depictions of sordid realities were designed to provoke pleasurable

screams of fear, rather than tears of compassion or pity.[10] In consequence, the Lord Chamberlain's examiners judged it to be meaningless
and excessive.

Assessment of the press coverage of the London Grand Guignol shows
that many critics shared this opinion. St John Ervine, drama critic at *The
Observer*, concluded that:

> I think we in these islands are right in our refusal to accept this sort of
> horror literature with anything but disrelish. The excitation of horror
> for the exclusive purpose of frightening the timid or of stimulating
> jaded emotions is a fundamentally immoral act.[11]

Again, the word 'exclusive' implies that horror might be acceptable in
other circumstances. From this perspective, performance was required
to have a *use*. Mere exhibition, or immersion in the world of the senses,
was unacceptable and could expect censorious suppression.

Here, Foucault's essay on the work of philosopher Georges Bataille,
'A Preface to Transgression', cited at the start of this chapter, suggests
both the predictability and the function of the outrage provoked by the
London Grand Guignol. Foucault notes that transgression and taboo
are closely linked: in order for there to be a crime, there has to be a
law. Contemplating Foucault's formulation of this relationship suggests
that disapprobation had an important part to play in the success that
Levy and the Thorndike-Casson family enjoyed with the plays they did
manage to stage at the Little Theatre. After all, as a genre, horror depends
upon transgression for its effects. Its imagery traces the boundaries of
taboo. In order to shock and thrill its audience it must affront our sense
of decency, outrage proprieties and challenge the civilised. So, it seems
that the London Grand Guignol was actually dependent upon the perception of a 'limit' of stage horror for the very effects that made it a
popular sensation. Indeed, examiners' reports on *Blind Man's Buff* and
Dr Goudron's System include reference to the 'permissible limit' and the
'legitimate limit of the horrible'.[12]

The *Sunday Times'* review of *The Old Women* suggests the other values
at work in the critical establishment's response to Levy's venture:

> Exhibitions of lunacy upon the public stage are pitiful admissions
> of theatrical incompetence. The moment an author has to drag a
> poor insane creature on the stage with the purpose of displaying his
> or her cerebral misfortune in all its tragical horror we may be sure
> he has either run short of material or is deliberately pandering to

human fears and inhuman curiosity. 'The Old Women' is so carefully prepared, so coldly calculated (it is a mysteriously premeditated and theatrically manufactured study of a whole madhouse) that it cannot be labelled for anything but what it is – a series of outrages. It is an outrage upon our senses, upon such taste as long study of the stage has left us, upon the intelligence we claim, and such decency as we profess. It is also an outrage upon religious feeling, for the lunatic asylum in question is kept, apparently, by Holy Sisters, whose prayers for the dead are of greater importance to them than regard for their living trusts. Three lunatics extract the eyes of a fourth with a knitting needle. Every possible detail to inspire terror and horror is thought of and included. The play is inartistic, because it is so obviously designed to make your flesh creep unendurably.[13]

This diatribe contains a telling contradiction. The reviewer declares at the start that the play is an example of 'theatrical incompetence' but then asserts that it has been 'carefully prepared', 'coldly calculated' and that attention has been given to 'every possible detail'. This apparent paradox seems to be a product of the logic that is voiced most plainly in the conclusion: the play is 'inartistic' because it is designed to provoke a visceral response.

The review also makes reference to another recurring theme in the critical response to the London Grand Guignol. The *Sunday Times*'s accusation that the play has been 'manufactured' is echoed by the writer at *The Spectator*, who announced that Levy:

is undertaking to supply London nightly with a certain well-known mixture of farce and horror (much as a chemist might undertake to supply it with malt and iron) which has hitherto been unattainable in England, and which he succinctly calls 'Grand Guignol Mixture, to be taken nightly in four doses'. People who go to him for poetry or profundity will of course be disappointed. It would be about as sensible to try the chemist for a Gainsborough. At the Little Theatre it is the 'Grand Guignol Mixture' that is being handed over the footlights, which are after all sometimes only a kind of illuminated counter, and it is by its efficacy or the reverse that we must judge the production.[14]

Describing the London Grand Guignol as a business venture, primarily concerned with profit, and categorising it as trivial, 'low' entertainment, allowed reviewers to exclude its work from serious criticism and withhold assessment of its artistic value. They still, however, had to find an explanation for its popularity.

Some critics attributed the London Grand Guignol's success to the quality of the acting at the Little Theatre. For some, this demonstration of ability mitigated its excesses, while others simply deplored the waste of talent. The theatre critic at *The Times* greeted a performance of *The Regiment* with the commentary: 'The terror is not the mind's terror but the body's; there is neither pity nor beauty in it: and there remains a regret that such brilliant performance should be given over to material so little worthy of it'.[15] This dismissive approach has a long legacy. Almost all of the critical coverage received by the French Grand Guignol since its closure in 1962 highlights the way it has been passed over as a legitimate subject for study in the past.[16] Writing in 1988, Mel Gordon proposes that theatre historians had ignored Grand Guignol until then because it was perceived as an exercise in popular escapism, peddled by business to tourists. He argues that it was ultimately judged to be 'little more than an unhealthy curiosity, unworthy of serious analysis or documentation'.[17] Of course, efforts to give obscure or forgotten phenomena a more prominent place in theatre history inevitably involve claims for their significance. Gordon foregrounds the Grand Guignol's popularity, whilst the latest reassessment of the genre by Richard J. Hand and Michael Wilson has attempted to rehabilitate Grand Guignol's reputation by challenging the notion that the performers were wasting their energies on second-rate material.

Hand and Wilson argue that the Grand Guignol was a writer's theatre, in which thrills were achieved by careful adherence to scripts that made use of sophisticated dramatic technique and meticulous timing in order to manipulate the imagination of the spectator. They propose that its continued association with bloody spectacles of violence is actually the product of a remarkably successful marketing myth created by the theatre's producers and that it was, in fact, 'a theatre of restraint rather than a theatre of excess'.[18] Nevertheless, by far the largest part of their analysis is dedicated to an exploration of the context of performance, acting techniques, stage design and special effects. Whilst their defence of the Grand Guignol rests upon reclaiming it as a 'writer's theatre', they have to acknowledge that the 'importance of physical action [...] cannot be denied'.[19] Hand and Wilson's desire to attribute much of the Grand Guignol's success to the literary sophistication of its writers on the one hand, whilst acknowledging the significance of its staging on the other, is reminiscent of the response of the theatre critic from *The Times*, when faced with a skilled cast of actors performing in a popular medium. It appears that we still find it difficult to accept that a brilliant performance may be 'given over to material so little worthy of it'.

The role and value of the text in Grand Guignol, and its relation-ship to the response to the form, has long been a matter of debate. French critics, for example, have speculated that the Grand Guignol failed to attract comprehensive coverage in the Parisian press because of its extra-textual qualities. Léon Métayer proposes that reviewers were uncomfortable when confronted with performances that placed more emphasis upon a totality of spectacle and action than text. He com-ments: 'for them, no text, no theatre'.[20] In Britain, the press were prepared to tackle the difficult task of reporting on the Grand Guignol, although its effects all but escaped linguistic description for some reviewers. When the reviewer for *The Era* reported on the Little Theatre's first season in September 1920, he attempted to outline the plot and action of *The Hand of Death* but was forced to acknowledge that he was unable to communicate its most important quality: 'Experiencing the thrill of it is essential; the thrill of it is indescribable.'[21] We will revisit the 'indescribable' thrill of the Grand Guignol but first need to consider Levy's negotiations with the Lord Chamberlain, which indicate the chal-lenge inherent in any attempt to assess the London Grand Guignol's appeal from a reading of its textual remnants.

The Lord Chamberlain: insuperable, insensible, invulnerable?

Levy complained that the Lord Chamberlain's reaction to the London Grand Guignol was unwarranted in the *Grand Guignol Annual Review*. He declaimed:

Censors are like the figures of 'Destiny' in Maeterlinck's 'The Betrothal'; 'insuperable, insensible, invulnerable, immutable, inex-orable, irresistible, invisible, inflexible and irrevocable!'[22]

Yet closer inspection of his dealings with the Lord Chamberlain reveals that the British censorship system was not as omniscient as this denun-ciation might suggest. With the help of the Thorndike-Cassons, Levy demonstrated that it was possible to foil the blue pencil. John Casson's biography of Sybil Thorndike reports on his family's anticipation of the Lord Chamberlain's reaction to their planned production of *The Old Women*. Casson recalls that they anticipated the Lord Chamberlain's likely refusal of the script and 'devised a cunning plan to dish the worthy censor'. Russell Thorndike submitted the script for performance, giving the location as St George's Hall, a parish centre in the small village of Wrotham in Kent. He correctly surmised that 'the psychological balance of the villagers of Wrotham was of no great concern to the Lord Chamberlain's office and the script was passed for their edification. And of course once a licence had been granted it was valid and legal for any other performance anywhere else.'[23] The play's similarity to the Grand Guignol did not go unnoticed at the office, but the Lord Chamberlain's examiner, George Street, noted that 'it is no worse than some of the Little Theatre plays' and recommended it for licence 'with great regret'.[24] He was later to have cause to reiterate this regret, acknowledging that his judgement was affected by the play's venue: 'I advised a licence for "The Old Women", when it was asked for a village hall, not anticipating that it would be worked into the horrible thing it was at "The Little Theatre".'[25]

This admission is indicative of the weaknesses inherent in this system of censorship. The Lord Chamberlain and his examiners struggled to proscribe performance because they were primarily dependent upon the script: only one element of a complex visual form. The examiners were aware of the shortcomings of this system, and, as Steve Nicholson notes, the office attended to costume, setting, gesture and movement, as well as adopting the strategy of sending a representative to rehearsals to assess pieces in performance from time to time.[26] But even this tactic could not expect to establish a definitive version of the performance, or to close down future interpretations of it, as Levy's defence of *The Old Women* reveals. A letter he wrote to the office shortly after a meeting at St James's Palace defends the play on the grounds that those who criticise it for excessive horror are victims of their own over-active imaginations:

> The play is being performed word for word as per the manuscript sent in and licensed by the Lord Chamberlain. From the dialogue it is impossible to determine that the old women stab the girl's eyes, and I was certainly surprised that most of the newspapers should have criticised it in this way. As a matter of fact, one or two of them suggested that the girl was being tortured. The action of the last act takes place completely in the dark and nothing whatever is seen, and we do not even bother to have a knitting needle as talked of in the dialogue as stage property. The three old women completely mask their victim and the whole incident is pure suggestion by acting.[27]

Figure 1.2 The 'eye-gouging' scene in *The Old Women*, 1921. Sybil Thorndike lies, eyes bandaged, below Russell Thorndike and Athene Seyler with Barbara Gott in the foreground.

Levy's emphasis upon the production's faithful adherence to the text demonstrates the difficulty facing the Lord Chamberlain and his examiners in their attempts to use licensed scripts to maintain control of a visual medium: no amount of intervention could check the audience's imaginative engagement with the piece.

The delusion of the eye and the denigration of vision

Certainly, it appears that the success of the French Grand Guignol was dependent on tightly organised artifice and illusion; performing in this theatre required the skill of a magician, great physical energy and consummate acting. It relied upon lighting effects, make-up and mirrors. These stage tricks and theatrical illusions were also set against a convincing backdrop: the Parisian Grand Guignol's attention to detail owed much to André Antoine's experiments with naturalism at the *Théâtre Libre* in Paris. This style of staging was designed to confuse and unsettle the audience, as it destabilised the status of the spectacle. Léon Métayer suggests that this kind of confusion was part of the appeal of the Grand Guignol, noting that its gruesome depictions of gore, madness and perversion were nothing if not convincing: 'The audience member was paying for the impression that it was really happening.'[28]

The plays produced at the Little Theatre appear to have been dependent upon a similar mixture of stage-craft and suggestion. Indeed, the confusion created by the conflation of artifice and reality afforded the performers some amusement. Casson recalls a humorous interlude:

> It was during 'The Kill' [...] that they received a visit from the R.S.P.C.A. Earlier in the play two real magnificent wolfhounds were brought onto the stage. Later during the 'kill' offstage the howling of the dogs was demoniacal. The R.S.P.C.A. inspector saw the show and demanded to be allowed back stage at the next performance. 'Nothing could make the dogs howl in this way,' he declared, 'except the most vicious cruelty'. I was there that night and I well remember his discomfiture. When the moment came he was shown [...] the stage manager standing in the wings baying like the hounds of hell.[29]

Casson's anecdote suggests that the inspector's dependence upon the evidence provided by his eyes – the appearance of the wolfhounds – meant that he failed to consider the possibility that the sound of howling came from another source. Hand and Wilson also draw upon Casson's biography and provide a convincing demonstration that the eye's unreliability was frequently exposed by the techniques of stage-craft employed at the Parisian Grand Guignol. They conclude that the genre's successful use of the power of suggestion confused the senses to such a degree that it allows 'the audience to see, or at least believe it has seen, what it clearly has not'.[30]

Grand Guignol's particular brand of horror also demonstrated the fallibility and limitations of the eye as an instrument of perception in more literal ways. The genre employed many different methods of murder, violation and disfigurement, but its playwrights seem to have been particularly preoccupied by the eye's physical vulnerability. Eyes were gouged out, stabbed and swallowed, while blind characters played a prominent role in the performances. It also played upon the fear that we may be misled by deceptive appearances. It did not contain monsters, ghosts, vampires or devils – easily recognisable embodiments of evil – instead placing its scenarios in quotidian settings inhabited by characters who initially appeared commonplace but were (more often than not) hiding homicidal tendencies. It exploited contemporary anxieties about contagious and inherited diseases, foreigners and the impact of technological and medical advances, focusing, above all, on madness and the threat posed by the indiscernibly mad to the sane. In these horrors, the eye of the victim cannot perceive the threat, nor does the eye of the murderer express it.

The genre also produced numerous disturbing images of public institutions that were purportedly all-seeing and all-knowing. This emphasis was due in no small part to the obsessions of André de Lorde, who provided the majority of the early scripts for the Parisian Grand Guignol. De Lorde was an amateur scientist, who spent considerable time visiting hospitals and mental asylums. His experiences appear to have undermined his faith in their work. Within de Lorde's paranoid fantasies, these institutions become traps for the defenceless or unwary: the isolated individual becomes a powerless victim in a brutal, dehumanising system. In these plays, the gaze captures and controls the subject, policing behaviour through invisible surveillance.

Here, Foucault's description of the development of the disciplinary society in the eighteenth and nineteenth centuries may provide a model for the operation of this form of power relation. In *Discipline and Punish: The Birth of the Prison*, Foucault argues that the architectural principles of philosopher Jeremy Bentham's Panopticon – a prison design in which the inmates do not know when they are being watched and when they are not – provide a blue-print for the operation of other disciplinary regime and institutions. This theory has come to be regularly – and perhaps too readily – applied to analyses of the operation of surveillance in contemporary society, but fear of the power of panoptic vision makes its presence felt throughout the Grand Guignol's horror repertoire and is clearly at work in *Dr Goudron's System* and *Blind Man's Buff*, both of which were banned outright by the Lord Chamberlain.[31]

De Lorde's play, *Dr Goudron's System*, is a reworking of a short story by Edgar Allan Poe, in which the patients of a mental hospital murder its director and take over the institution, posing as doctors. They then turn on two hapless journalists who are visiting the hospital, threatening one and gouging out the eyes of the other. *Blind Man's Buff* enacts a similar story, only here the residents of a home for the blind put out the eyes of a mysteriously silent new arrival. The fact that their victim was both deaf and dumb is only revealed to them after this grisly denouement. Their theme is shared by *The Old Women*, which is set in a mental asylum, where a young female patient – who is about to be released – is set upon by three old women who terrify her and finally gouge her eyes out with a knitting needle. All three plays concentrate on the paranoia produced by being under constant, though unverifiable, surveillance, and the attacks on vision contained within plays such as *Dr Goudron's System, Blind Man's Buff* and *The Old Women* point to a deep suspicion of the repressive, silent and invisible presence of panoptic authority.

   Grand Guignol's emphasis upon the eye as a vulnerable object and its ambivalence about the controlling gaze are illuminated by Judith Still's discussion of the fiction of the philosopher Bataille, whose pornographic work, *Histoire de l'oeil*, was written shortly after the closure of the London Grand Guignol and shares the genre's interest in sado-masochism and ocularcentrism.[32] Still argues that Bataille's philosophical attacks on the value of rational, scientific observation find figurative expression in the repeated degradation of the eye in this story of debauchery and excess. She proposes that emphasis on the materiality of the eye – its status as an object and its violation – undermines cultural deference to vision as the foundation of 'enlightened' or 'speculative' knowledge: once an eye has been removed from its socket, it is no longer an instrument of perception, but that which is perceived.[33] But Bataille's attack on the eye does not only serve to undermine the basis of sight and the reliability of vision as a sense, as Foucault observed in 'A Preface to Transgression'. He asserts that Bataille's vicious fictional assaults upon the eye seek to destroy its traditional connection with consciousness: a bloody eyeball, removed from its socket, can no longer be figured as a window to the soul.[34]

   The Grand Guignol presents a similar challenge to our cultural deference to vision. Its brutal attacks upon the eye highlight the organ's physical vulnerability, whilst its hapless victims are often undone by their eyes' inability to perceive hidden danger. The form's utilisation of the illusions of stagecraft demonstrated that the eye could be easily deluded, and its plots often explored the fallibility of the panoptic discipline of enlightenment institutions, like the asylum. Moreover, the history of the London Grand Guignol exposes the limitations of the powers of other institutions. The way in which it exploited the power of the imagination and explored invisible threats highlighted the weaknesses inherent in the British system of censorship, whilst it seems that two other text-driven institutions – the media and academia – have struggled with their response to the form.

'The thrill of it': audience response

This admission by the reviewer at *The Era* that 'the thrill of it is indescribable' (cited above) indicates the problems associated with any assessment of Grand Guignol's appeal today. Yet this 'indescribable' thrill was central to its attraction, and the London Grand Guignol undoubtedly possessed an affective immediacy that produced a physical, rather than an intellectual response. John Casson relates one audience member's behaviour and its impact on the performers:

> During one performance a gentleman stood up in the stalls and shouted: 'This is monstrous.' He then rushed out and was sick on the mat in the foyer. The actors were all delighted at the effect of their artistry and of course the indignation of many other intrepid theatre-goers was excellent publicity.[35]

The actors and management evidently considered this reaction to *The Old Women* to be a success; and in some ways, Levy and his company were correct to judge their performances by their physical effect on their audience. Some commentators have concluded that a physiological reaction is the very essence of horror.[36] The genre relies on the involuntary physical reflexes of its audience or readership for its effects, displaying the invasion and violation of the body in order to produce a sympathetic frisson amongst those who witness it. The Grand Guignol's reputation for inducing a physical response seems to have been one of its main attractions, as the poster below shows.

It also seems that the Lord Chamberlain's examiners blamed the audience for the Grand Guignol's excesses as much as the performers or producers. Following the production of *The Old Women*, and the subsequent media furore, examiner Street noted in a memo: 'These horrors are revolting and to the last degree inartistic and it is deplorable that there should be a public for them.'[37] Street's disapproval would no doubt have been heightened had he been able to anticipate future analyses of the appeal of the French Grand Guignol. Theatre historian Agnès Pierron asks why the audience members fainted at the Parisian Grand Guignol: was it because the images were unwatchable, unbearable or from too much pleasure?[38] Her modest speculation was more

Figure 1.3   This publicity poster by Aubrey Hammond shows the management of the London Grand Guignol were happy to capitalise on the promise of a truly shocking performance.

fully explored in a short television documentary on the Parisian Grand Guignol which included testimony from actors who had performed in Rue Chaptal. They recalled that the management were happy to cater to their customers who were sexually stimulated by watching horror: the seating area of the auditorium included private boxes at the back, fronted with wire mesh, which couples used 'as an alternative hotel room'. The actors did not speculate about the feelings of the cleaning ladies, who had the unenviable job of scrubbing away the 'traces of sexual pleasure' that these audience members left behind.[39] Both Léon Métayer and Pierron conclude that the Grand Guignol entertained its audience with spectacles of physical violence that were designed to create sexual excitement.[40] As Fredric Jameson's introduction to *Signatures of the Visible* notes, 'The visual is *essentially* pornographic, which is to say that it has its end in rapt, mindless fascination.'[41] While some members of the Parisian audience may have experienced disgust or revulsion on exposure to Grand Guignol's horrors, it appears that others enjoyed its covert eroticism.

Figure 1.4 Sybil Thorndike appearing as Daisy in M.F. Maltby's *The Person Unknown*, 1921.

There is no evidence that the audience at the Little Theatre included copulating couples. But it seems that the effect of acting in the Grand Guignol could provide similar satisfaction. Sybil Thorndike believed that she experienced a kind of 'release' during her performances at the Little Theatre, and that the audience shared this experience:

> I discussed the sense of release I got when I was in Guignol with a doctor once, and he quite understood, but thought it was rather hard luck on the audience to work all that off on them. I was able to tell him that it worked that way for the audience too.[42]

After this admission, reviews which comment on Sybil Thorndike's acting style make interesting reading. The critic at *The Era* praised

Thorndike's 'display of nervous emotion' in *Private Room No. 6*, as she depicted: 'The excitement, the terror, that underlay the superficial gaiety were admirable, and the white, quivering face and shaking lips, as she strangled her victim, made us shake and quiver in sympathy.'[43] This review bears witness to the empathetic response such performances were able to invoke.

Simon Shepherd takes this insight further, intimating that the popularity of this mixture of cruelty and pleasure can be explained by the dark impulses of sado-masochism. Analysing the popularity of nineteenth-century melodrama, he comments:

> A scenario that is terrifying and cruel can at the same time be hypnotically necessary and deeply pleasurable. A sado-masochistic scene is acted out between people who have agreed conventions, so that there is a safe framework within which deep psychic memories are explored and replayed. Highly charged material is recovered, negotiated and put back again. Its cruelty is its necessity is its pleasure.[44]

Figure 1.5 Sybil Thorndike and George Bealby as Lea and Gregorff in *Private Room No. 6*, 1920.

The conventions governing the relationship between audience and performance were still under negotiation in the Little Theatre, however.
Sybil Thorndike acknowledged that both the Lord Chamberlain's and
the actors' boundaries had been reached, though the audience was still
hungry for more:

> We could have gone on forever changing the bill if the audience
> hadn't demanded that each new play must be more terrifying than
> the one before, and we found it impossible to beat a masterpiece like
> *The Old Women*, which was the best of all. In addition to this, the Lord
> Chamberlain's office was becoming all the time more censorious on
> the grounds that it wasn't good for people to be too much frightened
> in a theatre.[45]

Russell Thorndike concurred: 'I think "The Old Women" was the highest
tide that Guignol could reach in a sea of horror. Other very excellent shockers seemed tame to our patrons afterwards.'[46] As Shepherd
observes, the Grand Guignol was trapped in a cycle of increasing expec-
tation, as it was 'moved always to overstep each new limit or stopping
point in order to excite the greatest number of people.'[47] Far from rejecting the form, as the reviewer at *The Stage* predicted before the opening
of the London Grand Guignol, it appears that London audiences had an
insatiable appetite for its horrors.

It seems, however, that the Grand Guignol was not able to keep pace
with this moving boundary: its power to cause genuine shock and alarm
was short-lived.[48] A reviewer at *The Stage*, reporting on a revival of *The
Hand of Death* performed during the final season of Grand Guignol at
the Little Theatre, observes:

> It is interesting to note that a second seeing of this Grand Guignol
> horror does not produce anything like the same thrill as the first.
> Thus Grand Guignol defeats its own object, just as potent sauces may
> ruin the palate. The tragedy of such stage realism is that it carries its
> own inoculation against its own effects.[49]

By 1932, when the Duke of York's Theatre launched a season of Grand
Guignol, the reviews record that it was greeted with hilarity, rather than
horror. One reviewer noted: 'Shame on London playgoers! They simply
will not be thrilled nowadays. [...] the more harrowing did the proceedings on stage become – corpses in cupboards, chopped-up bodies
in chests, blood-stained carpets – the more did the shameless audience

give vent to gurgles of delight!'[50] Even the Lord Chamberlain's office had changed its attitude towards Grand Guignol plays by 1945. After attending a private performance of *Coals of Fire* (which was refused a licence in 1922), examiner Henry Game reported on the effect of its grisly denouement: 'I regret to say that I and my companion, a distinguished critic, merely laughed – the realistic fizzling was too much for us! One just couldn't believe that the charming Miss Nora Swinburne, who played the girl, was having her face roasted on the coals.'[51] The play was subsequently licensed.

This change in attitudes reveals the fact that any good censor will seek to conceal: the boundaries marking the limits of propriety, taste and judgement are always provisional. The reception of the London Grand Guignol's spectacles of murder and mutilation demonstrates that the limits of dramatic representation were under constant negotiation during this period, not only between the Lord Chamberlain, his examiners, and the practitioners and producer of the Little Theatre but also between a demanding audience and the press. The press coverage indicates that censorious attitudes towards the staging of violence and beliefs about the 'proper' function of theatre were shared by many of the period's reviewers, whilst efforts to rehabilitate the Grand Guignol's reputation and assert the genre's artistic value suggest that the earlier trivialisation of the form still troubles those who write about it today. In addition, the production history of *The Old Women* exposes the limitations of a text-based system of licensing and shows that the authority exercised by the Lord Chamberlain over the theatre was partial, rather than absolute. Finally, the London Grand Guignol's exploitation of the powers of the imagination and the reports of the visceral thrills enjoyed by its audiences also provide a valuable reminder of the challenges inherent in any retrospective analysis of performance.

2
The Representation of Reproduction: Marie Stopes and the Female Body

Looking back at historical examples of censorship can provide stark evidence of social change, demonstrating that taboos and prejudices are under constant revision. Nowhere are the constantly shifting borders of social mores and morality more evident in Britain than in our changing attitudes towards sexuality and its representation, and the response to the plays written by birth control campaigner Marie Stopes vividly illustrates the profound transformations that attitudes towards sex have undergone since the 1920s. Stopes's insistence that women must have access to information about sex and contraception, and that they could and should expect sex to be a pleasurable experience, was highly controversial and provoked strong opposition – reactions that seem extraordinary today.

Yet many of the problems Stopes addressed are still with us. Britain still seems to be dogged by the combination of ignorance and embarrassment that she was fighting in the 1920s, despite the ready availability of information about sex and explicit sexual imagery. The UK continues to have Western Europe's highest teenage pregnancy rate, and recent years have seen growing concern over increases in sexually transmitted diseases amongst teenagers. Many argue that the British approach to sex education compares unfavourably to the full, frank and early discussion of sex in schools in the Netherlands and Germany; that we give our children and teenagers too little information, too late.[1] Marie Stopes International – the healthcare charity which developed out of the organisation Stopes set up – still delivers UK-based campaigns on early sex education and the terms of access to cervical screening, emergency contraception and abortion.[2] So, returning to Stopes's largely futile efforts to place the sticky subjects of contraception, childbirth and impotence upon the stage illuminates some of the cultural concerns which continue to haunt us today. Returning to these plays, and the debate that surrounded them, also makes a useful contribution to our understanding of censorship, as the ambiguities and contradictions they contain unsettle assumptions about the relationship between censor and censored. As we shall see, both Stopes and the Lord Chamberlain's examiners employ regulatory processes that are founded upon fear of uncontrolled reproduction, as they contrast the verbal to the physical, the corporeal to the linguistic, and the page to the stage.

Liberation through control: Stopes's radicalism

First, however, it is important to appreciate how radical Stopes's efforts to discuss the biological realities of reproduction were at the time. There was simply no respectable language or vocabulary for the experiences that Stopes was attempting to describe. Abortion was illegal and practical advice about birth control almost non-existent. Consequently, it is hard to discount the impact of her work. Stopes definitely did not do so. Her assessment of the influence of her first educational monograph, *Married Love* – first published in 1918 – is fair, though hyperbolic:

> It crashed into English society like a bombshell [...] its explosively contagious main theme – that woman like man has the same physiological reaction, a reciprocal need for enjoyment and benefit from union in marriage distinct from the exercise of maternal functions – made Victorian husbands gasp.[3]

The shock which she describes was unquestionably felt at St James's Palace. The Lord Chamberlain's examiners suffered from acute sensitivity towards any discussion of the management of reproduction, sexually transmitted disease or sexual problems. Performances which addressed 'delicate subjects', such as contraception, impotence and sterility, were simply unthinkable. Squire Bancroft, a member of the Advisory Board, was so shocked by one of Stopes's plays that he tendered his resignation from the Board after reading it.[4]

Stopes's interest in the theatre was explicitly pedagogic, but in contrast to the examiners' pronouncements on Grand Guignol – which often conceded that staged horror might be justified if it had a use – it was clear that they would be making no such allowances in the case of the representation of reproduction.[5] They acknowledged the educational impetus of Stopes's work but refused to give it special consideration.[6] *Vectia* and *Cleansing Circles*, which were submitted for licensing in 1924 and 1926 respectively, were banned outright. A revised version of *Cleansing Circles*, titled *The Vortex Damned*, was also refused a licence in 1930. *Our Ostriches*, submitted in 1923, was only licensed after substantial cuts.

This response needs to be placed in the context of the broader opprobrium Stopes attracted, which is indicated by the unsolicited letters contained within the Lord Chamberlain's correspondence files. Members of the public wrote to the Lord Chamberlain, begging him to ban Stopes's plays. The file on *Our Ostriches* contains one such missive from a C. Saville, who attacks Stopes for fostering immorality and unpatriotic sentiment:

> All who value morality and national greatness will share my horror at the proposed propaganda [...] the stage censorship of unEnglish and immoral plays might do something to stem the flood [...] why encourage her and all the revolutionary and defeatist elements by quixotically giving her unlimited licence and free advertisement. How can pre-natal murder (*the real baby killing*) be Racial Progress?[7]

The Lord Chamberlain also received a letter complaining about the play from one W.P. Mara, the Honorary Secretary of the Westminster Catholic Federation. His objections are more focused, though no less vitriolic:

> My committee wishes me to point out that this play is simply a part of the birth control propaganda which Mrs Marie Stopes has made notorious through certain offensive books. The two are intimately connected, and therefore, apart from any objectionable features in the play itself, the performance should be condemned as an item in the most deadly propaganda which has ever been agitated in this country. [...] My Committee thinks that you will not resent a protest against the production of theatrical performances designed to forward a camaign [*sic*] in favour of contraceptives, the evil of which is obviously greater than that of any ordinary immoral play.[8]

Members of the Roman Catholic Church were perhaps the most vocal of Stopes's opponents, but they were not the only source of disapproval. Conservative anti-feminists opposed sex education, information about birth control and provision of contraception on the grounds that women would be likely to reject their roles as mothers and wives if they gained control over their fertility, leading to under-population and the decline of the family.[9] Presumably C. Saville's letter – which conflated Stopes's birth control campaign with an attack upon 'national greatness' – was motivated by similar beliefs.

The management of reproduction was already a controversial issue in the public sphere when Stopes published *Married Love* in 1918: a campaign for 'voluntary motherhood' had proposed abstinence as a method of control in the 1870s; and the Malthusian League, formed in 1877, promoted itself as the first birth control organisation in the world. But Stopes was approaching the question of birth control from a new and challenging perspective. While the voluntary motherhood campaign had depicted women as asexual, and the Neo-Malthusians emphasised the pernicious effects of over-population, Stopes initially sought to celebrate female desire. This represented an important departure from the Victorian myth of the respectable woman's asexuality, as it presented the value of birth control in both pragmatic and romantic terms, depicting it as a positive development which would enable married couples to enjoy greater sexual pleasure. This was to be a continuing obsession for Stopes; most of her prose works, including *Married Love, Radiant Motherhood* and *Enduring Passion*, idealised the joys of sexual satisfaction within loving marriages. They focused on the benefits of personal fulfilment, rather than the possibility of resolving poverty through elimination of unwanted pregnancies.

Stopes's work was certainly controversial, but there can be no question that the nation desperately needed basic information about sex and contraception. A massive epistolary outpouring followed the publication of *Married Love*, which sold 2000 copies within two weeks of publication and ran to seven editions in its first year in print.[10] The Marie Stopes Papers Collection, held at the British Library, includes 60 archive boxes, which hold 300 files, containing tens of thousands of letters.[11] This archive records the desperation and confusion of thousands of men and women who had no access to practical advice and reliable information about contraception and sexual problems.

Stopes's reaction to the Lord Chamberlain's first outright refusal to license one of her plays reflects her sense of the urgency and importance of her campaign. She was infuriated by his decision to ban *Vectia* and requested an interview with the Lord Chamberlain. Unusually, a note describing this meeting has been preserved in the Lord Chamberlain's correspondence files. Stopes's outspoken critique obviously justified a record, which other, presumably less heated, exchanges did not:

> Dr Stopes was of the opinion that the theme of the play (a man's impotence) was a perfectly proper one for public representation,

much more proper, in fact, than many plays licensed by the Lord Chamberlain, such as 'Our Betters' and 'The Vortex'. She further said that all plays were considered from the man's point of view, and that anything derogatory to men was refused licence.[12]

This response seems to prove Stopes's point. The way in which the above comment identifies the theme of *Vectia* as 'a man's impotence' – which is an important plot point, though hardly central to the play – confirms Stopes's observation that the licensing system proceeded from 'the man's point of view'.

Stopes decided to present her objections to the Lord Chamberlain's ban to the public and published *Vectia* under the title *A Banned Play and a Preface on Censorship*. The preface reveals Stopes's fundamental dissatisfaction with the sexual status quo, as she criticises the Lord Chamberlain's decision, accurately asserting that comedies that dealt with sex in a light-hearted way were much more likely to receive a licence than serious attempts to stage sexual issues.[13] Stopes then assesses the numerous pressures that inhibit creative expression amongst women, responding to her own question, 'What is the woman dramatist up against today?' with the powerful answer:

Men managers, men producers, men theatre owners, men newspaper proprietors, men critics, men censors, a man-made code of so-called current morality [...] Yet against the current code woman's voice is scarcely ever heard, because even if it is raised it is not adequately transmitted through the press or the pulpit because of her economic weakness and dependence. Seldom is a woman's voice even raised, because her motherhood has tended on the whole to stultify woman's public intelligence to coercing her to a private and individual struggle to save, if she can, her own children, her own position.[14]

Her speculations about the impact of censorship upon female creativity have particular resonance:

I wonder how many other serious plays by women have been destroyed before ever they came into being? It would be interesting, were it possible, to assemble all the plays or parts of plays by women directly or indirectly denied existence by men. I fancy the collection would be scarifying. Women's creative work still does not get a fair chance, for women have things to say which men have not the ears to hear.[15]

Stopes – quite rightly – reasons that the censorship of *Vectia* is the product of deep-seated gender inequality. Evidence of this can be found in the Lord Chamberlain's correspondence file on *Our Ostriches*, which demonstrates the prejudice that women writers faced when attempting to tackle serious issues. Notes in the file show that the gender and the relative youth of the play's female protagonist contributed to the Advisory Board's disapprobation. A report from advisor Sir Douglas Dawson grants that the play is written with serious intent but argues that the play's pedagogic purpose would 'be lost sight of in the feeling of horror that a young lady, just engaged to be married, should air such views in public'.[16]

Still, the censorious response to these plays cannot be simply attributed to the youth or gender of the writer or the protagonist. When Stopes submitted *Cleansing Circles* for licensing under the name Clifford Cooper in 1926 – appointing the business manager of the Strand theatre to deal with the correspondence – George Street's report concluded: 'this is a quite impossible play to licence.'[17] This statement rests upon an unspoken set of assumptions, and raises more questions than it answers; what, exactly, was so 'impossible' about the play? Why were light-hearted sex comedies acceptable, whilst Stopes's plays were not?

Janet Price and Margrit Shildrick's introduction to *Feminist Theory and the Body* may provide us with some answers. They suggest that the female body has been the source of particular cultural anxiety, because the biological processes of reproduction disturb the boundaries of the body and blur the distinctions between self and other. They assert:

> The very fact that women are able in general to menstruate, to develop another body unseen within their own, to give birth, and to lactate is enough to suggest a potentially dangerous volatility that marks the female body as out of control, beyond, and set against, the force of reason.[18]

This analysis owes a considerable debt to Julia Kristeva's theorisation of the relationship between the formation of subjectivity, the maternal body, and impulses of disavowal and repulsion, which she describes in terms of 'abjection'.[19]

Abjection – the experience of disgust and physical nausea – is frequently associated with encounters with displaced bodily fluids, such as blood, mucous or urine, which are often figured as metaphorical pollutants, threatening to defile and contaminate. Kristeva cautions, however:

> It is [...] not lack of cleanliness or health that causes abjection but what disturbs identity, system, order. What does not respect borders, positions, rules. The in-between, the ambiguous, the composite.[20]

Abjection is produced, according to Kristeva, by the way in which children develop their own body image – and subsequently identity – through a rejection of the maternal body. In consequence, states and objects that suggest confusion between inside and outside, or the blurring of boundaries experienced in pregnancy and maternity, generate anxiety. So, blood or mucous create anxiety because they represent the transgression of bodily margins.

Kristeva also observes that our relationship to the abject is never one of straightforward repudiation, noting in *Powers of Horror*, 'It is something rejected from which one does not part. [...] abject is above all ambiguity.'[21] For Kristeva, the abject is an intrinsic, albeit unstable, part of the self, and encounters with it will always involve attraction as well as repulsion. Negotiation of these disturbing forces is central to the maintenance of the subject's identity and necessitates ongoing systems of control and exclusion.[22] Kristeva's theories provide us with one explanation for the attitudes of the Lord Chamberlain, his examiners and the Advisory Board towards the messy practicalities of reproduction. What's more, Stopes cannot have been immune to the anxieties created by the encounters with the abject. Here, we need to bear in mind an observation made by Harrison in *Circles of Censorship*: 'Once one allows for ambiguities and contradictions in the theory and practice of the censor, one must allow also for ambiguities and contradictions in the object of censorship.'[23]

The reiteration of regulation

Upon initial inspection, Stopes appears to have promoted a pragmatic feminism, and her vitriolic response to the decision to ban *Vectia* from public performance might well encourage us to identify her as a groundbreaking feminist: a judgement likely to be reinforced by the Lord Chamberlain's decision to ban her plays despite their pedagogic purpose. Yet we should avoid assuming that her work was particularly liberal or progressive because she experienced censorious intervention. As Harrison notes, the straightforward alignment of the censor with reaction and oppression, and the censored with the forces of liberation, has always been an attractive but reductive rhetorical trope. He cautions:

> discourses which offend against censors or would-be censors can no longer be assumed [...] to be opening up a new space from which oppressive, univocal authority is challenged. [...] This is partly because the censor cannot be relied upon to know in whose interests he or she is working, partly because those interests may, in fact, be legitimate, or contradictory, to a greater or lesser extent.[24]

A close reading of Stopes's plays and prose reveals that her political agenda was deeply conservative, and her arguments were constructed around eugenicist ideology, class discrimination and notions of racial purity. Far from 'opening up a new space' for the challenge of authority, her work reinscribes the controls and interdictions that surround the reproductive female body.

Stopes's prose initially sought to deal with the challenges of procreation by containing it within marriage. She dedicated *Married Love* to 'young husbands and all those who are betrothed in love', suggesting that women should fulfil their biological obligations as well as achieving a greater level of independence through management of their fertility. Indeed, Stopes had always been keen to establish the propriety and respectability of her writing. In another educational monograph, *Wise Parenthood*, she states: 'My object is not to make sex-experience a danger-free indulgence, but to raise the sense of responsibility, the standard of self-control and knowledge which goes with maturity, and consequently the ultimate health and happiness of those who mate.'[25]

The limitations of Stopes's radicalism are even more clearly indicated in her plays. The nascent feminism present in the introduction to *A Banned Play and a Preface on Censorship* is curiously absent in *Vectia*, the play it was designed to defend. *Vectia* concentrates upon the eponymous heroine's desperate desire to have a baby, which has been frustrated by her husband's impotence. In the final scene, she is forced to choose between her husband and the attentions of a male friend, who is presumably more virile. Unable to dispute the biological imperative, Vectia rejects her husband in favour of the more potent suitor. Curiously, given her emphasis upon sexual pleasure in *Married Love, Vectia* characterises women's sexuality as defined by desire for children, while marriage's role is to provide a safe space for reproduction. Vectia's interest in sex, so abhorred by her 'maimed' husband, is ultimately motivated by the

need to procreate, reinscribing reproduction as the primary aim of inter-
course. Her own sexual needs are neither discussed nor alluded to. She
is completely in thrall to the biological urge to procreate.

Stopes recognised the conservatism of the play in the introduction
to *A Banned Play and a Preface on Censorship*. She records her reaction
upon hearing that the play was to be refused a licence, describing her
'disappointment and incredulity':

> The play's ruin grieved me as would an injury done to a child. The
> play was in rehearsal, the producer enthusiastic, the actors engaged,
> the scenery built [...] it seemed to all of us obvious that a play in
> which there is no adultery, no prostitute, no illegitimate child, no
> erotic intensity, no sex vice of any sort, of which the theme is the
> desire of a sweet girl wife to have a baby by her husband and to carry
> on the race, was (and is) essentially in line with the objects desired by
> officialdom and held as our social ideal. Hence we expected it to be
> welcomed warmly. The possibility of its being disapproved of never
> crossed any of our minds.[26]

This final sentence seems somewhat disingenuous, but her argument is
sound. The play's message was 'essentially in line' with the dominant
ideology of the time. The Lord Chamberlain's refusal to contemplate
licensing it simply demonstrates the strength of the taboo against
discussion of such issues in public.

If Stopes's prose work *Married Love* celebrated the joys of sexuality
and presented birth control as a constructive, rather than a repressive
development, and *Vectia* sought respectability by reconnecting sexuality with reproduction, the focus of Stopes's practical interventions
reveals a different story again. While her drama and prose were designed
to appeal to the educated middle classes, her practical work in the
1920s was focused on working-class mothers. This concentration on the
reproductive rates of the lower classes can be seen as an inheritance
of Malthusianism, which proposed that overpopulation itself was the
major cause of poverty. Its theories were built around the anxiety that
unfettered population growth would create a situation where mush-
rooming numbers would result in the escalation of economic and social
problems.

Our Ostriches indicates her concern with these issues as it reflects the
degradation and poverty experienced by the lower-class urban population. The play portrays the differing fortunes of two separate families.
We are invited to compare the small, well-managed Ross family with

the Flinkers. Numerous pregnancies have left Mrs Flinker ill, exhausted and unable to cope with her large and growing brood. The play focuses on its young protagonist, Evadne, whose privileged background has not prepared her for what she sees in the slums when she visits a poverty-stricken neighbourhood. Evadne is unmistakably Stopes's mouthpiece. The play encourages straightforward identification with the idealistic heroine, as her shock and outrage provide a guide for audience reaction. Evadne berates the Flinker's family priest, Father Rawn, and gives evidence to an unheeding governmental committee on birth control policy. She throws herself into a lonely and strenuous battle against the Roman Catholic Church, social indifference and outmoded scientific models.

Our Ostriches demands symptomatic reading. Ostensibly, its concern lies with working-class mothers and children, caught in a cycle of poverty and ignorance; though it seems that the heroine's determined interventions mask other interests. We are asked to believe that Evadne's sympathies have been aroused by her exposure to the difficulty of life in the slums, though her concerns do not appear to lie with the individuals involved. She is preoccupied with the effect such unregulated reproduction is having on the state's infrastructure, and describes the poor in terms of misery, waste and disease:

> EVADNE: I cannot see what good to the state diseased, miserable people who lead miserable lives can ever do; it's waste, waste. [...] Do not you see the workhouses and the hospitals and the lunatic asylums filling up, filling up with these wretched lives you are forcing upon the world.[27]

A sympathetic medical representative, Dr Verro Hodges, echoes her views. When Evadne remarks that unwanted children suffer, he concurs: 'Ah, not only the child; it is the community that suffers. The community has to have that burden, that *contaminating disease spot* in its midst' (my emphasis).[28] Such metaphors reveal the play's real agenda. The ostensible humanitarian concern of Evadne and Hodges is undermined by the value judgements performed by their language.

The Lord Chamberlain eventually agreed to give the play a licence once all attacks on the Catholic Church were excised, along with its references to syphilis and sterilisation. It opened at the Royal Court Theatre on 14 November 1923 and ran for twelve weeks, with a considerable injection of cash from Stopes. Intriguingly, it seems that the performance of the play brought its subtext to the surface. The reviewer at *Punch*

LONDON SPARROWS AND AN OSTRICH.

Figure 2.1 Haselden's cartoon for *Punch* indicates the children's affection for Brother Rawn.

observed that it was telling that, although Evadne claimed to be deeply concerned about the plight of the children of the slum, she did not appear to have any affection for them nor they for her, while the priest, Father Rawn, seemed to be adored by them.[29]

Our Ostriches' hidden agenda is spelt out boldly in Stopes's prose work, *Wise Parenthood*, which was dedicated to 'all who wish to see our race grow in strength and beauty'. Stopes characterised the populous lower classes as parasitically dependent, draining society's energy and resources:

> The *numbers* of our population increasingly tend to be made up from the less thrifty and the less conscientious. Were this only a superficial matter, it would concern the race but little, but it is penetratingly profound and far-reaching. The thriftless who breed so rapidly tend by that very fact to bring forth children who are weakened and handicapped by physical as well as mental warping and weakness, and at the same time to demand their support from the sound and thrifty.[30]

Her primary concern, it seems, is not with the lower classes that her heroine, Evadne, professes to care so much for. In fact, Stopes's interest in eugenics, and the possibility of removing such unhealthy characteristics from the nation's population, had been long established, as *Wise Parenthood* attests:

> Whatever theory of the transmission of characteristics scientists may ultimately adopt, there can be little doubt in the minds of rational people that heredity *does* tell, and that children who descend from a double line of healthy and intelligent parents are better equipped to face whatever difficulties in their environment may later arise than are children from unsound stock. As Sir James Barr said in the *British Medical Journal*, 1918: 'There is no equality in nature among children nor among adults, and if there is to be a much-needed improvement in the race, we must breed from the physically, morally and intellectually fit.'[31]

Many successful, well-educated middle-class scientists, physicians, academicians and churchmen shared Stopes's eugenicist leanings. These establishment figures afforded the movement a social and scientific respectability that the Neo-Malthusian campaign had never enjoyed. The movement was fuelled by anxiety surrounding a collection of demographic issues, including the impact of rural depopulation, emigration and female emancipation. Underlying the debate was Britain's perceived inferiority to the growth of newly aggressive competitors, such as the United States.[32]

While these anxieties may have been triggered by the declining birth rate – a demographic trend begun in the late Victorian era – eugenics' primary preoccupation was not with numbers. Its basic doctrine was quality, rather than quantity. While statistics indicate a rapid drop in the birth rate during the first 20 years of the twentieth century, they also show a significant reduction in the reproductive rate amongst the higher socio-economic classes, compared to lower classes, where the birth rate remained high.[33] This information was to influence the focus of birth control campaigns. Stopes had always stated that an important aim of her Society for Constructive Birth Control and Racial Progress was to end the association of birth control with the negative connotations of Neo-Malthusianism's family limitation plans. However, the first birth control clinic she opened in 1921 was situated in Holloway and was intended to serve the poor. Her practical work was directed towards controlling the reproductive rate of the working class.

Such practical measures may seem relatively innocuous alongside the later excesses of the eugenicist project. Nonetheless, Stopes allows her fictional counterpart to go further on stage than she did in her practical projects or prose. Evadne's frank, outspoken discussion of the benefits of sterilisation was obviously too much for the Lord Chamberlain's examiners. Her suggestion that the government should sterilise people with mental disabilities and her outrage at the Church's apparent acceptance of the production of children with syphilis were considered worthy of special attention from the blue pencil.[34]

Stopes's next attempt to gain theatrical publicity for her views on good breeding approached the issue from a different angle. *Cleansing Circles*, which was submitted for licensing in 1926, was addressed to the middle and upper classes. Written in response to Noel Coward's *The Vortex*, it focuses on a wealthy but dysfunctional upper-class family. Sexually transmitted disease, sterility and drug addiction are paraded as part of a 'modern vortex of degeneracy and beastliness', before the family is finally reconciled in a melodramatic scene between Denis (the wayward father) and his son, Frank:

FRANK: But don't our lives mean the race. My generation is beginning to forget it, plunging into filth and beastliness, smashing up the traditions for centuries handed down! [...] but now, as it is, here's a job for me. To close the vicious circle and set the next generation on its feet...clean! A man's job for me...at last!

DENIS: You're right Frank! That's a fine thought...A man's thought. *(with intense yearning)* the line restored! The race cleansed![35]

It seems that what the poor lack in self-control, the educated elite may make up for with increased rates of reproduction.

The Lord Chamberlain's censorious response to Stopes's work might encourage us to interpret her theatrical examination of the issues raised by reproduction as a straightforward challenge to the authority he represented. But with hindsight, the Lord Chamberlain's vigorous suppression of Stopes's plays seems unnecessary, even self-defeating. Stopes's work is deeply conventional and conservative in many ways. Her interrogations of the practicalities of reproduction were accompanied by a complex system of exclusion. She was keen to establish her propriety and respectability, characterising her treatment of 'delicate' subjects as respectful and modest, in comparison to the crude, popular representations of sexuality on stage. Her work also surrounds the female body with systems of control and constraint. Sex and procreation were to be contained within marriage, whilst the birth rate of the 'diseased, miserable' and 'thriftless' lower class was to be strictly regulated.[36]

Concern for the control and regulation of the body also influenced Stopes's use of the theatrical medium. In *A Banned Play and Preface on Censorship* she emphasises that her work does not exploit the physicality of performance, insisting that its power is of a verbal, rather than a corporeal, nature:

> *Vectia* is a play of a type not yet very common, one in which the deeper mainsprings of action are of a nature to be *discussed* rather than to be represented by physical bodies being transported or hurling themselves about.[37]

Stopes declares that the body is self-effacing, still and orderly in her dramatic work. She indicates that whilst her plays are locked into speech, discussion and language, her work remains respectable and controllable, regardless of its controversial content. Given her commitment to the regulation and organisation of the functions of the reproductive body, this is unsurprising.

What is more remarkable about Stopes's repudiation of theatre's inherent physicality, and its potential to explore the possibilities of non-verbal communication, is that she is subjecting her work to a similar disciplinary model as that of the licensing system she criticised. The Lord Chamberlain's licensing system focused its energies upon the policing of performance, rather than publication, and placed its faith in the regulation of an approved text. Stopes's clear repudiation of performance's physicality and her commitment to containing educational enactment within discourse demonstrates the essential conservatism of her plays. They promoted control over the body and positioned themselves firmly against excessive reproduction in all its forms. In this instance, it appears that the cultural anxieties surrounding the female reproductive body are shared by examiner and playwright alike.

3
Suppressed Desire: Dramatic Inscriptions of Lesbianism

Now that gay couples have the right to civil partnership and adoption, and gay lifestyles provide material for mainstream television programmes, it is hard to imagine a time when the slightest suggestion of same-sex desire in a play would justify a ban on its public performance.[1] But this chapter returns to just such a time: the first few years of the 1930s. It examines the theatrical representation of lesbian sexuality, focusing upon six plays which were subject to censorious scrutiny from 1930 to 1935.

As we shall see, discourses surrounding lesbianism were in flux during this period, and the assessment of these plays caused considerable anxiety at St James's Palace. Keeping up with the radical social transformations of the twentieth century was one of the most troublesome aspects of the work of theatrical licensing. Castigated on both sides by those who found his examiners' judgements either too lenient or too strict, the Lord Chamberlain struggled to find a middle way. Part of the difficulty of this balancing act was the need to maintain the illusion that the decisions taken were based upon the authority of distinct moral values and that the Lord Chamberlain was protecting and maintaining a clear 'line in the sand'. But, as this chapter indicates, all censors are troubled by the impossibility of exact or enduring definitions of obscenity, propriety and – most significantly here – sexual identity.

Five of the six plays discussed in this chapter were banned completely by the Lord Chamberlain, and, unlike many of the other examples of censorship cited in this book, their silencing occasioned little – if any – comment. And, unlike the Grand Guignol, the critical attention which these long-buried scripts have attracted has not been grounded on claims about their value as dramatic literature or about the significance of their contribution to the development of performance practices. Instead, work in the archives in this field is often motivated by the desire to reclaim women writers and their work as lesbian and the wish to remedy a long history of silencing, denial, invisibility and erasure.[2] This reflects the way in which the scholarly focus upon the historical representation of gay lives and the development of queer theory has been tightly bound up with a history of activism and the fight for public acceptance and equal rights.

However, some of the problems generated by returning to the theatrical past in search of material which could make a useful contribution to a present-day project of lesbian self-affirmation are demonstrated by Jill Davis's introduction to the first published anthology of British Lesbian plays, which reflects upon the collection's limitations. Davis states:

> In editing this volume I would like very much to have included a play by, about, for lesbian women written before 1945. I haven't found one. I am not surprised, since theatre is the most public of all art forms and I doubt that such a play would have received a licence for performance. Having failed to receive a performance its chances of an after-life, through publication, are small.[3]

Davis's assessment of the likelihood of such a play receiving a licence is accurate. Nevertheless, the Lord Chamberlain's Plays collection – which was not publicly available when Davis published her anthology – does provide an unperformed play with a type of 'after-life' and shows that there were attempts to place lesbianism on the stage before 1945. Yet Davis's criteria for inclusion – the fact that she was looking for a play 'by, about, [and] for lesbian women' – might also explain why she was unable to find a suitable script to include. These criteria display signs of the critical blindness that often afflicts the reading of lesbian texts – a blindness that can trouble censor and critic alike.

Even identifying a script written *by* a lesbian woman, ostensibly the most straightforward of Davis's three criteria, is rather more complicated than it might at first appear. That the Lord Chamberlain's staff and advisors often had trouble deciding whether or not the play they were reading was actually *about* lesbianism indicates some of the difficulties raised by the second of these criteria, whilst Davis's final requirement – a play *for* lesbian women – is perhaps the most problematic of all. In fact, the scripts discussed in this chapter do not provide straightforward support for a project of lesbian validation that seeks to find positive historical images of lesbian identity. Instead they demonstrate that dramatic images of lesbian desire created during the first half of the twentieth century were often homophobic, prurient and deeply conventional in their reinstatement of the heterosexual norm. This chapter contemplates the difficulty of responding to images which seem to reflect a form of deeply ingrained self-censorship, and considers the way Foucault's critique of the repressive hypothesis and Judith Butler's examination of the melancholic structure of sexual identity may be used to gain a better understanding of this material.

Invisibility and emergence

Getting to grips with the censorious response to the theatrical portrayal of the lesbian involves returning to a collection of scripts which can be frustratingly enigmatic. The ambiguous and oblique imagery they contain presents today's reader with a considerable interpretative challenge. The Lord Chamberlain's correspondence files show that his examiners struggled with the same problem. In this period, the concerns felt in St James's Palace over the representation of lesbianism centred upon the difficulty of estimation and assessment: these scripts must have been an unwelcome reminder that the work of a censor is, ultimately, all about interpretation, as the meaning of the Latin base of the word 'censorship', *censere* – 'to estimate, rate, assess, to be of opinion' – reveals.[4] This task of interpretation was further complicated by the way in which the conceptual categorisation of lesbianism was undergoing rapid development during this period.

A measure of the speed of this development is indicated by the House of Lords' infamous decision to reject a bill designed to criminalise lesbianism in 1921, on the grounds that the very discussion of lesbianism, even for an act of public prohibition, was more dangerous than the benefits of containment through legislation. Lord Desart, the director of public prosecutions, voiced his opposition to the bill on the grounds that: 'You are going to tell the whole world that there is such an offence, to bring it to the notice of women who have never heard of it, never thought of it, never dreamt of it. I think that is a very great mischief.' The Lord Chancellor was of the same opinion, declaring: 'I would be bold enough to say that of every thousand women, taken as a whole, 999 have never even heard a whisper of these practices.'[5] Evidently, we might question whether these men were best placed to pass judgement on the content of women's dreams and whispers; but it certainly seems that the public was largely unaware of lesbianism before this period or at least had never heard it named. The opinion of the theatre critic

St John Ervine illustrates this perception of public naiveté. Writing in 1933, he observed: 'I doubt if there was one person in a thousand who, before 1914, knew the meaning of the word Lesbian.'[6]

This climate of ignorance helps to explain the response of the Lord Chamberlain's examiners and his Advisory Board when confronted with *Children in Uniform*. This translation of Christa Winsloe's play tells the story of 15-year-old Manuela, who is sent to a boarding school. She falls in love with a popular teacher, Fraulein von Bernberg, and an affectionate relationship develops between teacher and pupil against a backdrop of harsh institutionalisation and strict discipline. The story does not end happily. Following her success in a school play, Manuela gets drunk and declares her devotion. Her behaviour is punished by complete isolation. Manuela commits suicide, believing that she will never see von Bernberg again.

Late twentieth-century criticism has labelled Winsloe's work strongly lesbian, but the Lord Chamberlain's staff and advisors were not sure what to make of the play.[7] The examiner, Street, thought that it should receive a licence, arguing that 'such an ordinary thing as the "passion" of a schoolgirl for a mistress' should not be confused with 'adult Lesbianism'.[8] All the same, he took the unusual step of calling for a second opinion, and the Lord Chamberlain's Advisory Board agreed with his verdict. The Lord Chamberlain concluded that the contents of *Children in Uniform* were harmless enough, and the play was subsequently licensed.

What are we to make of their judgement? Here the writings of sexologist Havelock Ellis, and research into the traditions of the British boarding school, may help explain the period's approach to such adolescent attachments. Ellis dismissed experiences such as Manuela's as short-lived and opportunistic – a product of the boarding school environment – rather than interpreting them as precursors of adult 'congenital abnormality'.[9] Similarly, Martha Vicinus's research into English boarding schools reveals that intense female friendships flourished in these institutions, and young women openly expressed affection for each other in language that replicated the romantic terms of heterosexual attachments.[10] This background helps to explain the Advisory Board's refusal to interpret Manuela's infatuation as lesbianism. As far as they were concerned, her passion could be dismissed as an immature, adolescent obsession: the product of the pressures of boarding school life. This decision to err on the side of leniency was uncharacteristic, however.

Decoding and definition

The Lord Chamberlain's treatment of *Love of Women*, written by Aimée and Philip Stuart in 1934, is more representative. His decision to ban the play came as a surprise to the couple, who had previously enjoyed a string of West End hits.[11] Aimée Stuart wrote to the Lord Chamberlain, asking him to give the matter his personal consideration. She protested: 'Ours is a delicate play – entirely on the side of conventional morality – about two women, who, because of the shortage of suitable men, live for work, for ideas, for friendship!'[12] The play's focus upon the intense friendship of Vere and Brigit – two young women who have chosen to live together – illustrates one of the main problems the licensing system faced: a script's ambiguity. The examiner who produced the initial report on the play pronounced: 'Unfortunately the whole play is dubious, to say the least, and one of the most difficult to report on I have ever had.'[13]

Part of the confusion may have been caused by the Stuarts' anticipation of the Lord Chamberlain's unsympathetic reaction to any mention of lesbianism. The reviewer for *The Daily Telegraph*, W.A. Darlington, voiced the suspicion that the authors had employed a degree of self-censorship when he reviewed the private production of the play in June 1935:

> There is interesting stuff here; but to be developed properly the whole case would have to be discussed in such detail as the Censor would surely never allow. Hampered by this official shadow, the authors skirt uneasily but inoffensively round their subject.[14]

By the time the play toured to New York at the end of 1937, the overall judgement of the American reviewers was that *Love of Women* had been so watered down, it had become unintelligible. *Variety* reported that the play 'flies over, under and around the Lesbian theme, but never alights directly on it'.[15] The reviewer for the *New York Sun* noted, 'It is always possible, incidentally, that someone has been doing house cleaning on the play, and left behind the confusion and muddle characteristic of house cleaning.'[16]

The reviewers' comments have some validity. From a twenty-first century perspective, the play seems to reveal lesbianism one minute, only to obscure it the next. It goes to considerable trouble to justify the women's unconventional domestic arrangements. *Love of Women* labours over the point that it is male shortcomings, rather than any 'abnormality' on the women's part, that has brought about this situation. Vere and Brigit explain at length that their commitment to each other is about work and companionship, not sex. This defence, and the broader critical response to the play, illustrate a radical shift in the perception of intimate female friendships.

Until the 1920s, it seems that affection between female friends was presented in positive terms. Critic Lillian Faderman indicates that the freshly labelled 'New Woman' was often depicted as turning to romantic friendship as an alternative to heterosexual relationships, but no shame or reticence was attached to these relationships at first.[17] The New Woman's espousal of progressive notions, adoption of emancipated habits and severe dress sense undoubtedly presented a radical subversion of normative femininity, however, and Viv Gardner's analysis of the theatrical portrayal of the New Woman concludes that her commitment to education and to financial independence was interpreted both as a rejection of a reproductive role and as a challenge to masculinity.[18] As a result, the New Woman became an object of satire and ridicule in the mainstream drama of the 1890s. Faderman and Gardner's work is supported by other critics who argue that the Victorian ideal of female innocence and asexuality was being displaced by condemnation of women who were actively choosing celibacy.[19]

However, neither Faderman nor any of the contributors to Gardner's collection, *The New Woman and Her Sisters,* detects an association of the New Woman with lesbianism in these early attacks. The definition had no social significance in the 1890s: the emergent discourse of sexology had begun to identify and label the female 'invert', but the general public had yet to do so. Still, this gap between scientific and social discourse could not last for long, and Faderman observes that images from the 1920s show that the Victorian model of female asexuality was being left behind: what would have been dismissed as innocent friendship in the 1890s began to be labelled as lesbianism. This categorisation was pejorative: the label indicated abnormality and peculiarity. Female autonomy gradually came to be equated with the stock figures of the frustrated spinster, selfish barren wife and predatory lesbian in popular culture.[20] This shift in the perception of the New Woman must have conditioned the contemporary response to the relationship portrayed in *Love of Women.* Within the play, Vere and Brigit's autonomous existence is curtailed by society's refusal to accept the two women's definition and explanation of the relationship, just as the Lord Chamberlain refused to accept Aimée Stuart's argument that this 'delicate play' merely represented women living 'for work, for ideas, for friendship'.

This development in the categorisation of female same-sex relation-ships demonstrates the complexity of any definition of lesbianism, historical or otherwise. The Lord Chamberlain's examiner may well have had trouble identifying the lesbian in this play, but this question of definition is not fully resolved today. Our interpretation of the nature of the relationship at the centre of *Love of Women* continues to be conditioned by contemporary definitions of lesbianism and the very contingencies of interpretation that so concerned the Lord Chamberlain and his staff. The word 'lesbian' does not indicate a fixed term but a definition being pulled to and fro in a conflicted space of opposing and contradictory forces.[21] Dealing with these contingencies, as well as ambiguity and obscurity, is an integral part of any assessment of the historical dramatisation of lesbian desire.

The death of the playwright

One way of responding to these challenges is to go in search of autho-rial intention. Indeed, it can sometimes appear that literary criticism is incapable of discussing the textual, dramatic or cinematic representa-tion of the lesbian without interrogating the sexual orientation of the subject at the artwork's source. This approach reflects a much wider popular interest with details of writers' and artists' lives; an interest which begins to border on obsession when it comes to those artists whose work explores sexuality. But this preoccupation is not only found in biography or journalism; its operation can also be detected in acts of censorship. The Lord Chamberlain's correspondence files show that factors taken into consideration in the analysis of a problematic script included the author's sincerity, motivation and commercial interests; as if the examiners wished to assess both the 'conscience' of the play and the individual who wrote it.[22] And, as Chapter 8 shows, the identity of the writer or artist remains central to debates about censorship today.

Still, the response to Lillian Hellman's play, *The Children's Hour*, indicates the problems inherent in this approach. Hellman's life has attracted close scrutiny, and critical commentary on the play seems obsessed with the question of her sexuality. Hellman insisted that *The Children's Hour* was 'really not a play about lesbianism, but about a lie', claiming that she had chosen the story because she could treat it with 'complete impersonality'.[23] This disavowal only encouraged fur-ther speculation. Some critics have suggested that the play is the product of a confused sexual identity, suggesting that its failure to restore the heterosexual social order in its final scene discloses Hellman's unresolved struggle with her sexuality.[24] Even the Lord Chamberlain, who first refused to license the play in 1935, could not resist passing judgement on Hellman's character. After meeting her in person, he noted: 'A nice woman [...] not quite what we expected.'[25] This surprise, and the confusion produced by other efforts to draw out connections between Lillian Hellman's biography and *The Children's Hour*, reflects the limitations of this approach. We will never know whether her oblique inscription of lesbianism was motivated by a belief that homosexuality is unspeakably horrific or whether it was the product of repressed desire.

Of course, this tendency to focus upon the author, or playwright, is grounded in a form of interpretation long since found wanting by literary criticism. Since the publication of Roland Barthes' influential essay 'The Death of the Author', theories which emphasise reception rather than authorial intention have transformed literary criticism.[26] Writing in 1992, Reina Lewis proposed that queer criticism should catch up with such thinking, as she gently explains:

> It does not mean that we think books write themselves; it means instead that we allow the gaps, suppressions and silences of texts to speak [...] This is an appropriate critical response for lesbian and gay readers and writers whose relationship to representation has traditionally been one of coding and subversion.[27]

It seems that we must leave behind the critical preoccupation with the authorial source and replace it with a commitment to reading against the grain of the text. As Lewis observes, this is a mode of reading which is ideally suited to the inscription of sexuality, as 'the assumption of a sexual identity of any sort is always and necessarily riddled with contradictions and denials, some of which will emerge at the level of the text signalled by the absence, emphasis or de-emphasis of sensitive material'.[28]

On the page, *The Children's Hour* demands the kind of symptomatic interpretation which Lewis calls for, as it circles around the unspoken and unspeakable. The script cannot be interpreted without a willingness to read between the lines; it teases its readers, inviting them to fill in the gaps, and to draw their own conclusions. It requires the kind of analytic approach which is capable of drawing out multiple layers of signification. But the literary emphasis of Lewis's critique cannot take the collective creativity of theatre into account. Her approach applies to the performance text and its audience, but the focus upon the playwright's sexual identity as a key to interpretation becomes unsustainable when we consider the creative contribution made to any theatre production by a team of director, designers, technicians and performers.

The particular and peculiar history of British theatre censorship also presents another challenge to author-led analysis. The obscurity of much of the censored material buried in the Lord Chamberlain's Plays and Correspondence Archives undermines the grounds for such biographical inquiry. Without the trail of biographical information left by famous or celebrated authors, the name on the script can tell us very little about the source of the material, and the use of authorial pseudonyms confounds judgement based on the playwrights' sexuality or their gender. After all, a name does not indicate whether a writer is male or female, straight or gay.[29]

The Children's Hour also exemplifies some of the difficulties inherent in any attempt to decide whether or not a play of this period could be described as a play *for* a lesbian audience. Lynda Hart's assessment of the canonisation of Hellman's play struggles with this issue. She laments the fact that *The Children's Hour*, the most well-known of all lesbian plays, appears to be so deeply homophobic. She concedes that we must avoid imposing our own expectations upon a text written in 1934 but then follows up with a contradictory proviso: 'I want to point out that Hellman chose to show the play's events from the perspective of the homophobic community. A lesbian writer might have found subversive ways to affirm the relationship, whereas Hellman simply kills Martha off.'[30] Her efforts to promote these two incompatible positions indicate the problems which attend all attempts to reclaim theatrical portrayals of lesbianism from this period as part of a project of political affirmation.

Nonetheless, some critics have moved away from preoccupation with the lived experience of the writer and have come to terms with the uncomfortable content of works such as *The Children's Hour*. Reina Lewis suggests that literary historians cease searching for undiscovered lesbian writers and heroines in literary history and accept this history's contradictory and often uncomfortable nature. She proposes that we focus our interpretations on 'the texts themselves, including those which are unsympathetic or written by men, as a transcript of society's attitudes to lesbians and women'.[31] Alan Sinfield echoes Lewis's call in *Out on Stage*. He proposes that critics stop wasting valuable time and energy on speculation about the sexuality of the playwright and spend it on analysing performance, representation and imagery instead. He comes to the same conclusion as Lewis:

> There is no correlation between the (reported) sexuality of the writer, director or performer and the way he or she represents homosexuality. On the one hand, lesbians and gay men have produced hostile representations, because that was how they saw themselves, or that was the best they could manage in those conditions, or they needed to work. [...] Queer history is not just that which we have made for ourselves and it is not composed only of positive images.[32]

Sinfield encourages his readers to consider the way in which the desire to salvage positive images from the past often results in the elision of material that today's gay community may find confusing or disagreeable. He also proposes that we discard the notion that the process of cultural closeting served to obscure gay identity and instead contemplate the idea that it created it.

Lesbian panic, conventional climaxes

The six plays under discussion here show that there is no shortage of disturbing imagery or unhappy endings available for analysis. *Love of Women* draws to a miserable close. Brigit leaves to marry a dashing young doctor, and the curtain falls on Vere, distraught and alone. Both *Children in Uniform* and *The Children's Hour* conclude with suicide, as did *Lady of the Sky*, which was also censored by the Lord Chamberlain in 1934. This play, written by Gilbert Wakefield, finishes with the spectacular demise of the eponymous heroine, who ends her independent existence by wilfully crashing her plane.

These plays would not be much use to an editor looking to put together a collection of early twentieth-century plays which present positive role models from a lost lesbian past. But their melancholy endings are a common theme in the representation of lesbianism on the stage during this period, as the lesbian is invariably assigned the role of tragic heroine who succumbs to madness or commits suicide. Certainly, Patricia Smith's identification of what she terms 'lesbian panic' appears to apply to *The Children's Hour*, *Children in Uniform*, *Love of Women* and *Lady of the Sky*:

> Typically, a female character, fearing discovery of her covert or unarticulated lesbian desires – whether by the object of her desires, by other characters, or even by herself [...] lashes out directly or indirectly at

another woman, resulting in emotional or physical harm to herself or others. This destructive reaction may be as sensational as suicide or homicide, or as subtle and vague as a generalised neurasthenic malaise. In any instance, the character is led by her sense of panic to commit irrational or illogical acts that inevitably work to the disadvantage or harm of herself and others.[33]

Smith's valuable analysis appeared in the same year as another convincing explanation of the miserable phenomenon of 'lesbian panic' evident in these scripts. Judith Butler's *The Psychic Life of Power*, which builds upon her earlier works *Gender Trouble*, *Bodies that Matter* and *Excitable Speech*, contends that gender and stable heterosexual identity are dependent upon the prohibition and repression of homosexual desire. In this publication, Butler encourages us to take account of the 'acts of self-reproach, conscience, and melancholia that work in tandem with processes of social regulation'.[34] Elsewhere, drawing upon Freudian texts including 'Mourning and Melancholia', and *The Ego and the Id*, Butler argues that the subject of desire is '*the product of a prohibition*' created by the taboo against the infant's incestuous desire for one or other of its parents.[35] She also suggests in *The Psychic Life of Power* that the stability of heterosexual identity, and its definition, are dependent upon the repudiation of homosexuality and, hence, its existence. She observes: 'the positions of "masculine" and "feminine" [...] are established in part through prohibitions which *demand the loss* of certain sexual attachments, and demand as well that those losses *not* be avowed, and *not* be grieved.' As a consequence, any intimation of homosexual desire 'panics gender'.[36]

The question of how best to respond to this panic and fear is highlighted by another play banned by the Lord Chamberlain in 1930 – *Alone*, Marion Norris's theatrical adaptation of Radclyffe Hall's novel, *The Well of Loneliness*. *Alone* was unusual in that it did not generate any concern at St James's Palace. The novel had been successfully prosecuted under the Obscene Publications Act in 1928, and the Lord Chamberlain's examiner, Street, was plainly very relieved to have a prior decision to defer to. In fact, his report is surprisingly favourable considering the media furore which accompanied the suppression of Hall's novel.[37] He describes the play as 'a study of a sexually abnormal woman and a protest against women similarly affected being regarded as pariahs and outcasts', observing that it is 'sincerely and sensitively written and quite free from offence in detail' and noting approvingly that the script does not suggest any 'definite physical action'.[38]

The lesbian critical community remain divided over the value of Hall's novel, however. Neither the novel, nor the stage adaptation, are works that seek to celebrate lesbian experience, and many critics have judged *The Well of Loneliness* to be a naively reactionary text. Radclyffe Hall's protagonist is tortured by her sexuality, and the novel seems to display many of the symptoms of 'lesbian panic' described by Smith and Butler. *Alone* is burdened by a tone of self-denial and abnegation, as the play reasserts the value and desirability of the heterosexual norm, emphasises the painfulness of the protagonist's struggle towards a lesbian identity and depicts the failure of her search for social acceptance.

The novel's conflation of lesbianism with affliction has produced particular disturbance amongst critics.[39] This approach can be attributed in part to the dissemination of the ideas of sexologists Richard von Krafft-Ebing and Havelock Ellis around the turn of the century, which are referred to in the novel. Their tracts sought to describe and classify the sexual invert, as they categorised the lesbian into types on a rising scale of inversion and degeneracy. Drawing on contemporary sexual ideology that associated active sexuality with the male, they linked female sexual deviancy with masculinisation and gender crossing.[40]

It is possible to interpret Hall's adoption of the sexologists' image of the invert as a constructive departure from the constricting, asexual convention of romantic friendship.[41] It is also possible that the increasing awareness of lesbianism produced by the sexologists' work may have encouraged women to identify themselves as lesbian, despite the system's emphasis upon abnormality. And, unlike the other plays considered here, *Alone* raises the issue of lesbianism in a direct fashion. Even had she wanted to, there is no way that the adaptor, Marion Norris, could have argued, post production or publication, that the play is actually about women's independence, the destructiveness of slander or a childish infatuation. It tackles the subject of lesbianism head on, providing a space for the consideration of the difficulty of social acceptance and the nature of homosexuality. In this light, condemnation of *Alone*'s adoption of the model of inversion as evidence of self-loathing or repression seems inappropriate. As Alan Sinfield points out, it may well have been more palatable for lesbians during the period to see themselves as gender inverts, rather than immoral or depraved. He comments: 'It was better to be a freak than to be wicked or not to exist at all.'[42]

Here, the influence of Foucauldian thought – specifically Foucault's critique of the 'repressive hypothesis', which he set out in the first volume of *The History of Sexuality* – is clear to see. In this work, Foucault uncouples the link between censorship and silencing, suggesting that we have misunderstood the relationship between sexuality and repression. He contends that histories which characterise the nineteenth century as an era of sexual prudery, modesty and prohibition fail to grasp that sexuality was produced by the discourses which sought to control it. He argues that sex became the object of obsessive amounts of attention during this period and that there was a

> multiplication of discourses concerning sex in the field of exercise of power itself: an institutional incitement to speak about it, and to do so more and more; a determination on the part of the agencies of power to hear it spoken about, and to cause *it* to speak through explicit articulation and endlessly accumulated detail.[43]

So, this explosion of discourse comes to constitute sexuality, just as it defines its boundaries. It also has the effect of making these prohibited, forbidden forms of sexuality desirable.

Sinfield interprets the Lord Chamberlain's attempts to suppress the representation of homosexuality along these lines. He argues that the system the Lord Chamberlain presided over merely produced a 'surface of decency', rather than ending the theatrical portrayal of homosexuality completely. He concludes:

> Censorship indicates an area of pressure, not an absence. The social order promoted same-sex awareness, as well as penalising it, through a continuous flirtation with the impermissible. To be sure, individuals were subjected to vicious penalties, but these too made homosexuality present, even while forbidding it.[44]

Commenting on the reception of Noel Coward's plays, Sinfield examines the way in which their semantic layering generated a split between two audiences, 'between the uninitiated and those in the know'. He observes:

> by suppressing irregular sexuality the chamberlain did not eliminate it; on the contrary, he implied that it was always about to irrupt into visibility. He was not just acknowledging its presence, he was helping to make theatre a place where sexuality lurked in forbidden forms.[45]

This conclusion seems convincing enough when applied to the work of one of the West End's most celebrated playwrights. But it is difficult to reproduce such positive thinking when faced with the successful suppression of the dramatisation of lesbianism during the 1930s, though Sinfield tries. Using the example of Mary's whispered accusations in *The Children's Hour,* he proposes that homosexuality was in effect an 'open secret'. This reading does not acknowledge, however, that *The Children's Hour* was banned by the Lord Chamberlain, despite the obliqueness of its reference to lesbianism. The uncompromising suppression of plays such as *Lady of the Sky*, in which lesbianism is all but submerged, reveals the limitations of Sinfield's analysis. As the public performance of these plays was stymied or postponed, for the most part contemporary audiences did not have the opportunity to question their conventional conclusions, and the development of a kind of knowing subculture amongst audiences for the legitimate, licensed stage was also delayed.

Having acknowledged the existence of lesbianism, the Lord Chamberlain would not contemplate any performance of lesbian desire on the public stage, no matter how oblique, or conventional, its presentation. The slightest inference of lesbianism was sufficient to justify suppression in the early 1930s. The decision to ban *Riviera* (written by Henry Broadwater) reflects this sensitivity. The play's inscription of lesbianism is indistinct to the point of invisibility. This script focuses upon the relationship between Madeleine and Elizabeth, who enjoyed a close friendship at boarding school. They have been separated for many years, but now recently widowed Elizabeth arrives in time to save her friend from a dismal marriage. This play presents a considerable interpretative challenge. The script gives next to nothing away. Even the strongest statements of emotional commitment are couched in ambiguous language.

Towards the end of the play, Madeleine is questioned about the character of their attachment. She observes: 'Friendship...the marriage of the soul...a tacit contract between two sensitive persons [...] we complete one another. (*Pause*) Our understanding is harmony itself.' She emphasises compassion and sympathy, as their mutual respect and understanding is contrasted with a series of duplicitous, abusive heterosexual couplings. Their relationship is also defined by reticence about its meaning and the depth of emotion experienced. Madeleine is asked if she loves Elizabeth. In response, she states simply: 'More than I could tell you'.[46] The phrase seems to sum up the delicate, private nature of their relationship. But these concluding exchanges were to seal the fate of *Riviera*. The Lord Chamberlain's note on the examiner's report states: 'The obvious Lesbian implication at the end of the play precludes me from granting its licence.'[47]

We may struggle to pin down the 'obvious' lesbianism in the above material, but the Lord Chamberlain was not alone in his assessment of *Riviera*. A memo to the Lord Chamberlain from one of his staff, C.L. Gordon, reveals that the play's producer shared his perspective:

> I interviewed Mr Peter Ridgeway, of the Play Society, in regard to the above Play today and explained to him that it could not be licensed as it stood in view of the Lesbian element introduced into it. Mr Ridgeway frankly admitted that that was his own view and that he had only submitted the play on the request of the author. Mr Ridgeway said that he thought that it was a poor play and he would be quite glad to be relieved of the responsibility of having anything to do with its production. I therefore arranged with him, subject to the Lord Chamberlain's approval, to send him a formal letter refusing a licence.[48]

That such a consensus could be reached is indicative of how much things had changed since the licensing of *Children in Uniform*. Gordon and the unsympathetic producer of *Riviera* not only concurred over the presence of lesbianism in an incredibly oblique text, but they also agreed on the desirability of its censorship. This surprising alliance suggests that an exponential increase in the awareness of lesbianism was accompanied by greater concern for its constraint and control.

Indeed, it seems that any inference of lesbianism was sufficient to justify suppression in the early 1930s. The Lord Chamberlain would not contemplate any performance of lesbian desire on the public stage, no matter how indistinct, or homophobic, its presentation. Reference to the correspondence files reveals that the Lord Chamberlain and his examiners were often convinced of the conservatism of these plays and chose to ban them regardless. The public was to be protected from representations of lesbianism at all costs. Passing judgement on *Lady of the Sky*, the Lord Chamberlain observed:

> The play may not be technically either indecent or demoralising, still [...] no matter what attempts are made to conceal it, this play's motif deals with one aspect of homosexuality, albeit the manner of presenting the theme is not offensive or blatant. Still, the germ is there and either in its female or male form I have no intention of seeing it fostered on the British stage if I can prevent it.[49]

As far as the Lord Chamberlain was concerned, *Lady of the Sky* may have been a decent, moral play (presumably because it results in the lesbian protagonist's death), but its infection with the 'germ' of homosexuality ruled out a licence.

Accounts of the silencing and censure of same-sex relationships are understandably keen to celebrate moments when censorship appears to be self-defeating, but the miserable conclusions of *Love of Women*, *The Children's Hour* and *Lady of the Sky* are difficult to equate with Sinfield's 'flirtation with the impermissible'. It is hard to detect the resistance built into Foucault's model of productive prohibition in their multiple silencings. Nevertheless, the Lord Chamberlain's examiners constant calls for second opinions, their decisions to refer plays to the Advisory Board and their adoption of an attitude of almost paranoiac sensitivity towards the depiction of lesbianism, indicates the depth of the investment in the protection of sexuality's borders.

This commitment to protect the public could only be fulfilled, however, if the Lord Chamberlain's examiners and advisors were able to recognise lesbianism, and their work of detection and decoding was problematised by the developing discourses surrounding lesbianism. In fact, the Lord Chamberlain and his staff were struggling to keep up as the sexologists' diagnoses of inversion, and Hall's depiction of a butch/femme relationship, displaced the convention of asexual, romantic friendship. These shifts in the understanding of lesbianism produced some seemingly anomalous decision-making. In 1932, Manuela's obsessional desire for a schoolmistress in *Children in Uniform* was dismissed as childish over-excitement, but by 1935, Elizabeth's protectiveness towards her friend, Madeleine, was interpreted as evidence of a lesbian relationship.

Today, it seems unimaginable that a suspicious censor could fail to interpret Manuela's devotion to her teacher as lesbian desire. The Lord Chamberlain's failure to do so indicates the importance of the prevailing constructions of homosexuality which condition our response to representations of lesbianism. The way in which analysis and interpretation of past inscriptions of sexual identity have moved away from fascination with the author towards interest in the wider discursive struggles between regulation and realisation is just one example of how these pressures inform our understanding.

What the Lord Chamberlain's response to these plays also shows us is that the lesbian's increasing visibility in the public sphere was accompanied by tighter regulation. Categorisation and labelling rendered her vulnerable to censorious control, and public exposure came at a price:

as the Lord Chamberlain's examiners came to anticipate public recognition of the lesbian, they became more confident in their exclusory judgements. I will return to the question of the value of visibility, and the significance of the belief that the public must be protected from the infectious 'germ' of homosexuality, when I examine much more recent efforts to control the representation of homosexuality in Chapter 6.

4
Soldiers: Playing with History

As the last three chapters have demonstrated, returning to past examples of censorship can be an uncomfortable business. The material that we uncover frequently fails to fit into a neat, conventional model in which censorship is imposed upon an individual by an external body, whether that be the state, an institution or another individual. This material can also prove inconvenient for rhetoric that places persecuted artists and injust, oppressive authorities on either side of a sharp divide. It reminds us that theatre has been known to trade upon transgression, and often shows that the cultural beliefs and values that motivate acts of censorship are shared by critics, other practitioners and sometimes even by the censored, too. The ambiguities and contradictions this material inevitably contains also present a challenge to projects which return to what remains of the censored past in the hope of finding forgotten images or silenced voices to celebrate. Sometimes the ideological content of what we unearth may make us uneasy, forcing us to confront the fact that an unwavering commitment to freedom of expression in all circumstances will involve supporting the utterance or display of statements and images which we may judge to be abusive, bigoted, offensive or simply false. These issues are highlighted in particularly stark ways by examination of the extraordinary controversy generated by Kenneth Tynan's determination to stage Rolf Hochhuth's play, *Soldiers*.

Soldiers caught Tynan's attention in late 1966, during his time as the literary manager at the National Theatre. The self-styled incendiary recognised a unique opportunity to goad the political and theatrical establishment. Hochhuth had a history of controversial work; *The Representative*, which suggested that Pope Pius XII had failed to exert his influence to protect the Jews from Hitler, had provoked riots in Berlin during its first production in 1963. *Soldiers* was no less contentious. The play revisits events that occurred during the Second World War, focusing closely upon Churchill, his advisors and his staff. It requires its audiences to consider the human cost of the war from a German perspective, and offers an impassioned critique of the bombing of civilians. This critique was, however, largely obscured by Hochhuth's decision to speculate upon the strategic importance of another, single death: that of the Polish President-in-exile, Wladyslaw Sikorski, who died in a plane crash in Gibraltar in 1943. The source of the controversy was Hochhuth's suggestion that Churchill was complicit in a successful conspiracy to assassinate Sikorski.

The scale of the scandal over *Soldiers* was due in part to Tynan's privileged position as a critic and cultural commentator. He ensured that his outrage at the National Theatre Board's refusal to stage the play was widely reported, as he condemned their decision as a case of the suppression of free speech; an attempt to undermine the artistic integrity of the National's artistic director, Laurence Olivier, and a devalorisation of the theatre's role as a forum for public debate.[1] Once the Lord Chamberlain had also demonstrated his unwillingness to license the play, Tynan raised the stakes still further. He denounced state censorship and championed Hochhuth's right to produce a play that questioned officially authorised versions of history, comparing the theatre establishment to the repressive totalitarian regimes of Eastern Europe.[2] In part, Tynan's rhetoric was so inflated because it had a role to play in a wider debate. The dates of the first attempt to obtain a licence for the play in December 1966, and its eventual production in December 1968, rest on either side of the introduction of the Theatres Act in September 1968, and the controversy over *Soldiers* was framed and focused by the larger battle over theatre censorship. As a result the struggle to stage the play presents us with an unusual opportunity to examine the consequences of the Lord Chamberlain's removal and illustrates the many types of censorship and control the theatre was subject to in the 1960s.

Moreover, the form of *Soldiers* raises issues that remain pertinent today. The play has an uneasy relationship with both fact and fiction. Balanced precariously between the two, it draws upon archival documentation and the conventions of historical research, whilst inventing incidents, dialogue and, arguably, historical events. In fact, the dissent that surrounded Hochhuth's work, and the censure the play received in the press exemplifies the tensions that attend current debate over documentary drama and 'verbatim' work, as critics continue to examine the nature of the ethical responsibilities inherent in theatre that claims to represent the real, as well as the propriety of particular forms of documentary drama.

These concerns are brought into focus by consideration of David Irving's close involvement with the play's development, realisation and promotion. The disgraced historian's support for the project encourages contemplation of the way in which we distinguish between a valuable reconsideration of the historical record and its unacceptable distortion, as Irving's subsequent career and his position in the continuing debates over censorship and freedom of speech destabilises the liberal certainties asserted in Tynan's rhetoric. Returning to the debate over the production reveals the ideological blind spots in liberal attitudes towards censorship, as well as deep and continuing unease about the advisability of 'playing with history'. It also encourages examination of the desire to return to the archive as a source of knowledge – a desire dissected by Derrida in *Archive Fever*. We will find plenty of evidence of what Derrida labels the *'mal d'archive'* – the need of archives – which he describes as 'an irrepressible desire to return to the origin, a homesickness, a nostalgia for the return to the most archaic place of absolute commencement'.[3]

Collusion and conspiracy: the old boys network

Tynan's plan to stage *Soldiers* at the National Theatre seems to have been designed to provoke controversy and confrontation with the establishment. Most British theatre boards would have been unsympathetic to Hochhuth's blackening of Churchill's reputation in 1966, given that the war leader had died only the year before, but any attempt to place *Soldiers* upon the stage of the National Theatre – giving it the royal stamp of approval in the state-sponsored flagship of national excellence – was certain to produce confrontation with the establishment. And Tynan faced a particular problem with this institution. The Chair of the National Theatre's Board, Lord Chandos, had served as a member of Churchill's War Cabinet in 1941–1942 and then as his Colonial Secretary. Consequently, he had been embroiled in the events depicted by Hochhuth.

Tynan anticipated resistance. He knew that staging the play at the National would involve a battle of wills, with the Board on one side, and himself and the National's artistic director, Laurence Olivier, on the other. His letters to Hochhuth indicate that he thought of his internal assault on the National Theatre institution as a military campaign.[4] He was also aware that getting the play past the Board was just the first step.

The Lord Chamberlain's office would still have to be reckoned with, regardless of the Board's decision.

The final years of responsibility for licensing were awkward ones for the Lord Chamberlain and his staff. The Joint Select Committee's ruling of 1909 had advised that the Lord Chamberlain should be able to ban plays on the grounds that they presented an 'invidious' portrayal of 'a living person or any person within fifty years of his death'.[5] As theatre began to display a growing interest in the staging of contemporary issues, such 'invidious' portrayals could hardly be avoided: a difficulty highlighted by Hochhuth's play. Ever anxious to evade controversy and press attention, the Lord Chamberlain and his staff had always been extremely careful to avoid any suggestion of overt political censorship. But Tynan's submission of the *Soldiers* script placed them in a difficult position. Should the play be licensed, it might appear that tacit Royal approval was being given to its opinions: a problem that had always dogged the Lord Chamberlain's staff.[6] On the other hand, a blunt refusal to license the play would undoubtedly produce accusations of egregious political intervention. *Soldiers* presented them with an uncomfortable choice. Any intervention would lay them open to charges of political bias, whilst granting a licence would give the play a spurious legitimacy.

The difficulty of the Lord Chamberlain's position in the late 1960s is spelt out in a note from the Lord Chamberlain's secretary, Ronald Hill, who, having read the synopsis of *Soldiers*, attempts to advise the Lord Chamberlain on a response to the play. While he feels able to state firmly that the play is a 'gross libel on Sir Winston Churchill dead for only two years', he also acknowledges that the increasing prevalence of documentary-type theatre places the Lord Chamberlain in a tricky position. The subtlety of his response makes it worth quoting at length:

I am not surprised that it [*Soldiers*] has been taken up by Mr Tynan since the latest aspect of the activities of the progressive theatre has been to move from the sphere of calculated indecency, through the 'Theatre of Cruelty', to plays which fictionalise real events, in the interests of a policy of antagonism of all in authority. [...] I know that where there is political context to a play the Lord Chamberlain is at his weakest; since the last thing he can afford to be accused of is political bias. Nevertheless he has a mandate from Parliament to forbid invidious representation – the whole of this play is imagination, and it is imagination projected as fact through the mouths of living or very recently dead notabilities, and I do not think it should be allowed. [...] If there is a case of improper behaviour let the facts be stated in a pamphlet or a book, the charges supported by evidence, and the matter submitted to the Courts if any of the accused are in a position to take action. I can see no future in the policy of giving official approval, if tacitly, to works of fiction, which since they impute words and actions to the living or recently dead, which they never uttered – must be untrue. I know that what I say would, if acted upon give rise to uproar, and I feel that the growth of this form of play constitutes a very cogent reason why the Lord Chamberlain should either lose the censorship or have his authority endorsed. I still feel that to allow the misrepresentation on the stage of the living or recently dead is wrong, and I would, if the synopsis truly represents the play, disallow it.[7]

Hill's report reflects the indefensible contradictions which dogged the licensing system during these last years. It also shows that Tynan's 'policy of antagonism' effectively highlighted the Lord Chamberlain's weaknesses. In consequence, this policy caused considerable disquiet behind the scenes, and the several files on *Soldiers* held in the archive reveal an extraordinary level of collusion between the theatre censor and the National Theatre. In a letter to Lord Chandos, the incumbent Lord Chamberlain, Lord Cobbold, observes that the play 'is obviously a difficult one for reasons which you, as a former colleague of some of the leading characters, will be the first to appreciate'. He then issues an invitation: 'I wonder if there is any chance of our having a private and informal word about it. If you are in London next week would you care to look in and have a word, or come and have a drink one evening at my house in St James's.'[8]

Tynan's notes reveal that he was aware of this behind-the-scenes contact and that he suspected the establishment of closing ranks to protect Churchill's reputation.[9] His anxieties were well founded. The Lord Chamberlain stalled, informing Tynan that no decision on licensing would be taken until the National Theatre had approved the production.[10] This was shortly followed by a unanimous decision by the National Theatre Board – which included representatives from all fields of the arts establishment – to reject the play as unsuitable for production.[11] At this point, the story broke in the press.

Staging public conflict

The first interviews granted to the press after this decision indicate the profound schism at the National created by Tynan's advocacy of the play. In an official statement, Lord Chandos coolly asserted that a play which suggested that Winston Churchill was complicit in the murder of General Sikorski was simply not suitable for the National Theatre.[12] Elsewhere, other board members, Sir Maurice Parisier and Victor Mischon, were less restrained. They were reported as condemning the play as 'repugnant' and 'a gross slander'.[13] In response, Tynan unleashed a storm of invective against censorship and political intervention in the theatre. No stranger to controversy, Tynan knew how to create a scandal. An interview in *The Times* reported that Tynan thought that the National's board had shown both 'a tragic failure of vision' and a 'remarkable lack of confidence' in Olivier's judgement as artistic director. Moreover, he claimed that the impasse 'brought into question the whole matter of the separation of powers within a subsidised theatre', arguing that although the board might have the right to establish the broad basis of the theatre's programming policy, decisions about which plays to programme, and which actors to cast, must remain the artistic director's prerogative.[14]

This sort of talk (together with the initial threat of resignations from both Tynan and Olivier) was bound to provoke a media furore. A plethora of cartoons appeared. Everyone seemed to have an opinion on the issue.[15] The print coverage was so extensive that in February 1969, Sean Day-Lewis observed in *Plays and Players* that it had been impossible to open a newspaper without finding some reference to the controversy for over two years.[16] The play attracted similar attention on the small screen, drawing attention to the different values governing each medium; *'Release'*, an arts programme, was able to show clips of the Berlin production of the play on BBC 2 on 14 October 1967, before it was possible to perform the play on stage in Britain.[17] David Frost also hosted two talk shows on the scandal, whose guests included Rolf Hochhuth, Edward Prchal (the Czech pilot of the plane in which Sikorski died) and Tynan.[18] The media interest was such that it even provoked questions in Parliament.[19]

Despite the play's high public profile, Tynan and Michael White (the producer who Tynan had convinced to take on a commercial production of the play) found London's main venues unexpectedly cool when they sought to stage the play following the abolition of the Lord Chamberlain's powers in September 1968. The Royal Court and the RSC refused it, explaining that their programmes were already fixed, and the West End also closed its doors.[20] Publicly, White speculated that financial caution had discouraged theatre managers from taking up the piece, but Tynan was happy to air his suspicion that the decision was primarily an ideological one. In an interview in the *Evening Standard*, he acknowledged that they could not hide the fact that he and White had not found a venue, arguing that they were facing a 'virtual boycott against the play', and that there were other reasons for the disinterest than the 'strict commercial considerations' being cited by the venue managers they had approached. He concluded: 'we appear to have got rid of a public censorship and replaced it with private censorship.'[21] Tynan's theory was supported by the content of an editorial in the *Evening Standard* the following day that included an interview with Bernard Delfont, manager of a West End conglomerate including the Shaftesbury, the Saville, the Comedy, the Prince of Wales and the Aldephi. Delfont commented that he was not prepared to see it staged at any of his theatres, regardless of its potential to be a commercial success, observing that: 'I may even have a theatre empty, but I still would not put it on.' This impasse effectively demonstrates the high level of control exerted by a small number of theatre managers over London's large stage spaces. The Lord Chamberlain's hold over the theatre may have been abolished, but the owners of its institutions had similar powers over programming. The editorial in the *Evening Standard* reflected upon this turn of events and the motives of theatre proprietors, proposing that they were simply responding to the loss of the legitimising safeguard which had been provided by the Lord Chamberlain's licence. The editorial concluded that the theatre had not been 'reborn entirely free from the censor's funeral pyre, it merely took a change of chains'.[22]

This editorial's speculation that the removal of the protection of the Lord Chamberlain's licence was the source of greater caution in programming may well be accurate, but its emphasis upon theatre's 'change of chains' is rather myopic. Control of performance had never been limited to the Lord Chamberlain's licensing powers, even while they were in operation. The comprehensive documentation contained in both Tynan's papers and the Lord Chamberlain's correspondence files bears witness to theatrical censorship's many different manifestations. The National Theatre Board's refusal to countenance the play's performance foregrounds the interference of management in artistic decisions regarding content, while the old boys' network served to mount a remarkable defence of Churchill's reputation. The theatre management structure also sided with the establishment, and demonstrated their control over much of London's stage space: a power they enjoyed both before and after the Lord Chamberlain's period of influence as censor.

Tynan and White did eventually find a venue, and the play opened at the New Theatre. But the controversy did not abate. In his memoirs,

White recalls the profound public disquiet the play provoked. He notes: 'It was hard going. Even my family disapproved of this play – the only time they ever criticised my activities. I was disturbed enough myself by then. I was beginning to get serious hate mail, postcards of Coventry after the Blitz, scrawls calling me a Nazi sympathiser.'[23] The press also voiced their disapproval in no uncertain terms. During its short four-month run reviewers expressed disquiet not only about the play's content but also about the medium of its expression. Philip Toynbee's review, which accuses Hochhuth of 'playing with history', and connects performance with emotive judgement and irrationality, is representative of this response. Toynbee asserted:

> There remains, of course, the last point of all: and a very important one it is. Did Churchill *in fact* murder Sikorski? Nearly all the historians seem to agree that he did not. And since it is at least highly probable that he did not I believe that Herr Hochhuth is on very shaky moral ground in using the stage as a means of claiming that he did. It is no use him answering that *he* believes in his thesis: the place for putting it forward is in a book, or a pamphlet, or a learned article. That is the proper way to carry out an historical argument, and the stage – where the case is inevitably assumed without being properly made; where the function of all the participants is to conjure emotions rather than to reason a case – is a most unsuitable vehicle for putting forward a fanciful theory of this kind. Hochhuth's real offence [...] is an offence against the properties of historiography: and that, to my mind, is a very grave offence indeed.[24]

Other reviewers seemed particularly concerned by the accuracy of actor John Colicos's convincing impersonation of Churchill, sensing an uneasy slippage between art and life. Lord Chandos also took the opportunity to hammer home his point about the inadvisability of plays such as *Soldiers* in *The Spectator*, claiming that when Hochhuth's theories were 'presented on the stage, and the characters are made up to resemble the real characters, the audience may be led to believe that they are being shown historical truth'.[25]

An editorial by reviewer Irving Wardle in *The Times* provides an insightful analysis of this reaction. He proposes that this response is evidence of theatre's continuing cultural power, arguing that the differentiation between legitimate criticism on the part of historians and unacceptable theatrical representation is the product of an enduring Puritan fear of the 'taboo-breaking' usurpation of identity realised

Figure 4.1   John Colicos as Churchill and George Coulouris as General Sikorski at the dress rehearsal for *Soldiers* at the New Theatre, 1968.

through acting. According to Wardle, this anxiety is to be celebrated. He concludes that Hochhuth's plays 'revive a certain awe for all forms of dramatic representation. The managements that locked their doors against him simply did not realise who their best friend was.'[26] Wardle's assessment definitely has some validity. The fascination with Colicos's accurate portrayal of the national icon seems to have been fuelled by a residual suspicion of theatre as a medium. Wardle was, however, less accurate in describing the 'taboo-breaking' of theatrical mimicry as the management's 'best friend', as taking responsibility for this transgressive performance was to prove both dangerous and expensive. The venue received bomb threats and was forced to adopt a range of security measures, including a nightly search before opening, whilst the pilot of the plane in which Sikorski was killed, Edward Prchal, was awarded £50,000 libel damages against Hochhuth in the High Court in 1972.[27] Prchal brought five legal actions in all, including cases against Clifford Williams as the director and Tynan and White as co-producers of the play. White settled out of court and ruefully described the successful litigation as 'the Lord Chamberlain's revenge'.[28]

'What happened happened'

Returning to past examples of censorship often tempts comparison between past illiberalism and today's tolerance: a comparison that bolsters our belief in the progressive forward march of history. This belief might seem to be strengthened by this case; *Soldiers* itself no longer has the power to outrage or shock, as demonstrated by the modest ripple of media commentary which accompanied the play's first revival in London at the Finborough Theatre in 2004.[29] The current British appetite for documentary and 'verbatim' plays might also seem to indicate that we are no longer troubled by the dramatisation of historical or even very recent events. But traces of unease remain, even amongst the most enthusiastic supporters of innovative contemporary theatre.

Comments from the academic and director Stephen Bottoms in an article for *TDR* on the current vogue for documentary theatre in 2006 might seem to indicate how far we have come from the outraged denunciations of the form in the 1960s, as he notes: 'there is nothing wrong, of course, with a writer presenting history as imaginative fiction'. Nonetheless it becomes clear that Bottoms is also profoundly troubled by the way in which many of these plays confuse realism with reality, arguing that they 'can too easily become disingenuous exercises in the presentation of "truth", failing (or refusing?) to acknowledge their own highly selective manipulation of opinion and rhetoric'. His analysis of David Hare's *Stuff Happens* (which opened at the National Theatre in 2004) reiterates the terms of the reviewers' objections to Hochhuth's play:

> the claim that 'what happened happened', that the events depicted are all 'true', is surely questionable when upwards of 80 percent of *Stuff Happens* takes place 'behind closed doors' – that is, on the stage of Hare's mind, in a series of conventionally realistic scenes depicting reimagined meetings. [...] it becomes impossible to tell with any reliability where factual reportage stops and political caricature starts: under Hare's all-seeing gaze, both acquire equal status as (dramatic) truth.[30]

Bottoms's important assessment of this production's dramatisation of the period before the invasion of Iraq in 2003 is, of course, a long way from Toynbee's assertions about the 'proper' place for historical argument, or Lord Chandos's vote of no confidence in the future of documentary theatre. His criticism precedes the proposal of a better way: an alternative theatrical form of self-conscious reflexivity which makes audiences aware of the complex and competing discourses which contribute to the construction of history. But his accusation that Hare 'fabricates his own evidence', his interrogation of the playwright's claims and criticism of the production's adoption of a 'realistic' style are grounded upon the same concern that audiences are being manipulated and misled.[31]

Placing Bottoms's concerns about the form taken by documentary and verbatim theatre today up against an analysis of Hochhuth's claims, the *Soldiers* scripts, and the play's British premiere, proves revealing. Hochhuth's descriptions of the process behind the creation of *Soldiers* promoted the play as a serious contribution to historical debate, drawing attention to the months he had spent consulting unpublished archival sources and carrying out interviews.[32] The weighty script submitted to the Lord Chamberlain for licensing highlights this laborious development process, including footnotes and extra information which encourages its readers to consider it not only as a play script, but also as a piece of historical research.[33] The published script is very much slimmer, but historical detail is crammed into dialogue instead. Characters assail one another with long speeches bursting with dates, names and statistics.[34] But Hochhuth did not wish to adopt the disinterested position of the traditional historian. He acknowledged that he saw the theatre as a moral forum and that he had written *Soldiers* with an explicitly interventionist agenda – to highlight the immorality of attacks upon civilian populations, unprotected by the Geneva Convention – even though he was pessimistic about the probability of effecting significant change.[35] Considering this commitment, and Hochhuth's adoption of a style that evoked the authenticating conventions of historical research, it is perhaps surprising that he did not choose to align his work with the emerging tradition of documentary theatre. Instead, Hochhuth sought to disassociate his work from the 'Theatre of Fact' or 'The Theatre of Documentation', commenting that he thought such labels meant very little. He argued: 'Pure documentation can never be more than a bunch of documents. Something must always be *added* to make a play.'[36]

These additions are most apparent in the prologue and epilogue which frame the historical action at the centre of the play. These portray a dress rehearsal for a modern production of *Everyman* set in the ruins of Coventry Cathedral in 1964 – the centenary year of the original Geneva Convention. This production includes several symbolic figures. Everyman appears as a soldier, while the other characters are actors, the director, and a series of national symbolic types, including a French General, a Russian military attaché and a Japanese Professor. Hochhuth recommends the doubling-up of the actor playing the West German and American military roles, observing that the actor should appear in both as a 'turn', rather than a character.[37] The play is presented as a trial of conscience for its director, Dorland, who seeks atonement for his previous career as a bomber pilot. So, the re-enactment of the central historical material is placed firmly within the theatrical realm. The performers are introduced as performers, and the historical content is explicitly framed as the projection of an individual's convictions and concerns.

The *verfremdungseffekt* evoked in this distinctly Brechtian structure is yet more apparent in the asides upon historiography, which appear regularly within the script. Its stage directions include detailed comments upon the nature of historical knowledge, and Hochhuth gives his characters speeches which reflect upon history's constructed nature, its foundation on subjective judgement and the uneven preservation of archival evidence, effectively emphasising the script's status as a reinterpretation of the past. Hochhuth highlights both the problems facing the researcher who attempts to examine material excluded by conventional historical narratives and the difficulty of reconstructing past events from their documentary traces. One of his characters comments: 'Do the documents merit closer attention than – the gaps? The relation of the document, if one may believe it, to the fact, is that of the fragment to the whole vase.'[38] This is representative of the way in which the script submitted for licensing foregrounded its status as a reinterpretation of the past. Even the conspiracy theory at the centre of the controversy – the implication that Churchill was complicit in the death of Sikorski – was tentatively advanced.

But the published play's subtleties did not survive its transition to the stage. The version directed by Clifford Williams at the New Theatre cut the framing prologue and the script's emphasis upon the contingent construction of history, reducing the play to the bare bones of plot and character. This severe reformulation of the play was the source of a great deal of critical consternation. Irving Wardle's review noted that we do not see 'a modern Everyman staged for the Red Cross centenary, but a straightforward drama of Churchill's conduct of the war during 1943.' He concluded that the production sacrificed argument to character, observing: 'Hochhuth may have set out to write a polemic against the bombing of non-combatants; but what he has produced is primarily an addition to the Churchill legend. [...] in theatrical terms, this material serves only as a pretext for showing John Colicos's Churchill in action.'[39]

This outcome cannot simply be blamed upon a reductive production. To some extent, it was inevitable: the play was unperformable as published. Not only was it prohibitively long, but the information Hochhuth had included in the stage directions would necessarily be lost in performance, something the Lord Chamberlain's examiner pointed out. What remained, once the script's textual trimmings and Brechtian frame had been stripped away, was a demand for emotional engagement with the human cost of war, a naturalistic preoccupation with the detail of historical events and a fascination with the actions of men in power.

The claims that Hochhuth made in the press after the National Theatre rejected the play suggest that these elements were indeed of central importance to the playwright. Despite his script's sophisticated negotiation of historiography's speculative, provisional and ultimately partial nature, and thoughtful self-reflexivity, Hochhuth asserted that the Sikorski subplot was absolutely true and could be proved by documentation that he had locked away in a Swiss bank vault. In fact, Hochhuth's letters to Tynan indicate that he had become convinced that the play's shadowy world of conspiracy was now his reality. In one particularly, anxious letter, he told Tynan that he would only name his sources in fifty years' time and described the six weeks he had spent recording the details of his research into the Sikorski case, which he now planned to deposit in three Bank vaults. He notes that he hid away while he was writing this report because he was convinced that he might be assassinated. He tells Tynan that the British Secret Service is taking an unhealthy interest in him and others involved in the project and warns him that he is in danger, as there are 'people' who would imagine that Tynan's death would prevent the play's performance in London. Not only does he warn Tynan about this undefined threat but he also suggests that that these 'people' may have read the letter before him.[40] How much of this anxiety was justified will no doubt remain a mystery. Nevertheless, this letter does indicate the depth of Hochhuth's problematic dependence upon the incontrovertible power of archival evidence, and the rhetoric of his public statements reveals his seduction by the archive's traditional association with truth, plausibility and authenticity.

Hochhuth's refusal to frame his work as imaginative speculation was the source of further critical dissent. For many reviewers, his insistence upon the existence of archival evidence which proved the play's allegations was too much to stomach. The reviewer for the *Sunday Times*, David Pyrce-Jones, concluded that it was simply lazy to 'dismiss the question of truth with an apology about the demands of drama, just as it is tendentious for Hochhuth to shelter behind information kept secret in a Swiss bank'.[41] It seems that the combination of these two strategies was one of the reasons for the lack of commercial interest in the play. In a letter to Tynan setting out the reasons for the Mermaid

Theatre's decision to turn it down, producer Bernard Miles reiterated just such concerns, arguing that he could have gone ahead with the production if the accusations against Churchill had been merely speculative. But he reports that Hochhuth's assertions that he had the evidence for Churchill's guilt locked in a Bank vault made the Mermaid's Board view the play negatively. He concludes: 'If a reputation is up for trial let's have the evidence and judge it, was the general verdict, otherwise don't touch it'.[42] In view of the contradictory messages being sent out by Hochhuth, it is hard not to sympathise with this attitude or to disagree with Eric Bentley's conclusion that both the play and Hochhuth's approach to it were 'confusing and confused'.[43]

Playing with history

One way of interpreting this confusion is to place it in the context of the range of attitudes towards historiography which were in circulation in the late 1960s. On the one hand, Hochhuth's claim that the truth of his account would be substantiated by the information he had locked away in a bank vault, and his insistence upon his painstaking consultation of unpublished material, evokes the long-established legitimacy of a model of research which dates back to the innovations of French sociologist, August Compte, and German historian, Leopold von Ranke, in the 1830s. Compte's prescriptions for a positivist methodology centred upon the painstaking accumulation of documentary evidence, followed by patient study and detailed comparative analysis: a slow process of collection, examination and interrogation which was inspired by the rigorous observation of phenomena privileged by the natural sciences. Scientific truth about the past came to be associated with a similar set of practices in the newly professionalised discipline of history, which were summed up by Ranke's three principles of historical investigation. These emphasised the objectivity of the historian, close analysis of archival material and the importance of '*Wie es eigentlich gewesen*' ('showing what actually happened/how it essentially was').[44] This model prevailed in historical research in the social sciences until the 1950s: long enough for the archive to become firmly established as a symbol of truth and authenticity.[45]

However, Hochhuth's acknowledgement of his own political agenda – and the way in which his script reflects upon the uneven preservation of archival evidence and the challenges inherent in reconstructing historical events from their documentary traces – suggests the impact of the sustained theoretical offensive against such empiricist approaches which took place in the latter half of the twentieth century. These aspects of his work reflect the radical reassessments of historical fact and personal memory that were beginning to take hold in the 1960s and which have now transformed our understanding of history and memory.

Psychoanalytic theory, for instance, questions whether memory contains an accurate reflection of past events, showing that its reliability is compromised by dubious distortion, selective recall and imaginative elaboration. As Jacques Lacan observes,

> The fact that the subject relives, comes to remember, in the intuitive sense of the word, the formative events of his existence, is not in itself so very important. What matters is what he reconstructs of it [...] when all is said and done, it is less a matter of remembering than of rewriting history.[46]

Analyses of historiography have effected a similar destablisation of the notion of objective analysis. Hayden White's work on historiography points out the discipline's reliance upon narrative forms and the tropes of fiction, and the way in which the past is transformed through our own investment in it, as he observes: 'all discourse constitutes the objects which it pretends only to describe realistically and to analyse objectively.'[47] Similarly, Foucault's Nietzschean concept of genealogy rests upon an acknowledgement that there are no facts as such but only interpretations of facts. His 'history of the present' highlights the link between knowledge and power, and acknowledges the political interests and position of the historian or critic.[48] Other historians, such as those in the French *Annales* School, have rejected the notion of a singular 'history' in favour of plural 'histories'.[49] Even archaeologists – whose painstaking recovery of material evidence might seem to lend itself most obviously to a positivist approach – have begun to discuss their work differently. Michael Shanks, for example, argues that archaeology is a 'practice of cultural production', proposing that the idea of a 'singular material record bequeathed to us from the past and from which meaning can be "read off" ' is no longer tenable.[50]

The details of these distinct approaches and the debates they have produced in their fields deserve a more thorough discussion than I can give here. But their implications are undoubtedly disconcerting. Full recognition of the roles imagination and repression play in our memories is deeply disturbing: to believe that you cannot rely on your memory is to experience a profound sense of disruption and imbalance, and to remember that one has forgotten, or to distrust the authenticity of your recollections, is an unsettling, vertiginous experience. Without the carefully constructed narrative of memory, how can we know who, or what, we are?

Acknowledgement of the indeterminacies inherent in the construction of any historical narrative seems to create similar anxiety. The censorious response to *Soldiers* certainly indicates that when it comes to national identity – the stories we tell ourselves about the construction of our communities – many crave the satisfying closure of a concluded narrative. Facing the provisionality and partiality of all accounts of the past is an uncomfortable business and raises many difficult issues. Derrida's *Archive Fever* reflects upon the results of our awareness of the contingency of historical narratives and concludes that they lead to:

> the archive fever or disorder we are experiencing today, concerning its lightest symptoms or the great holocaustic tragedies of our modern history and historiography: concerning all the detestable revisionisms as well as the most legitimate, necessary and courageous rewritings of history.[51]

Before we consider the vexed question of how we distinguish between 'detestable revisionisms' and 'courageous rewritings' – a question posed, but not answered, by Derrida's text – we must turn our attention briefly to David Irving's contribution to the development and defence of *Soldiers*, and his subsequent career.

This career is perhaps best summed up by the outcome of Irving's unsuccessful libel action in 2000 against Penguin publishers and Deborah Lipstadt for comments made in her book *Denying the Holocaust*, which gave a court an opportunity to examine Irving's politics, prejudices and historical methods. In his summing up, the judge, Mr Justice Gray, stated that 'Irving has for his own ideological reasons persistently and deliberately misrepresented and manipulated historical evidence' and that 'for the same reasons, he had portrayed Hitler in an unwarrantedly favourable light, principally in relation to his attitude towards and responsibility for the treatment of the Jews.' He concluded that Irving was 'an active Holocaust denier; that he is anti-Semitic and racist and that he associates with right-wing extremists who promote neo-Nazism'.[52] This damning verdict – which was upheld on appeal – has done little to dissuade Irving, and he was sentenced to three years in prison following his arrest in 2005 in Austria for holocaust denial.

Of course, it is important to remember that although Irving was a controversial figure in the late 1960s – subject to denunciations by

"My next play will be all about those horrifying concentration camps run by Billy Butlin!"

Figure 4.2   Jak's cartoon ridicules David Irving's defence of Hochhuth at the play's Berlin premiere press conference.

historians, and libel actions – he was not yet a pariah, as his close involvement with *Soldiers* shows. Programme notes for the play state that Hochhuth was inspired by reading *The Destruction of Dresden* by Irving, and, perhaps most significantly, Tynan's papers show that Irving had helped Hochhuth with his research in the four years before the historian's publication of *Accident: The Death of General Sikorski* in 1967.[53] As the scandal developed, Irving took every opportunity to defend the play publicly: writing letters to newspapers and articles in support of Hochhuth; appearing at the press conference for the play's Berlin premiere; and arguing the case for the play on David Frost's television talk show. He also provided financial backing for the production at the New Theatre.[54]

The ethical questions raised by *Soldiers* are brought into sharp relief by consideration of Irving's contribution to the play's conception, development, defence and practical realisation. Looking back at the scandal over the play with the knowledge of Irving's subsequent disgrace provides a new perspective on its contents and the debate over its propriety. The stark polarity of Tynan's black and white portrait of the battle between repressive state and persecuted artist seems less plausible, and his liberal certainties leave some awkward questions unanswered. Today, would we be as quick as Tynan to champion theatre's right to question officially authorised versions of history, if we knew Irving was involved in the production's development? Would we be prepared to defend a play that questioned the existence of the holocaust?

This last question was answered, in part, by the notable lack of protest from human rights organisations and the British press over Irving's arrest in 2005 and his conviction for Holocaust denial in 2006. This silence was all the more striking in the context of the ongoing controversy over the Racial and Religious Hatred Bill in the UK and the global outcry over the Danish cartoons of the prophet Muhammad. The way in which the right of freedom of speech was employed across Europe to justify the publication of the cartoons, whilst Austria escaped censure for its laws against Holocaust denial, made the limitations of the right to freedom of speech starkly apparent.[55]

Irving's tendency to misrepresent archival documentation in support of his fascist politics in his writing has been repeatedly demonstrated in court, but our commitment to the right of freedom of expression should, in theory, protect his right to make these statements, no matter how misleading, distasteful or infuriating we may find them. It seems that the grounds upon which we distinguish 'courageous rewritings' (which require protection) from 'detestable revisionisms' (which can be safely silenced) are often ideological. 'Courageous rewritings' are likely to be those versions of the past which chime with our political allegiances; 'detestable revisionisms' are those which we find unpalatable.

Finally, we might wish to consider what all of this might have to tell us about the British public's current appetite for documentary and verbatim work. In an insightful analysis of the resurgence of interest in this form, Janelle Reinelt makes reference to the difficult issues posed by Holocaust denial and argues that the public's enthusiasm for documentary plays reflects 'a deep collective urge for the link between knowledge and truth'. She avers that this is produced in response to 'the fear of total fiction', and despite our awareness of the contingencies of historiography, just as Derrida's *Archive Fever* argues that the contemporary awareness of historical indeterminacy is central to our continued attachment to the historical record.[56] It seems that the current popularity of the documentary form indicates the strength of this desire, as does the extraordinary controversy over *Soldiers*. Hochhuth's paradoxical dependence upon and destabilisation of 'the archive' displays all the symptoms of the 'fever' described by Derrida. Both are a product of enduring concern about the problems of 'playing with history', which lies at the heart of censorious responses to plays such as *Soldiers*.

5
Mary Whitehouse, *The Romans in Britain*, and 'The Rape of Our Senses'

Howard Brenton and Judith Butler provide us with two different ways of thinking about the impact of overt acts of censorship. Butler's argument, developed in the context of her work on hate speech, pornography and obscenity in *Excitable Speech*, proposes that explicit censorship is caught in a self-defeating Catch 22. She argues:

> Explicit forms of censorship are exposed to a certain vulnerability precisely through being more readily legible. The regulation that *states what it does not want stated* thwarts its own desire, conducting a performative contradiction [...] Such efforts [...] are also compelled to restage in the spectacles of public denunciations they perform the very utterances they seek to banish from public life. Language that is compelled to repeat what it seeks to constrain invariably reproduces and restages the very speech that it seeks to shut down.[1]

Building upon the Foucauldian critique of the repressive hypothesis, she analyses the paradoxical outcomes of many acts of open intervention: the reiteration of the discourse they ostensibly aim to silence. For Butler, this space of repetition and citation – where slippage in meaning necessarily occurs – is figured as the space of agency: an opportunity for change and the development of a 'counter-discourse' which challenges the censorious logic of the original attempt at silencing. Brenton's take on the publicity which attends high-profile controversies over censorship is much less positive. Discussing *The Romans in Britain* in 2006, he noted:

> Notoriety is destructive in the arts. The work disappears in the strobelight barrage of scandal, moral hysteria and media frenzy [...] As for

the play, it became 'reified', as the philosophers say: turned into something it is not. It was no longer a piece of theatre – it was either a cause or an outrage.[2]

Brenton views the proliferation of discourse which occurs as reductive and distorting, as the art work is obscured by its reappearance as a point of debate in arguments over the rights and wrongs of censorship.

The censorship of *The Romans in Britain* provides us with an excellent opportunity to consider the impact of what he refers to as the 'strobe-light barrage' of media attention. Before the closure of Gurpreet Kaur Bhatti's play *Behzti* following riots outside the Birmingham Rep in 2004, the court case brought against the director of the premiere of *The Romans in Britain*, Michael Bogdanov, in 1981 was the most regularly cited example of post-1968 censorship in the theatre. It has created as much belated critical commentary as contemporary column inches, and as a consequence the coverage of the first major professional revival of the play in 2006 – which took place in the midst of broader debates over censorship, freedom of speech and civil liberties – was framed and focused by the earlier controversy.[3] Together, analysis of the original scandal and the response to the revival (which was directed by Sam West at the Sheffield Crucible) provide us with the opportunity to consider whether the attempted silencing of *The Romans in Britain* was successful or unsuccessful as an act of censorship and to assess the long-term effects of the original controversy.

But before addressing the question of whether *The Romans in Britain* was successfully censored, we need to ask ourselves what a successful act of censorship might be. How might we recognise it? What criteria would we be using to calculate this success? In this case, the obvious place to start is with the statements made by the person who is now thought of as being central to the controversy – Mary Whitehouse. Whitehouse – who was then Chair of the National Viewers and Listeners' Association and a vociferous campaigner against televised sex and violence – based her objections to the play upon its representation of male rape and well-worn anxieties over theatre's ability to influence and arouse its audience. She seemed to suggest that the play was a titillating provocation to paedophiles, stating: 'One is concerned about protecting the citizen and, in particular, young people. I'm talking about men being so stimulated by the play that they will commit attacks on young boys.'[4] If we begin by measuring the success of Whitehouse's actions against her own statements about her reasons for condemning the play, we might well consider her intervention to have been unsuccessful on the most basic level: it did not stop thousands of male theatre-goers being exposed to the scene of anal rape during the play's run at the National Theatre. Yet the immediate closure of the play was something Whitehouse could never have hoped to achieve, and the complex legal manoeuvres she set in motion aimed to curtail future performances of the play. These manoeuvres, however, resulted in some outcomes which she could not have anticipated. An explanation requires a short description of the curious operations of the law.

Having failed to convince the Director of Public Prosecutions to recommend a public prosecution of the play, and having been refused permission to instigate a private prosecution of the play under the 1968 Theatres Act by the Attorney General, Whitehouse's solicitor took advantage of a legal loophole in the 1968 Theatres Act. This enabled him to bring a summons against Bogdanov for procuring an act of gross indecency between actors Peter Sproule and Greg Hicks on the stage of the National Theatre under Section 13 of the 1956 Sexual Offences Act in January 1981.[5] This piece of legislation was designed to facilitate prosecution of homosexual behaviour in public lavatories, and the prosecution's case relied on the supposition that the theatre could not be judged outside the general law of the land. Whitehouse's prosecution of the play rested on the notion that the context of the rape within the play, or the fact that it was simulated as part of a performance, was unimportant.[6] Ultimately, the prosecution was based on the notion that an act of simulated indecency was the same as an *actual* act of gross indecency, effectively conflating performance and the real. This approach left Bogdanov's lawyers with none of the defences that were built into the 1968 Theatres Act, which declared that no scene should be considered out of context and that a production should not be convicted if it was judged to be in the interests of drama or learning – 'the public good'. Whether Brenton had intended to shock the audience – in the interest of the public good – was to be of no concern to the court. Bogdanov's defence were left with the argument that a simulated rape is not grossly indecent. Legally, this was a difficult position to defend.

The court case did not play out as Whitehouse might have hoped, however. Not only did the prosecution fail to deliver a final judgement upon the play's indecency and impropriety, but the extraordinary legal performances which it entailed made Whitehouse and her legal team look ridiculous, as the law's seemingly nonsensical conflation of performance and reality was held up to ridicule in the newspapers. Whitehouse's commentary in her autobiography, *A Most Dangerous Woman?*, demonstrates the difficult position she found herself in:

I must say that of all the silly things which were said by what one might call 'the theatre lobby' the silliest surely was Marius Goring's claim that if the judge thought that an act of simulated homosexual rape on stage was the same as actual homosexual rape in the context at point, then Macbeth involved a handful of (presumably prose-cutable) murders. But that which makes the simulated and actual acts the same in this particular context clearly does not apply in the case of murder. If one were to ask where the gulf lies for an audience when it comes to distinguishing the obscenity of an actual rape on stage and a simulated one, the distinction must be nice indeed. Hardly so between real and simulated murder.[7]

As Whitehouse was to discover in court, the distinction was to be an important one.

The defence rested on the assertion that the act of rape was an illusion, a piece of performance trickery. In order to demonstrate this, the art of the theatre entered the court arena. This was complicated by the fact that the rules of evidence meant that the jury were neither permitted to see the play nor a video of it or even to read the script.[8] They had to depend on the memory of the prosecution's eyewitness, Mary Whitehouse's solicitor, Graham Ross-Cornes. Geoffrey Robertson attests to the successful strategy of Jeremy Hutchison, QC, who led the National's defence. The theatricality of his performance, in court, demonstrated the theatre's power to delude its witnesses.

Hutchison faced the job of undermining Ross-Cornes's seemingly unshakeable assertion that he had seen an actor – playing a Roman soldier – place his erect penis against the buttocks of another actor – dressed as a Celtic Druid. Having established that the solicitor watched the performance from the back row of the auditorium, Hutchison then launched a devastating cross-examination, recorded here by Robertson:

'Do you go to the theatre *much*, Mr Ross-Cornes?' Jeremy inquired sweetly. The witness confirms that he does go to the theatre, but not much. 'I go to pantomimes and such like.'

Q: You know that theatre is the *art of illusion*?
A: If you say so, Lord Hutchison.
Q: And, as part of that illusion, actors use physical gestures to *convey impressions* to an audience?
A: Yes, I would accept that.

> Q: And from the *back row, 90 yards from the stage*, you can be *certain*
> that what you saw was the tip of the actor's penis?
> A: Well, if you put it that way, I can't be absolutely certain. But
> what else could it have been?
>
> [...] Jeremy stood to his full height, 6 ft 3 in in his wig, and pushing
> aside his lectern with his left hand, he held out towards the jury his
> clenched right fist. 'What you saw, I suggest, was the tip of the actor's
> *thumb...*' (he slowly raised his right thumb, until it stood erect, pro-
> truding an inch from his fist) 'as he held his fist over his groin – like
> *this*.' Jeremy flung open his silk gown with his left hand while placing
> his right fist, thumb erect, over his own groin. [...] The jurors stared
> transfixedly at the QC's simulated erection.[9]

Ross-Cornes was forced to admit that he could have seen a thumb, rather
than a penis. Whitehouse remained unimpressed by this argument. She
acknowledged that the act of buggery was simulated, but that 'it was
simulated to make it so real that the impact on the audience was as if it
really was happening.'[10] Despite her protestations, the point had been
made, and her prosecution of Bogdanov ended in a fiasco. The prosecution decided that they did not want the case to go before a jury and
wished to terminate the prosecution. The judge was forced to acknowledge that this brought about a legal impasse, and the Attorney General
registered a result of *nolle prosequi*. Bogdanov was acquitted: his costs
were paid from public funds. Whitehouse had to pay her own costs.[11]

   This legal escapade could hardly be described as a victory for
Whitehouse. The prosecution failed, her solicitor had been made to
look ridiculous, and her actions had increased the amount of exposure
the play received. Upon initial inspection it seems to be an excellent
example of the performative contradiction which dogs acts of overt censorship, as identified by Judith Butler in *Excitable Speech*. But Brenton's
claim that notoriety can be destructive also requires due consideration.

Recontextualising the rape

Brenton's argument that scandal turned *The Romans in Britain* 'into
something it is not' may seem to invite critique. Its emphasis upon
the destructiveness of the play's transformation into 'a cause or an
outrage' might appear to suggest that there is a singular form of the
play, and a correct interpretation of it, which require protection and
respect – a claim which would elide the diverse and multiple acts of

interpretation through which any play is realised by directors, designers, performers and audience. Yet Brenton's protest is not about inaccurate interpretation or distorting description, which would require engagement with the content of the play and its staging. What concerns him is the possibility that the play is no longer considered a 'piece of theatre'.

Infamously, Whitehouse launched her attack upon *The Romans in Britain* without having seen the play. As a result, she could not possibly address the symbolic significance of the rape scene or its broader context within the production. The prosecution's ability to consider the staging of the rape out of context exacerbated this effect, as did most of the media coverage of the dispute, as we shall see. This does the play a great disservice. Examining this depiction of violent sexual assault within the context of Brenton's earlier work and the play's epic historical scope demonstrates its illustrative function and Brenton's broader political agenda. Brenton had already confirmed his commitment to shock tactics; the physical violence contained within his plays during this period invoked the Brechtian traditions of alienation and estrangement. A knowledgeable audience would expect his work to force them out of customary, comfortable positions and into difficult, painful confrontations with previously unsuspected truths.[12]

In *The Romans in Britain*, Brenton juxtaposes contemporary events in Northern Ireland with scenes from earlier moments in British history, in order to trouble myths of imperial glory and to encourage critical reflection upon the contemporary political scene in Northern Ireland. The first section of the play presents Britain in 54 BC, in the historical moment immediately preceding the Roman invasion. This section is concluded when British soldiers from the 1970s walk into this ancient Celtic civilisation and shoot a slave. This confusing temporal overlap occurs again when a modern undercover agent, Chichester, lurks on stage while Britons from 515 AD make their entrance.

Brenton hammers home the significance of this historical montage when Chichester attempts to explain his seemingly nonsensical decision to announce his identity to Republican terrorists. He describes his vision in terms that universalise historical conflicts over territory:

> I keep on seeing the dead. A field in Ireland, a field in England. And faces like wood. Charred wood, set in the ground. Staring at me./The faces of our forefathers./[...] They stare at me in terror./Because in my hand there's a Roman spear. A Saxon axe. A British Army machine-gun./The weapons of Rome, invaders, Empire.[13]

The play's inclusion of such explicit statements, which reflect upon the reccurring violence that has accompanied historical acts of invasion, mean that the symbolic significance of the rape is not difficult to interpret. It is hard to equate the sexual violence in *The Romans in Britain* with anything other than the literal invasion of one culture by another. Brenton reinforces this association through a series of symbolic substitutions; knives stand in for penises, and vice-versa, throughout. Within this context, it is clear that the brutal, if unsuccessful, rape of the Celt symbolises the more general destruction of the Celtic culture and way of life following the Roman invasion.

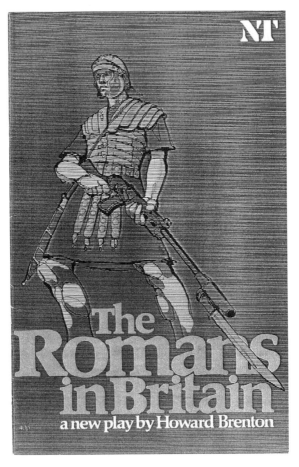

Figure 5.1   Richard Bird's programme cover for *The Romans in Britain* indicates the centrality of knives as props and metaphors in the play.

Brenton's play is also driven by an ethical imperative based upon the body. His vision of life in Britain's past foregrounds corporeal experience, drawing out the physical hardship of life in earlier times and treating the past with an aesthetic that is base and scatological. The characters' language is dominated by talk of their most basic physical needs. They are preoccupied with hunger, exhaustion and pain. We see them fighting, eating, sleeping, drinking and vomiting. The universal here is pain, whether it is the product of wounds, disease or injuries. All are vulnerable to infection and affliction, regardless of class or privilege. This history – in Fredric Jameson's words – is 'what hurts'.[14] Chichester's vision of himself as Roman, Saxon and modern day British soldier invites a reading that places the body at the ethical base of that performative paradigm. In this context, the attempted rape is presented as an image of universal suffering and unconscionable violation.

This image, of course, was only available to those who saw the play: Whitehouse's characterisation of the rape encouraged a wider public audience to imagine it as a titillating provocation to paedophilia. And although the prosecution raised general awareness of the play, Whitehouse's focus upon the rape and her purported concern about its stimulating effect obscured its symbolic function and Brenton's broader political agenda. This focus on sexuality had a further effect. It not only displaced Brenton's political agenda but also elided the political aspect of Whitehouse's own intervention. Her retrospective comments on the controversy indicate that her actions were motivated by unease over the political ramifications of the material, as well as concern over the exposure of sexually explicit material. At the end of Bogdanov's trial, *The Times* reported that the main reason for her private prosecution against Michael Bogdanov was her desire to protect Britain's image abroad and quoted Whitehouse as saying that 'the key point' to her actions was the fact that the show was being performed at 'the National Theatre [...] the theatre that belongs to all of us, which gives an image of Britain to the whole world'.[15] This point is reiterated in her autobiography, in which Whitehouse emphasises that the images performed on the National's stage should be of interest to every tax-paying citizen:

> The National Theatre is the *National* theatre. It is financed by our money, therefore we all have a responsibility for what is done on that stage. If no action is taken, without doubt 'the boat' will be pushed even further out. It is our culture as much as our national morality which is at stake, and that is important to us all, whether or not we go anywhere near the theatre.[16]

Figure 5.2   Merrily Harpur's cartoon for *The Guardian* illustrates the difficulties inherent in any staging of challenging material at the National Theatre.

A letter to *The Times*, written at the time of the production, voices the objection to the politics of the play in clearer terms. Its author, John Southam, observes that it is not the sexual element of the play which gives offence, but its political content. He wrote:

> Sir, if the sexual habits of the Roman army are portrayed by [...] any other theatre, I do not give a hoot. But I object strongly to the National Theatre being used to launch an attack on a national policy, and on the difficult and dangerous role of the British Army in carrying it into effect.[17]

For Whitehouse and Southam, it was clear that the national stage should support governmental policy and nationalistic ideals, rather than questioning them. These issues were largely masked, however, by Whitehouse's emphasis upon the impropriety of the staged rape. So, despite the tardiness of Whitehouse's intervention, the ridicule visited upon her hapless legal counsel and the huge amount of publicity generated for the play, it appears that this exposure did not serve to promote Brenton's political agenda, nor did it highlight the patriotism which informed Whitehouse's actions.

The outcome of the prosecution could not be interpreted as a victory for the theatre. The consequences of Whitehouse's legal manoeuvring were serious, both for those immediately involved and for the theatre industry more generally. For Bogdanov, there was a long wait between the initial summons in January 1981 and the start of his trial in March 1982, and during this time he had to cope with the threat of a possible two-year prison sentence and an unlimited fine, as well as dealing with the distress suffered by his family, who suffered excrement posted through their letterbox, threatening phone calls and bullying at school.[18] While the collapse of Whitehouse's case represented an immediate release from the threat of punishment for Bogdanov, the implications for the theatre were less comforting. The judge, Mr Justice Staughton, had already ruled that there was evidence to consider under Section 13 of the 1956 Sexual Offences Act and that this law could be applied to dramatic performance. Staughton's ruling clearly went against the spirit and intention of the 1968 Theatres Act, overturning assurances given by the then Home Secretary, Roy Jenkins, and Home Office representatives that there would be no private prosecutions of theatres and that the Sexual Offences Act would not be applicable to the theatre.[19] Yet the Attorney-General, Sir Michael Havers, refused to give an assurance that a judgement of *nolle prosequi* would be entered in similar prosecutions in the future nor that there would be no more private prosecutions of the theatre under statutory law.

The impact of 'the strobe-light barrage'

By 2006, this detail was lost on many critics as they assessed Sam West's new production of the play at the Sheffield Crucible. For example, Philip Hensher expressed surprise that *The Romans in Britain* had not received a full-scale professional production on a major, mainstream stage during the twenty-five years since its premiere at the National and that the play's notoriety had not generated interest amongst other producers at the time. He observed: 'It might be imagined that if a new play had that degree of publicity [...] every theatre in the country would have queued up to stage [it]'.[20] But Hensher seems unaware of the legal uncertainty surrounding the play. Far from being free from risk of prosecution, as he avers, the judge's decision that there was a case to answer meant that legal action could be brought on the same grounds in the future.

This question mark over potential prosecution may well have discouraged directors and producers contemplating revivals of the play. Amateur productions by university students, planned in the early 1980s, were halted after threats of prosecution and intervention by university authorities, and some anxiety appeared to remain about the play's vulnerability in 2006.[21] Those who had a direct involvement in the scandal of the 1980s seemed to believe that West's production would renew the controversy. Bogdanov voiced his concern that there would be further demonstrations, whilst John Beyer, the director of Mediawatch UK (successor to the National Viewers' and Listeners' Association) used an interview with *The Sunday Telegraph* to remind the Crucible that any production of *The Romans in Britain* had to abide by the law of the land.[22]

It might seem hard to take Beyer's veiled threat seriously, given that the-atrical stagings of simulated rape or sex have not attracted prosecution since the collapse of Whitehouse's case in 1982.[23] All the same, Angela Galvin, Chief Executive of Sheffield Theatres, confirmed that they had sought legal advice before deciding to take on the production.[24]

This cautious approach reflects the long-term consequences of the scandal surrounding Whitehouse's intervention. As Steve Nicholson has pointed out, censorious intervention has not necessarily been unsuc-cessful if it draws attention to the performance that it seeks to silence, as this controversy may have an impact upon the choices taken by writ-ers and producers in the future.[25] Still, it would be incorrect to conclude that Whitehouse's abortive legal action put paid to all productions of the play between 1981 and 2006. There have been revivals of the play since, including student productions in Cambridge, Bristol, Melbourne, and Berkeley, California, and a small production at the Man in the Moon pub theatre on London's Kings Road in 2000.[26] So, there may be other reasons for the show's absence from Britain's major professional stages.

The play's critique of the British presence in Northern Ireland was a response to a particular historical moment, addressing those circum-stances in a way that may not have seemed politically resonant again until now. And although almost all reviewers praised West's production, many seemed unconvinced by the quality of the play itself, as we shall see. Perhaps the single most tangible reason for the play's absence from the professional stage, however, would seem to be its epic scale. West managed to present its fifty-eight characters through inventive doubling with seventeen performers; but the financial risk involved in producing a challenging, non-canonical play, which requires a large cast and is notorious for scenes of sexual violence, must surely have made the play unattractive to many producing houses.[27] So, it seems that Whitehouse's intervention is one of several reasons for the play's relative obscurity.

What we can be sure of is that the controversy her actions gener-ated has had a lasting and profound impact upon the reception of the play. This controversy dominated the media's response to West's pro-duction at the Sheffield Crucible, frustrating his hope that it would now be possible to forget the legal case and focus on the play.[28] Previews of the production were framed by reference to Whitehouse's prosecution, whilst most reviewers began their commentary with a statement that the scandal had made the play difficult to assess.[29]

In fact, the media's continuing preoccupation with Whitehouse's intervention does not only obscure the play itself but also the complex-ity of the original response to it in the 1980s. There can be no doubt that her tenacity in pursuing the case and the resulting prosecution were exceptional, but emphasis upon her actions prevents analysis of other forces at work, just as an exclusive focus upon the Lord Chamberlain elides the influence of other agencies in the pre-1968 period. Despite the way in which the complexities of the controversy were set out in Mark Lawson's 2005 radio drama documentary, *The Third Soldier Holds His Thighs*, subsequent coverage has lost sight of the fact that Whitehouse was not alone in her anxiety over Brenton's representation of rape.

Returning to the production's original reception, and records of its development, reveals that there were concerns about the rape in the highest quarters. Peter Hall's account of the production in his autobiography records that, as director of the National Theatre, he was unsure about the wisdom of the explicit staging of the rape scene. He recalls that after seeing the first preview, he asked Brenton and Bogdanov if the rape might take place out of view, rather than at the front of the stage. He rationalised that this would ensure that the play would be more likely to be taken seriously and noted his concerns that the rape would dominate the critical coverage.[30] Hall's fears turned out to be well founded, and he found himself defending the scene in the press. *The Daily Telegraph* reported his support for Brenton and Bogdanov:

> Certainly the director and actors knew what they were doing and I endorsed it,' said Sir Peter. He added that during rehearsals the play's director, Michael Bogdanov, had asked him whether it was right to do the scene in full light. 'I said it was right because the scene is meant to horrify, and if it had been done in half-light, behind a tree, it would have titillated. In the context of the play it is not indecent. It is horrifying, it is anti-violence, it is anti-buggery – which is a metaphor for invasion. By the interval the morality is understood by the audience.[31]

Unfortunately for Bogdanov, the subsequent controversy indicated that Hall's original fears were justified. Preoccupation with the rape did indeed obscure the play's political critique.

Hall's concerns were not a matter of public knowledge at the time, but another member of the National Theatre Board, Sir Horace Cutler, the Conservative leader of the Greater London Council (the GLC), was not so discreet. Cutler, who was on the board as a result of the GLC's £650,000 annual grant to the theatre, walked out of a preview of the play and released a telegram of complaint to Hall to the press, which described *The Romans in Britain* as 'a disgrace to the National Theatre' which showed 'a singular lack of judgement' on Hall's part. He concluded 'the GLC will be considering its position *vis-à-vis* the National Theatre at an early date.'[32] This threat found form in the GLC's decision to freeze its grant to the theatre in March 1981 – a drop of 15% in its subsidy in real terms.[33]

Other public protests followed – both inside and outside the theatre. The National Front protested outside the building, whilst one show was interrupted by a small number of audience members (calling themselves the South London Action Group) who threw eggs, flour and fireworks at the stage.[34] The media emphasis upon Whitehouse's subsequent pursuit of Bogdanov through the courts ignores all of this. It also conceals the way in which her actions were *preceded* by a media furore of extraordinary proportions and, to a certain extent, that they were *orchestrated* by the media. Journalists from the *Daily Mirror* had contacted Cutler to ask for his views on the production, thus precipitating his visit to the theatre to see the show.[35] Whitehouse was also contacted: no doubt in the hope of provoking her outrage and furthering the scandal.[36]

The play also received damning notices and copious critical commentary in the broadsheets and in periodicals. The newspaper reviewers responded to the play with indictments of the quality of the writing, Brenton's use of 'shock tactics' and the physicality of the performance. Reviewers such as Michael Billington acknowledged Brenton's intent to deliver a serious message but savaged the form it arrived in. Writing in *The Guardian*, Billington declared that the play was simplistic in its treatment of complex historical realities: 'I accept totally that Mr Brenton finds the hunger for empire anathema; but in order to savage such a crucial historical phenomenon I suggest you first have to understand it.'[37] *Punch* was more cutting, stating that the play was 'an underwritten and overproduced pageant which would look inadequate if performed as a school play.'[38] In addition, Brenton and his play were accused of immaturity in *The Times*, whose reviewer objected to the play's inclusion of 'homosexual rape, bloody violence, frequent obscenity and political signifying', concluding 'so many of his parallels are driven home with a bludgeon that his regard for an adult audience must be questioned.'[39]

The play's many detractors focused on the production's exposure of an instance of sexual violence to the exclusion of the political elements of Brenton's work, whilst his emphasis upon corporeal experience generated much of the hostility in the press. He was accused of alienating and assaulting the audience in *The Daily Telegraph*:

"*Of course, we were terribly lucky with the notices.*"

Figure 5.3 Ben Shailo's cartoon for *The Daily Telegraph* illustrates the counter-productive potential of explicit acts of censorship.

The serious evangelist – Mr Brenton is nothing if not serious – should realise that they cannot get their precious messages across if they drive people from their seats in disgust [...] Caesar's marauders [...] specialise in the rape of naked young men, while the play specialises in the rape of our senses.[40]

The response of *Country Life*'s reviewer, Ian Stewart, sums up the attitudes expressed in the press and is worth quoting at length.

The play contains no argument, only attitudes (primitively expressed) and instincts (vulgarly demonstrated): imperialism may be brutal but that idea is not convincingly argued by the crude sexual assault on a young Druid by a Roman soldier, or by the facile analogy implied when we see Caesar and his men doubling as British soldiers in Ulster. [...Brenton's work aims to] demonstrate man's inability to learn from history. *Demonstrate* seems the right word, for there is another approach to the question of the right form or medium for an artist to work in. Mr Brenton may be thought of as a writer who thinks in pictures, if that is not a contradiction in terms. The images here are mostly violent – torture, rape, murder, suicide – and the play proceeds through a sequence of exhibits rather than by exposition. One may also think in terms of sound pictures since there is so much grunting and groaning. Inevitably the text is meagre and rudimentary – what can a playwright who disarms himself in this way make his characters *say*? Gut response is not enough, and though this very silly play may not prove to be a waste of money, I believe it to be a waste of time and of the talents of a large cast.[41]

Stewart rehearses the age-old responses of anti-theatrical prejudice, as he rails against theatre's inherent physicality, its visual form, its wasteful expenditure of time and energy and its potential to have a powerful – and seemingly corporeal – impact upon its audience.

Twenty-five years later...

These critical prejudices live on. In 2006, Billington reiterated his view that 'the real problem with the play is [...] the way it substitutes images for argument and poetry for politics.'[42] He was not alone in his estimation that the play lacked serious debate, and whilst none of the reviewers went so far as to claim that the play amounted to a 'rape of our senses', Paul Taylor did follow his observation that it failed to subject 'the imperialistic impulse to intelligent analysis' with the conclusion: 'you end up feeling battered rather than enlightened.'[43] The reviewers' evaluations of West's staging of the rape scene also indicate a critical preference for tasteful veiling, rather than 'vulgar', or explicit, demonstration. West was judged to have taken a wise decision in staging the rape half-submerged in the pool in the centre of the set, rather than placing it in full view as Bogdanov had chosen to do.[44] Paul Taylor sums up these assessments, as he argues that this change, far from being simply 'prudish', instead ensured that 'the audience is not distracted from the human import of the scene by prurient technical curiosity.'[45]

Intriguingly, when pressed to explain the way in which his directorial approach differed from Bogdanov, West seemed to accept that physical display was a distraction, rather than an integral or significant element of the play. Citing his experience in rehearsal for his decision to limit the amount of nudity in the production, he compared his staging to Bogdanov's production, observing: 'There's less nudity [...] There's a scene where the boys come naked out of the water, for example, and in our production they eventually get dressed, because I realised that – how shall I put this? – no one was listening to the dialogue!'[46] Nonetheless, reviewers in 2006 did acknowledge that the play was *designed* to alarm and disturb, unlike their colleagues twenty-five years earlier. There was broad acceptance that Brenton was utilising the shock value of violent sexual assault and murder in order to make a point. As Benedict Nightingale pointed out, the rape: 'was unpleasant then, is unpleasant now, and is meant to be unpleasant'.[47]

The play's political agenda also received comprehensive critical coverage in 2006. This may be partly explained by the efforts made by both Brenton and West to direct their audience towards the contemporary relevance of the play's depiction of the brutal realities of invasion and occupation. The Crucible's programme included photographs of American troops in Iraq and Israeli forces in Gaza, whilst Brenton hammered home the point in interviews. Referring to the situation in Iraq, he observed:

> Is America our Rome? The Trinovantes, a powerful tribe in what is now Essex and Suffolk, were in an abject alliance with the Romans, just as we are with Washington today. All the way from here to the Iraq-Iran border, an imperial power is barging around the world believing that it alone holds the keys of 'civilisation', as dangerous as Caesar's legions.[48]

West argued likewise: 'it can't not be about Afghanistan, Iraq, Abu Ghraib, Iran, and the imperial attitude that says it's OK to go into another country without being asked.'[49] These parallels were accepted and reiterated by reviewers, almost all of whom made references to the assaults by American soldiers upon Iraqi prisoners in Abu Ghraib prison.

The major contrast between the critical coverage of 1980 and 2006, however, was the overall consensus in 2006 that the revival actually failed to shock.[50] The reviewer for *The Daily Telegraph*, Susan Irvine, noted that West's production was not brutal or shocking enough to communicate the horror of its subject matter, whilst Thomas Sutcliffe commented in *The Independent* that while he would have liked to report that the rape scene horrified him, 'the truth is that I looked on rather dispassionately. If there were emotions in place they were an odd compound of embarrassment and historical curiosity.'[51] Sutcliffe speculated that failure to be shocked by the violence on stage reflected a growing desensitisation to images of violence, suggesting that this lack of strong emotional response might be evidence of the commonplace and widespread representation of scenes of violence in literature, computer games, video and film. Whatever else may have changed, concern over the deleterious effect of exposure to representations of violence remains.

Perhaps this attempt to ascertain whether Whitehouse's intervention into the debate over *The Romans in Britain* can be considered successful or unsuccessful merely demonstrates the inevitable frustration of such an enquiry. On the one hand, her abortive, and much ridiculed, prosecution unquestionably increased general public awareness of Bogdanov's production and did not prevent the show being seen by thousands of theatre-goers during its run at the National. On the other, it seems that fear of prosecution may have been a significant factor in the show's twenty-five year wait for a major professional revival. Whitehouse's lack of engagement with the actual play also raises the possibility that those responsible for explicit acts of censorship may not, in fact, be measuring the success of their intervention in terms of its impact upon the supposed object of their outrage. The success of their actions may instead be calculated in terms of the amount of publicity they generate for their cause or the number of supporters they mobilise.

What we can be sure of, however, is that although state censorship of the theatre had been dismantled, many of its discursive tactics remained in circulation. The rhetoric surrounding *The Romans in Britain* in the early 1980s utilises many of the justificatory strategies employed by the Lord Chamberlain and his staff, as the disapprobation and polemic that greeted Brenton's play reiterates censorious concerns over performance's potential to influence its audience. Whitehouse's denunciation of Bogdanov's production shows that the anxiety that mimesis will turn into mimicry and spill out into real life has been an enduring one.

Moreover, the media's focus upon Whitehouse's objection to the sexually explicit elements of Bogdanov's production obscured both the play's political content and the political agenda of those who called for its removal from the National, just as the Lord Chamberlain's apparent preoccupation with sex served to mask his political interests.[52] The mythology which has grown up around Whitehouse's prosecution has also obscured the other censorious forces at work in the early 1980s: within the National Theatre itself; within the organisations that funded the theatre; within the audience; and, perhaps most importantly, within the media, who were responsible for creating the controversy over the play in the first place.

Comparing the coverage of the play in 1980 with the critical response in 2006 shows us that whilst the play's political agenda has been acknowledged, and Brenton's shock tactics are now considered a legitimate theatrical strategy, the critical establishment continues to show signs of anti-theatrical prejudice and displays enduring concern over the representation of violence. Furthermore, even after a major revival, the play remains synonymous with Whitehouse's prosecution and debates over censorship. Sadly for Brenton, its association with scandal, moral hysteria and media frenzy seems likely to be the most enduring thing about it. The next chapter, however, provides us with a more convincing example of Butler's theory of performative contradiction.

6
Section 28: Contagion, Control and Protest

Section 28 of the British government's 1988 Local Government Act stated that:

(1) A local authority shall not

  a) intentionally promote homosexuality or publish material with the intention of promoting homosexuality;
  b) promote the teaching in any maintained school of the acceptability of homosexuality as a pretended family relationship.

(2) Nothing in subsection (1) shall be taken to prohibit the doing of anything for the purpose of treating or preventing the spread of disease.[1]

With hindsight, this legislation appears crude, badly worded and legally impossible to enforce.[2] For the gay community, however, the message of the legislation was clear; the country's elected representatives were not yet ready to accept the legitimacy of gay lives and would much prefer it if gay men and lesbians returned to the closet.[3] As the first new legal restriction on homosexuality since the nineteenth century, Section 28 was viewed as an example of active discrimination created and sanctioned by government; an endorsement of prejudice, bigotry and homophobia; and as a symbol of the second-class status of gay men and lesbians in society.

The circumstances which led to the introduction of Section 28, and the subsequent reactions to it, have a lot to tell us about why we censor and about the outcomes of censorship. This chapter assesses the impact of the legislation upon theatre, the gay community's reaction to Section 28 and the metaphorical model of communicative efficacy that fuels such acts of censorship. The rationale behind the introduction of Section 28 reveals the broad ideological investment in the metaphors of contagion that we use to discuss the adoption of controversial ideas or identities, whilst the reception of Section 28 indicates the unpredictable – and often paradoxical – results of censorship. On the one hand, examples of the effective silencing of publicly funded gay theatre following the introduction of the legislation indicate the power of constitutive censorship, whilst on the other, the vulnerability of regulative intervention is revealed by the concurrent upsurge in performative protest.

Disease and metaphor

The introduction of Section 28 was closely intertwined with the radical right wing agenda of the Thatcher administration and the vagaries of party politics. Margaret Thatcher's years as Conservative party leader were characterised by an emphasis on moral conservatism that sought to celebrate 'traditional family values'. This was inspired by the 'Victorian values' of self-discipline and restraint and was bound up with opposition to pornography, permissive attitudes towards sexuality and liberal sex education. Until their third term in office, however, Conservative support for this moral agenda had been limited to rhetoric. But warning signs that this hot air might solidify into legislation were present in Mrs Thatcher's address to the Conservative party conference in October 1987. She proclaimed: 'Children who need to be taught to respect traditional moral values are being taught that they have an inalienable right to be gay.'[4]

Conservative party politics were, of course, informed by a wider political climate, and Thatcher may have felt that the homophobic sentiments of Section 28 were likely to prove popular with the electorate during the panicked atmosphere generated by the discovery of the HIV virus. Section 28 also presented the Conservatives with an opportunity to embarrass the Labour party and to limit the powers of local authorities in metropolitan centres such as Manchester and London. Following the example of the Greater London Council, some local authorities had introduced equal opportunities policies for gay and lesbians, and funding for gay and lesbian centres and helplines. Clearly, this was out of step with the government's moral agenda. The Conservatives succeeded in abolishing the Greater London Council in 1986, and in the same year the tabloid press reported that some 'loony left' Labour councils had been funding the distribution of information that presented positive images of gay men and lesbian women.[5] Section 28 can be interpreted as the result of the combination of the Conservative's desire to curb the remaining powers of Labour local authorities and the need to score party political points in the media.

The legislation was controversial from the first. Concerns were raised that the many theatres, arts centres, galleries and cinemas owned or subsidised by local authorities could find themselves subject to legal action, if they happened to stock, display or programme material that might be judged to 'promote' homosexuality. The Arts Council informed Nicholas Ridley, the Environment Secretary, that the proposed legislation was 'dangerously imprecise' and provided him with an alternative wording, which would protect freedom of artistic expression and exclude material which served an artistic, scientific or educational purpose.[6] Significantly, the proposed amendment omitted the word 'promote' – one of the most controversial aspects of Section 28.[7] Critics were swift to pour ridicule on the notion that it is possible to 'promote' homosexuality, asserting that it is impossible to change a young person's sexuality through representation and images.[8] But the wording of the legislation was based upon a deep-seated suspicion of the power of mimesis. This long-established prejudice is sustained by the belief that images are, in some way, contagious: that their influence passes from the fictional or artistic sphere out into the world like a disease or a virus. The habits of language trace this conceptual connection between disease and the object of censorship, as censorious statements surround proscribed material with a terminology of contagion and infection: we talk of being *infected* or *corrupted* by the *diseased* work of a *sick* mind. The superstitious simplicity of this logic may seem easy to reject, and sociological research has long since dispensed with the 'effects model' which attempts to identify a straightforward relationship between stimulus and response in favour of a more sophisticated understanding of the uses that audiences may find for various media they watch, listen to, and read.[9] Conservatives who wish to sanitise representation – cleansing museums, cinemas, broadcasting, music and literature of 'undesirable images' – accredit imagery with remarkable power; equating mimesis with mimicry, and communication with contagion. The result of this schematic logic is increased constraints upon 'undesirable' (or perhaps all too desirable) representations.

Section 28's dependence on this logic was mirrored a few years later by the announcement of a North American congressional statute – discussed by Butler in *Excitable Speech* – which required that homosexuals in the American military should adopt a 'don't ask, don't tell' policy.

This prohibition upon 'coming out' figured, as Butler puts it, 'the very word as a contagious substance, a dangerous fluid'. It conflated speech with conduct, proposing that the statement 'I am a homosexual' is an act and, moreover, an act that that must be proscribed due to its potential to open 'the floodgates' and inspire a compulsive, uncontrollable repetition of further homosexual acts.[10]

Butler's reading of this statute draws upon Freud's analysis of the contagious effect of the breaking of taboo in *Totem and Taboo*, where he notes (in typically androcentric style): 'Anyone who has violated a taboo becomes taboo himself because he possesses the dangerous quality of tempting others to follow his example [...] Thus he is truly contagious in that every example encourages imitation.'[11] But Butler also acknowledges that the logic of contagion which lies behind the statute is based upon fear of Aids. Here Susan Sontag's assessment of disease's double life as metaphor, *Illness as Metaphor* and *Aids and its Metaphors*, may help us understand the reasons for deep-rooted belief in this model of contagious representation, the media hysteria that surrounded the discovery of Aids and the thinking behind both the military statute discussed by Butler and the Section 28 legislation.

Sontag explores the suspicion and superstition that surround ill health and the way in which it is associated with corruption, pollution, decay and weakness. She argues that the metaphorical baggage which accompanies disease is ultimately unhelpful to the sufferer, observing that this process of misguided labelling and categorisation has been exacerbated by the increasing popularity of quasi-psychological interpretations of illness in which disease is seen as speaking through the body, dramatising internal conflict.[12] These interpretations – which ostensibly aim to identify the origin of illness and thus provide a cure – often end up placing blame. Ill health becomes figured as a form of punishment, connected to deficiencies of character, which effectively places responsibility for the ailment upon the patient. Sontag's reading of the response to Aids reflects upon the particularly heavy metaphorical burden carried by outbreaks of disease that are labelled epidemics. She explores the way in which highly contagious diseases become figured as a secret invasion of the body politic by a ruthless, insidious enemy; as an evil, invincible predator, colonising its host and assaulting its defences. Sontag also indicates that epidemics are equated with social disorder and moral corruption – the inheritance, perhaps, of the ancient world's tendency to interpret disease as an instrument of divine wrath and retribution.[13]

In fact, the epidemic carries such weight as a metaphor, that any social problem – drug addiction, alcohol abuse, paedophilia, divorce – can find itself labelled as one. This labelling is used to signal the perceived difference between past health and present sickness, and anxiety about the uncontrollable and inexorable spread of these phenomena. In drawing on this language of contagion and communicability, we are utilising a particular apparatus and logic – a specific method of producing and organising bodies politically. Epidemics demand control, action from the authorities and a forceful effort of management to curtail their spread. Consequently, this metaphor is more than a useful descriptive tool. Describing an outbreak of disease as an epidemic provides a rationale for intervention and surveillance. Insights into this process are to be found in Foucault's work, *Discipline and Punish*, where he cites 'fear of the plague' as the source of the need to classify, categorise, order and oversee.[14] These tactics were plainly at work in the initial response to Aids and were intensified by the way in which the disease often lies dormant for a period before making its presence known. The consequent difficulties in testing for it led to the proposal of extraordinary measures, including compulsory testing, quarantine, mandatory notification of sexual partners and tattooing.[15] This is Foucauldian bio-power at work, as an epidemic provides justification for intervention in everyday life, giving the authorities access to bodies and a rationale for inscribing them.

The potency of the metaphorical language surrounding Aids – which the media initially referred to as the 'gay plague' – should not be underestimated. The word plague, from the Latin *plaga* (stroke, wound), resounds with apocalyptic references. Plague traditionally marks the nadir of calamity – a time of anarchy and chaos, in which fear and death overcome all prior laws and prohibitions. The disorderly antithesis of discipline, it is a synonym for a collective experience of social and psychic catastrophe. Plagues are never simply a medical problem. They pervade the fabric of everyday existence, demanding a reassessment of taken-for-granted habits, values, practices and pleasures. They are also generally characterised as unwelcome imports from abroad and as being fundamentally 'Other'. Aids is no exception. It was branded a tropical disease, spreading from the third to the first world: from Africa via Haiti to the US and then Europe. It was an ideal focus for First World political paranoia, becoming figured as the ultimate illegal immigrant, the quintessential invader from the Third World.

Plague presents us with meaningless death and suffering on a grand scale. In response, many conservative positions are offered as a form of explanatory closure. Not least amongst these rationalisations were assessments of Aids that portrayed the disease as a form of retributive justice, providing a rationale, a form or order to what would appear to be an entirely indifferent spread of contagion.[16] The transmission routes of the disease focused attention on the way our culture has historically constructed and valued sex, and in consequence, conservatives were able to utilise the atmosphere of anxiety in order to reassess the sexual revolution of the 1960s, taking the opportunity to mount a defence of 'family values' – back to basics, no less. Aids was, therefore, figured as the consequence of moral bankruptcy or degeneracy, the result of unsafe behaviour or the product of indulgence and delinquency – addictions to illegal chemicals and/or deviant sex. But as the disease revealed itself as a problem for heterosexuals as well as homosexuals, the convenient labelling of Aids as a disease of 'the Other' – the foreigner or the deviant – came unstuck. Boundary membranes in the body politic – like those in the body personal – were revealed as semipermeable; innocuous, everyday acts found themselves re-categorised as 'risk-taking'; and the distinction between 'us' and 'them', 'Other' and 'Same', could not be maintained. This potent mixture of belief in the influence of imagery, fear of disease and anxiety over the permeability of personal and political boundaries goes some way to explaining the Conservative government's introduction of Section 28. Their rationale: if the virus itself could not be controlled, then the 'promotion' of the lifestyles that were being blamed for it could be.

Constitutive censorship: a climate of uncertainty and caution

Playwrights were swift to anticipate the effect Section 28 could have on their work. Noel Greig, director of the theatre company Gay Sweatshop between 1977–1987, wrote to *The Guardian* in December 1987 in order to register his concern over the possible impact of the proposed legislation on the work he created for theatre-in-education companies. He argued that the Local Government Bill would jeopardise the school tours of his plays planned for the following year and prophesied a wave of bannings and funding cuts.[17] Six weeks later, playwright David Edgar also wrote to protest, taking issue with comments made by Conservative MP David Wilshire, who introduced the Bill in Parliament:

> While confirming that Local Authorities have the right to censor works of art whose production they enable, Mr Wilshire said that his clause was intended to attack only the promotion of homosexuality by publicly funded bodies, but not (of course) its portrayal. The

difference between the two was obvious, he said [...] Well, it may be clear in Mr Wilshire's dictionary, but as a practising playwright I have to tell him that it isn't in mine.

Edgar compared the playwright's art to that of the novelist, observing that the dramatic medium was designed to question different positions and ethics, rather than supplying its audience with a clear-cut moral position:

> Without the comforting authority of the authorial voice, playwrights find themselves in even more difficult territory. [...] not only is it hard to draw the line between presenting, defending, and promoting a character (or a relationship) but often that ambiguity is at the very heart of the dramatic project.[18]

Unsurprisingly, the Conservative government did not pay much attention to these complaints. The amendments proposed by the Arts Council were not incorporated into Section 28, which became law on 24 May 1988.[19]

Section 28 was to have a negative impact upon some forms of theatre, as Noel Greig and David Edgar predicted. Whilst mainstream theatre appeared to be largely unaffected by the legislation, it did create a climate of uncertainty and caution amongst local authorities and schools. Some began to turn down plays and performances that contained gay characters or addressed the issue of homosexuality.[20] Theatre-in-education companies were particularly vulnerable to such decision-making. A report produced in 1997 by Jennifer Edwards, director of the National Campaign for the Arts, outlined Section 28's pernicious legacy. She concluded that theatre-in-education companies had reacted to the legislation by avoiding work by gay writers or plays that represented gay characters or relationships, effectively employing self-censorship.[21] *The Stage* supported Edwards in their leader column, calling for the repeal of the law and observing that the fact that Section 28 had never been used in court actually made it more difficult to tackle. Without recourse to a framework of legal precedent, and lacking expert knowledge in the nuances of theatre-in-education programming, the editorial observed that 'the average councillor' was likely to adopt a policy of 'when in doubt, just say no.' It concluded: 'Section 28's effectiveness has always derived from fear of what it might do, not what it has done.'[22] Of course, theatre companies that included a variety of subjects in their repertoire were free to alter the content of their plays in response to such timidity. A company which concentrated solely on the exploration of gay and lesbian issues would have much greater difficulty overcoming such problems.

In 1990, Gay Sweatshop was the only British theatre company dedicated to the performance of plays about gay and lesbian experience. Founded in 1975, it toured its productions of new writing by gay and lesbian playwrights, performed by all gay and lesbian casts, to small provincial towns. As Philip Osment's history of the company shows, they had become accustomed to dealing with prejudice, bigotry and ignorance.[23] But, writing in 1989, Osment correctly predicted trouble ahead:

> What is certain is that how the company fares in the nineties is very dependent on funding. [...] The Arts Council is currently encouraging their clients to seek out other forms of sponsorship. This is difficult enough for companies that are much more prestigious and much less controversial. It is hard to imagine that commercial sponsorship companies will find kudos in sponsoring Gay Sweatshop. [...] Without adequate Arts Council subsidy there is no guarantee that there will be an ongoing thread of work from these artists in this country.[24]

As Osment foresaw, the Arts Council's decision not to grant the company revenue funding in 1990 resulted in the company's closure. Joint artistic director, David Benedict, was unequivocal in placing the blame for the company's demise on local authorities' increasing unease about being seen to provide support for gay theatre. He observed that bookings from theatres being supported by funding from city councils had become increasingly difficult to obtain, and argued that: 'The creation of gay work [...] is even less prevalent than before [Section 28]. There just aren't gay plays being written [...] Section 28 has legitimised organisations thinking they needn't fund gay work.'[25]

The paradox: performative protest

Butler's observation that repression, exclusion, erasure and abjection are central to the construction of the subject, and her proposal that sexual identities are formed through repudiation, loss and guilt may help us understand the continuing existence of homophobic attitudes and the introduction of censorious legislation such as Section 28. The outcomes of the introduction of Section 28 are, however, not limited to the negative impact they had upon the dramatic representation of gay experience. Section 28 provides us with an excellent example of the performative contradiction which Butler claims is inherent in the regulation that *'states what it does not want stated'* and the vulnerability of explicit acts of prohibition.[26] This act of prohibition resulted in a proliferation of public debate and discourse, in much the same way as the North American congressional statute discussed above, which Butler argues made the term 'homosexual': 'more speakable rather than less'.[27]

Butler's interpretation of the response to this statue is informed by Foucault's formulation of power as productive, rather than simply repressive. After Foucault, Butler argues that power should be understood as a 'a field of productive, regulatory, and contestatory relations', which 'not only consists in the reiterated elaboration of norms or interpellating demands', but is also 'formative or productive, malleable, multiple, proliferative, and conflictual'.[28] Accordingly, Butler's work provides a convincing description of the operation of self-regulation and self-censorship, yet also leaves room for the possibility of resistance and social change, as her understanding of the relationship between power and resistance draws upon Foucault's assertion that 'There are no relations of power without resistances, and these resistances are formed precisely where power is being exercised.'[29] Butler's engagement with this approach to power leads her to conclude that explicit acts of censorship may have inadvertent outcomes. This is undoubtedly true of Section 28.

While Gay Sweatshop and conventional theatre education certainly appear to have been detrimentally affected by the introduction of Section 28, other forms of performance received a positive boost. The legislation provoked vocal opposition from the start. At the bill's first reading, more than 700 gay and lesbian activists gathered at Westminster to lobby their MPs.[30] The next few months were to see a flurry of protest. Large public demonstrations were held across the country, culminating in a march attended by approximately 30,000 protestors in London on 2 May 1988.[31] Protestors even managed to get their voices heard within Parliament. On 3 February 1988, three women abseiled into the House of Lords debating chamber from the public gallery, shouting slogans in protest.[32] When the bill received Royal Assent on 24 May, a similar protest targeted another institution – the Six O'Clock News. *The Guardian* reported:

> The BBC news presenter Sue Lawley calmly brought the nation news [...] last night while her co-presenter Nicholas Witchell was sitting

on a lesbian protestor attempting to stifle her shouts about Clause 28. 'We have rather been invaded', Ms Lawley announced, as the viewers heard muffled shouts, thumps, and the picture began to shake.[33]

Section 28 precipitated the emergence of several pressure groups such as ACT-UP, OutRage! and The Lesbian Avengers, which adopted these confrontational tactics, taking their grievances to the streets in a highly performative, theatrical manner.

ACT-UP was an import from North America, where its logo – a pink triangle on a black background alongside the ultimate anti-censorship statement, 'SILENCE = DEATH' – first appeared in New York in 1986. Their performative protests presented a challenging engagement with the politics of epidemiology, aiming to give a positive voice to a constituency that could easily be positioned as traumatised victims. Initially, the group focused their 'zaps' – swiftly organised and orchestrated theatrical protests – on specific targets, including drugs company Burroughs Wellcome and the American government agency responsible for licensing new drugs, with the intention of drawing the public's attention to the role of the government and the pharmaceutical industry in the development of a cure for Aids.

The movement grew quickly, and the first meeting of the London chapter of ACT-UP took place in January 1989. Their first action also focused upon Burroughs Wellcome, as they invaded the company's Annual General Meeting at Park Lane's Grosvenor House Hotel. The next protest was designed to publicise the Home Office's refusal to fund research on drug taking and homosexuality in prisons. Activists attached safe-sex literature to helium-filled condoms and floated them over the walls of Pentonville Prison. This was followed by actions against targets including the *Daily Mail* (which printed the virulently anti-gay views of columnist George Gale), Benetton for a controversial advertising campaign and Texaco for enforcing HIV testing for all employees. The variety of these targets indicates the broad scope of ACT-UP's ambitions. Focusing on pressing material issues (including extortionate drug pricing, the inaccessibility of drug trials and inadequacy of funding for medical research), they also tackled cultural targets, taking on the weighty issue of biased media coverage. Their activity began to be characterised by a concern with contesting negative, conventional images of those in communities threatened by Aids. For a short period, the organisation succeeded in drawing attention to its message as it disrupted everyday life in the capital. In his account of the British response to Aids, *The End of Innocence*, Simon Garfield recalls Whitehall being brought to a standstill by a demonstration outside the Department of Social Security which was designed to draw attention to inadequate disability benefit and Westminster Bridge being blocked with protestors demonstrating about the closure of the Health Education Authority's Aids unit.[34]

Other organisations picked up where ACT-UP left off in 1990. OutRage! was formed with the stated aim of raising public awareness of issues affecting lesbians and gay men, which were being ignored by the national government and media. Dominated by the figure of political activist Peter Tatchell, they relied heavily on a combination of bold slogans and outrageous events. Their activities were carefully orchestrated in order to include photo opportunities for the press, who were informed of the event and its aims through detailed press releases and handouts.

Humour also had a large part to play in OutRage! demonstrations. They developed a camp and parodic style, which was designed to draw in as many participants as possible, as well as playing to the media gallery. Their approach acknowledged that their demonstrations needed to be highly visual – theatrical, even – in order to catch the attention of

Figure 6.1   OutRage! protest at the Labour Government's failure to deliver equal age of consent legislation at the Pride March in London, 3 July 1999.

news programmers, hence the dramatic, colourful and inventive nature of these protests, in which costume and props played an important role.[35] Whether these organisations were throwing blood at insurance companies, unfurling giant condoms or holding die-ins, the packaging of their message was paramount. As Simon Garfield observes, these protests needed to be simple, witty and disruptive to attract media attention. A few arrests were also useful in this respect.[36]

Some protests also seemed to be using other tactics. Events organised by Outrage! sought to draw attention to institutionalised prejudice and homophobia, and the inequality of British legislation. Couples performing public vows at a queer mass wedding in London's Trafalgar Square on 12 June 1991 made their desire for equal rights clear, both through their presence in a symbolic public space and through the demands their vows included:

> We want the right to cherish each other and legally be each other's next of kin [...]
> We want the right to have and to hold anywhere in the world with full immigration rights
> We want to love each other in sickness and in health with hospital visitation rights
> For richer for poorer with partner's rights and pension rights and insurance schemes
> For better or for worse with full adoption rights
> Until death us do part with full inheritance and tenancy rights.[37]

Earlier in the same year, OutRage! organised a mass 'turn-in' at Bow Street police station, designed to highlight gay men's status as 'sex criminals' under British law. Over 300 protestors attended the demonstration, and 16 men attempted to 'give themselves up' to the police for the 'sex crimes' of soliciting in the street, procuring, and having sex with other men before the legal age of consent.[38]

Here, Butler's redeployment of J.L. Austin's speech act theory provides a useful frame for analysis of these parodic citations of the law. Butler's influential utilisation of Austin's category of the performative in her description of the cultural construction of gender proposes that its dependence upon the repetition – or reiteration – of conventions of behaviour and appearance opens it up to potential re-inscription and reinvention, through which the 'rules' of sexual and gendered identities can be challenged and changed. Butler's later work on hate speech in *The Psychic Life of Power* and *Excitable Speech* extends this concept to propose that terms of abuse such as 'queer' may be reclaimed and restaged, effecting a 'subversive reterritorialisation'.[39] She argues:

> By understanding the false or wrong invocations as reiterations, we see how the form of social institutions undergoes change and alteration and how an invocation that has no prior legitimacy can have the effect of challenging existing forms of legitimacy, breaking open the possibility of future forms.[40]

One of Austin's favourite examples of a successful performative is the wedding vow, as he demonstrates its dependence upon a wider framework of convention. In these protests, the participants' failure to command the power of the law – to bring about the weddings and arrests their actions invoke – provides an eloquent critique of the law's shortcomings.

Aspects of Butler's theories – including the limitations of this form of subversion – have attracted criticism, and they demand more discussion than I can give them here. It is, however, important to remember that Butler recognises the difficulty of working through the traumatic history carried by some terms, which may prove particularly resistant to this work of 'reterritorialisation'.[41] She also observes that the re-citation of reactionary terms does not necessarily result in progressive resignification, acknowledging that the 'risk of renormalisation' always exists.[42]

A sense of these problems is noticeably present in the debate which raged in the gay community over the value of spectacular, attention-seeking protest. One side of this debate is voiced in a substantial article in *The Guardian* on The Lesbian Avengers, an exclusively lesbian pressure group, which was set up in August 1994 with the aim of promoting lesbian visibility. Many of their actions were carried out in reaction to the perceived media misrepresentation of the lesbian community, but they also took a more proactive approach on occasion. In May 1995, they hired an open-top bus and toured the West End to mark Section 28's seventh anniversary. About 50 women participated, making a very public declaration of their sexuality, targeting individual shoppers with remarks directed through a megaphone. As Alex Spillius remarked on his report on the group, their behaviour could hardly be described as evidence of the love that dare not speak its name. It was instead 'one that shouts it full blast from the top of a Routemaster'. Spillius's report reveals the ambivalent reactions to such forms of protest. He reported that other gay activists had questioned the value of the group's activities, airing accusations that without a specific grievance, or anti-lesbian legislation to oppose, its campaigns for lesbian visibility had turned 'into a freak show on wheels'. He also records such responses as: 'What's the point of behaving like football supporters, chanting, "We're lesbian, we're lesbian"? It's just exhibitionism. It doesn't do anything for anybody.'[43]

The tone of Spillius's report is dismissive, and the responses he quotes do not contain any great insight into the issues raised by such activism. But the vagaries of the media's reception and presentation of such protests became the focus of much dissent and disagreement amongst the gay community. Some sections of the community claimed that the protests' reliance upon flamboyance, provocation and transgression alienated potentially sympathetic elements of the general public. Divisions developed between those who supported a measured, assimilationist approach (characterised by Stonewall's discreet lobbying) and those who preferred the more confrontational tactics associated with public demonstrations. The two stances are diametrically opposed; one values adaptation, the other celebrates difference and transgression. Some disowned the actions of ACT-UP and OutRage!, claiming that their extremity generated adverse publicity for the cause of equal rights. These critics were in favour of the use of more conventional forms of protest: campaigning and lobbying. They argued that the strategies of civil disobedience and 'in-your-face' exposure misrepresented gay identity and served to cement homophobic prejudice rather than disarming it.[44]

This dissent over techniques of self-representation represents an important interrogation of simplistic representational politics that relate visibility to empowerment and indicates awareness of the double-edged nature of representation: an issue addressed by Peggy Phelan's work, *Unmarked: the Politics of Performance*. Phelan rejects the simple 'greater visibility, greater empowerment' equation, in favour of assessing the underlying links which exist between political power and the achievement of visibility in the representational sphere. She suggests that we have set up a false binary opposition between the power of visibility and the impotency of invisibility, as she argues that the disclosure of previously unseen imagery of other cultures, identities and practices can work as a form of hegemonic control and that inappropriate display can result in a speedy and negative reification of the newly exposed.[45] As we saw in chapter three, the increasing visibility of lesbianism in the public sphere during the 1930s was accompanied by tighter regulation, and the images of lesbian and gay protest which circulated in the media during the 1980s often seemed to support the Conservative case for Section 28, rather than the campaign against it. *The Star*, for example, greeted the protest on the Six O'Clock News with the headline: 'Loony Lezzies Attack TV Sue'.[46] The value of such coverage is surely questionable, as it may be seen to reinforce prejudice rather than combating it. Visibility can have disadvantages. As Phelan observes, before exposure, we should ask the questions: 'Visible to whom? Who is looking and who is seen?'[47]

In a reading which draws upon feminist theories of spectatorship and the male gaze, Phelan argues that invisibility is usually associated with ideological centre-point or the masculine norm. Phelan aligns the invisible position with masculinity, and the visible Other with femininity, as she observes:

> Cultural reproduction takes she who is unmarked and re-marks her, rhetorically and imagistically, while he who is marked with value is left unremarked, in discursive paradigms and visual fields. He is the norm and therefore unremarkable; as the Other, it is she whom he marks.[48]

Phelan asks us to think again about the relationship between the visible and the invisible, and the power inherent in each position, suggesting that visibility should not be celebrated as a value in and of itself. But what are we to do with this insight? Despite the vulnerability and risk inherent in public exposure, it would be pointless to suggest that gay men and lesbians return to the closet. The gay community would have been incapable of contesting the introduction of Section 28 from such a location. Consequently, it seems that valorisation of invisibility is the weak point in Peggy Phelan's work, *Unmarked*. Not everyone has a choice about whether to remain visible or invisible, and as a consequence debates over whether the marked or unmarked position is stronger politically are rather compromised by their assumption that this is a matter of strategy. Similarly, those who have never enjoyed the luxury of self-expression may not be so enthusiastic about silence.

Phelan is aware of this argument and concedes, 'there is no real power in remaining unmarked.' She also acknowledges the pragmatic appeal of visibility politics:

> There is a deeply ethical appeal in the desire for a more inclusive representational landscape and certainly under-represented communities can be empowered by enhanced visibility, [...] Visibility politics

have practical consequences; a line can be drawn between a practice (getting someone seen or read) and a theory (if you are seen it is harder for 'them' to ignore you, [...]); the two can be reproductive.[49]

The swell of activism that followed the introduction of Section 28 disrupted the legislation's wider aim: the removal of representations of gay identity from the public sphere. Retrospective assessments of this period agree that it was characterised by greater public visibility of gay and lesbian identities. Celebrities such as Ian McKellen took the opportunity to 'come out' in solidarity with the cause, whilst the wider gay community also decided to exercise its political muscle.[50] The consensus seems to be that the gay community has actually been strengthened by the adversity they experienced in the 1980s. Philip Osment, theatre practitioner and former member of Gay Sweatshop observes:

> Gay people are now presenting culture about our lives with a new assurance which is without any trace of apology. This confidence arises out of a shared awareness of our worth that the Aids crisis and Section 28 have only made stronger.[51]

The continuing success of annual Pride festivals in metropolitan centres across the country provides a visible register of this new sense of confidence, and in 1998, Mark Watson, Stonewall's campaign director, observed that Section 28 'had the reverse effect of what Thatcher intended [...] She hoped that we would quietly disappear. Instead, we became more visible than ever.' Correspondingly, Martin Bowley, QC and chairman of the Bar Lesbian and Gay Group, commented that – quite inadvertently – the Conservative government had 'unleashed an unstoppable momentum for reform'.[52]

These reforms have seen the removal of Section 28, which was repealed in Scotland in 2000 and in England and Wales in 2003, and recent years have seen a move towards the lifting of legislation that may be interpreted as using sexual preference as grounds for discrimination. The gay age of consent was brought down to sixteen in 2000, and 2005 saw the introduction of the Civil Partnerships Act, giving gay and lesbian couples who choose to register their relationship the legal rights which the Outrage! mass wedding had demanded back in 1991. In 2007, the introduction of legislation which would outlaw the incitement of hatred against lesbians and gays was proposed by the government.[53]

The picture is not entirely rosy, however. Critics recorded the 'uneven development' of the lesbian and gay movement during the 1990s,

Figure 6.2   OutRage! protest at the House of Lords' blockage of the equal age of consent legislation at the Pride March in London, 3 July 1999.

measuring activism's success in raising the profile of gay men and lesbians against an increase in 'queer bashing'.[54] Twenty years after the introduction of Section 28, homophobia still makes its presence felt in brutal crimes such as the murder of Jody Dobrowski on Clapham

Common in October 2005.[55] Even the legislation which has been passed in recent years has been subject to sustained opposition in Parliament: the Labour government invoked the rarely used Parliament Act in 2000 to force the long-delayed Sexual Offences (Amendment) Act – which brought the gay age of consent down to 16 – through an uncooperative House of Lords. Section 28 also remained controversial to the last. Its repeal in Scotland in 2000 was preceded by a 'Keep the Clause' campaign and a privately organised referendum. In England and Wales the new 2003 Local Government Act, which finally repealed the Section, was obstructed in the House of Lords.

Of course, there is real difficulty in establishing a direct link between public protest and changes in government policy or shifts in wider social attitudes. Such changes are unlikely to follow on directly from any given campaign or event, and even seemingly speedy legislative progress may be precipitated by other concerns on the part of the policy makers. This indeterminacy of influence is the element ignored by metaphors of contagion and contamination. No matter how prescriptive the words or images we produce, we cannot predict how they will be received or what action they may precipitate. This resistance to empirical measurement provides both the most satisfying repudiation of models of communicative contagion and the most profound challenge to the activists who have to trust that their plural acts of resistance will have the desired outcome.

7
Capital Constraint: The Right to Choose?

Overlooking the impact and influence of capital would be to ignore one of the most significant constitutive factors conditioning the realisation of every theatrical production. Theatre has always been dependent upon a mixture of commercial backing, charitable support, governmental funding and the financial commitment of the individuals who create it. Our mixed economy supports a complicated, heterogeneous network of funding institutions who may work to support and sustain, on the one hand, whilst also constraining and conditioning, on the other. Most theatre-goers, however, cannot be expected to know much about the financial framework behind the spectacle on stage. Acknowledgements and advertisements in programmes may indicate who the parties involved are, and yet the drama of pursuit and negotiation between artists and funders remains a largely private affair; the exact nature of the support given, and the compromises that had to be made in order to secure it, are usually not public knowledge. We may even attend venues that are named after individuals, families or companies without a moment's reflection on the provenance of the names that hang above their doors.

The detail of theatre's financial arrangements usually only enters the public realm when reductions in state funding become a pressing issue for the theatre industry. As a result, the relationship between funding and creativity is often presented in terms of straightforward cause and effect, in rhetoric that paints a stark picture of the disastrous results of funding cuts. This was evident in the reaction to the announcement of a 35% – or £29,000,000 – drop in the Arts Council's Grants for the Arts scheme in March 2007, which was swiftly followed by warnings that this cut would have a cataclysmic effect on the infrastructure of British theatre, resulting in the devastation of the national touring network and the destruction of opportunities for the development of new work.[1] The employment of a mechanistic model of cause and effect is entirely understandable in the context of a vociferous campaign against cuts. But it skates over the difficulties of establishing the links between finance, content and creativity. It may be relatively straightforward to come up with a set of figures, but it is much more challenging to ascertain the exact impact and influence of funding upon content.

This chapter's case studies concentrate upon three unusual moments in 1998 and 1999 when the links between finance and content were exposed to public scrutiny, providing us with the opportunity to examine their relationship. The first covers the reaction of Calder's Cream Ale to the adverse media coverage attracted by Diane Dubois's play, *Myra and Me*, which was programmed at a venue they were sponsoring at the Edinburgh Festival Fringe. This illustrates business's potential to function as censor once given a sponsorship role. The second case study assesses the Arts Council of Northern Ireland's (ACNI's) decision to remove funding from a piece of community drama, *Forced Upon Us*; while the third scrutinises the relationship between the Jerwood Foundation and the Royal Court Theatre, demonstrating that even charitable institutions can operate as agents of constraint. These case studies indicate the need for a full-scale study into the economics of the British theatre industry in the twentieth and twenty-first centuries; a study that would provide comprehensive assessment and analysis of business correspondence, financial reports, contracts and records of incorporation. Tracy C. Davis's *The Economics of the British Stage* provides a model for this kind of research, and her introduction to this detailed investigation into the economics of the nineteenth-century theatre delivers eloquent advocacy of the importance of finance in theatre history. As she notes, 'Pretending that representation is not in league with markets, promoters, and technologies – the usual purview of business and economic history – and that capital is not behind them all, is to clash the cymbals [. . . and] throw a handful of fairy dust.'[2] Full engagement with the economics of the British stage during this period lies beyond the scope of this chapter, but the impact and influence of capital is too central to the study of theatre and censorship to be omitted here.

It is important to acknowledge, however, that describing decisions over funding as censorship can be divisive, as indicated by the heated debate which greeted Howard Barker's claim that he and his company, the Wrestling School, had been made victims of censorship following the removal of their Arts Council grant in June 2007.[3] Some contributors to this debate spoke up in support of Barker's position; others argued that the Arts Council's decision to cut this grant was the result of their failure to value Barker's work, rather than a desire to see it silenced, and that the removal of funding should not be equated with censorship in any case. Others asserted that subsidy is not a right or an entitlement but a gift and a privilege, and applying the term in this way detracted from genuine acts of censorship. As Rae Langton puts it,

> If censorship is everywhere, there is no point in making distinctions. If censorship is everywhere, there is no point in saying that some people are silenced, some are not; some are silenced at some times, not at others; some are silenced here, but not there; some are silenced in a bad way, some in an innocent way. If censorship is everywhere, it might as well be nowhere.[4]

One way of responding to this accusation would be to create an analytical distinction between 'hard' and 'soft', or explicit and implicit, forms of censorship. Yet Butler argues persuasively against setting up such a conceptual division. She suggests that we think of different forms of censorship existing on a continuum, partly because there are many examples of censorship that rest in the middle of this range, including both explicit and implicit aspects. She also proposes that this middle ground requires particular attention, observing that:

> the masquerading or fugitive forms of censorship that have both explicit and implicit dimensions are perhaps the most conceptually confusing, and, by virtue of that confusion, may be most politically effective. When we cannot tell whether or not speech is censorious, whether it is the vehicle for censorship, that is precisely the occasion in which it works its way unwittingly.[5]

In the area of theatre finance it is often difficult to tell whether speech is censorious, and it is easy to see how taking decisions to remove controversial claims, or sexually explicit or violent scenes, may be named or labelled as something else: good business sense, reasonable co-operation with funding bodies or sensitive negotiation of the demands of the market. These strategic elisions, however, only serve to obscure the enormous influence wielded by funding bodies and sponsors. Nevertheless, the case studies covered in this chapter raise the question of the definition of censorship perhaps more starkly than any other controversy discussed in this book and require us to engage with the problems raised by such a broad definition of censorship.

The removal of Owen O'Neill's comic monologue, *Off My Face*, from the Manchester Irish Festival programme in March 1998 following objections from the festival's sponsors, Guinness, highlights these problems and raises the question of whether we are describing a coherent ontological category when we declare an act or decision as censorious or whether we are judging those who are responsible for it. O'Neill's monologue addressed the comedian's problems with alcoholism, and Guinness presented their decision as good business sense: the natural reaction of an industry protecting its commercial interests. A spokesperson for the Association for Business Sponsorship of the Arts justified the company's actions in terms of their 'rights', observing that companies have the right to choose which projects they wish to support.[6] This may seem unarguable. But whether we accept that an individual or an institution has the 'right to choose' is, of course, central to definitions of censorship.

Frederick Schauer's acute analysis of the operation of constitutive forms of censorship highlights this issue, as he asks why some acts of selection and editing are deemed appropriate and uncontroversial, and others attract condemnation. Using the examples of librarians, curators in museums and galleries, and teachers and professors, he demonstrates that certain professions are assigned the right to determine content: the right to make some books, artworks, artefacts and information publicly available whilst excluding others. The perceived autonomy of educational and artistic institutions, and the authority of professional expertise, legitimate these acts of exclusion: when we do not recognise the authority of the individual or institution involved we label similar acts censorship.[7] Schauer's analysis explains why the three diverse cases outlined in this chapter generated such controversy. In each, the autonomy of an artistic institution is apparently threatened by the imposition of commercial, moral or political considerations: concern over adverse press coverage; the protection of commercial interests; or the support of a broader social policy. Schauer's discussion usefully reminds us, however, that academic or artistic institutions are not ideologically neutral zones. Certainly, the examination of moments where partnerships between arts organisations and funding institutions have soured indicates that both funders and theatre practitioners have their own distinct ideological agendas. Even the criteria we use to describe artistic excellence are the product of a particular politics. Perhaps we only judge institutions to be operating autonomously when their values are so in tune with our own that they have become invisible to us.

Consequently, it is significant that the controversies over public and private funding considered in this chapter took place at a moment of political change, when public debates over how the arts should be financed had a particular urgency. Theatre practitioners, venue managers and producers the country over were waiting to see whether the new Labour government's apparent enthusiasm for the arts would translate into a more generous approach to subsidy. They had good reason to expect significant change. The Conservative party's arrival in power, nearly twenty years earlier, had resulted in a substantive shift in policy. Just three months after the election in 1979, the Conservative arts minister Norman St John Stevas announced that the arts world needed to accept the fact that government policy had 'decisively tilted away from the expansion of the public to the private sector'. Though he insisted that the government intended to continue to support the arts, he observed: 'we look to the private sphere to meet any shortfall and to provide immediate means of increase.'[8]

His party did its best to live up to this early rhetoric. During the long period of Conservative rule centralised state subsidy for the arts – which had risen steadily during the 1960s and 1970s – was reduced through cuts and funding freezes. At the same time, corporate patronage and business sponsorship were encouraged, leading to substantial increases in business involvement in arts funding. In 1976, business sponsorship of the arts was reported as a mere £600,000. By 2000, the figure being cited was £150 million.[9]

During this period these figures – and others like them – were frequently cited in the context of largely futile protests about the deleterious effects of cuts in state funding. These complaints were made with renewed vigour as the arts industry lobbied the new Labour government, making a strong case for future increases in public subsidy and careful reassessment of the role of business sponsorship. In 1998, the National Campaign for the Arts presented the new Labour government with a report titled 'Theatre in Crisis'. It argues that small companies and regional repertory theatres had been particularly hard hit by a succession of grant cuts, the systematic removal of project funding and the 'stand still' funding freezes of the early 1990s. The report's authors assert that the regional reps are now at crisis point, losing both their local, regional flavour and control of their creativity as they are forced to cut back on education and outreach work, as well as new productions and cast sizes. They argue that theatres are shelving experimental work in favour of less risky ventures and relying upon filling programmes with touring companies rather than producing their own material. The report warns that the repertory theatre's special position as a focus for the local community – engaging with local issues and working with children and young people – is being undermined by these efforts to control costs.[10] The report's conclusions were echoed in 1999 in a briefing from the Theatres Trust, and then again in the Boyden Report, commissioned by Arts Council England, which followed a year later. Both advised that the steady erosion of public funding was turning the theatre into a conservative and formulaic medium.[11]

It is hard to argue with the conclusions of these reports, and most academic discussion of the period does not do so. Retrospective analysis of the relationship between economics and the theatre has been profoundly influenced by enduring resentment of the policies implemented by the Conservatives during their time in office from 1979 to 1997. Keith Peacock's *Thatcher's Theatre*, John Bull's *Stage Right* and John McGrath's *The Bone Won't Break: On Theatre and Hope in Hard Times* are representative of a deep sense of the destructiveness of the Thatcherite approach to arts funding. Bull lays the blame for British theatre's 'malaise' in the early 1990s directly at the door of the government's monetarist policies, and McGrath accuses the Thatcher government of 'cultural terrorism', as he describes the changes wrought in the cultural landscape:

> The source of funding and guidance for most of the new theatre work of the 70s, the Arts Council, was gutted from top to bottom, and left, gutless, in the life-extinguishing grip of the then Sir William Rees-Mogg. The whole blossoming bough of popular theatre, which was all set to achieve so much for British theatre, was clumsily hacked off. Ideological repression and fiscal misery combined to change the geography of the arts.[12]

Thatcher's emphasis upon commerce was never popular in the arts world. Even those at the centre of the British theatre establishment shared McGrath's perspective. Richard Eyre (artistic director of the National Theatre for the period 1988–1997) proposed that the ideological beliefs of the Conservative party were inimical to the preservation of local or regional theatre work. He foregrounded the incompatibility of Thatcherite values and the concept of subsidised theatre in an interview in *The Observer*, in which he concentrates on the negative impact of monetarist ideology and, like McGrath, draws upon an environmental metaphor:

> The whole network of publicly funded theatre is based on the notion of community – within a region, within a town. But that notion has been eroded by a society in which the very molecules in the air are charged with avarice and self-interest. People have been encouraged to view the notion of public funding as old hat and contemptible [...] Now more than ever, we who work in publicly funded theatre inhabit a uniquely impossible financial ecology.[13]

These responses reflect an abiding resistance to the notion of business involvement in theatre and are representative of the deeply ingrained liberal-humanist belief that the arts require protection from market forces and political interference, because they are both morally and spiritually improving: that their value cannot and should not be reduced to pounds and pence.[14]

The idea that theatre's value was to be defined by a free market philosophy of self-sufficiency and profit making was anathema to many practitioners and cultural commentators, who saw the ideological shift towards the commodification of culture as a form of corruption. Writing in 1985, reviewer Michael Billington complained that the way in which the term 'investment' was coming to replace 'subsidy' amounted to a debasement of the language of the arts.[15] And it was not only a matter of the language being used. Business involvement was seen by some to be inimical to the creation of controversial, challenging work. In *Stage Right*, Bull maintains that business's preoccupation with profit makes it intrinsically incompatible with theatre that seeks to disrupt the status quo. He observes that the presence of corporate sponsorship in the subsidised sector is likely to have serious implications for politically committed theatre, noting 'it is difficult to imagine a multinational company fronting the production of a play that was, let us say, overtly critical of the workings of multinational capitalism.'[16]

A lot has changed since the publication of Bull's book in 1994. Today, young British theatre practitioners are happy to discuss their involvement with big business.[17] But the depth of our attachment to the notion that there should be a separation between the spheres of business and art is indicated by the way this belief persists, even when radical thought eschews other orthodoxies. Baz Kershaw, for example, rejects simplistic models of economic cause and cultural effect in his carefully considered article, 'Discouraging Democracy: British Theatre and Economics, 1979–1999'. He presents several different ways of interpreting the outcomes of arts policies during this period and concludes that the story of British theatre and economics:

> would be more reassuring if it had shown straightforward causal effects in operation, for instance state fiscal policies producing structural economic change in the theatre sectors. But in a globalised world everything is part of a complex interdependence which renders nothing straightforward, so that it becomes increasingly difficult to identify primary controlling factors – whether in the theatre or the economy – with any confidence.[18]

Kershaw's conclusions were echoed a few years later by critic Aleks Sierz. Writing in 2003 – when British theatre was dealing with a sudden abundance of funding, rather than shortages – Sierz troubles the commonsense notion that there is 'a direct relation between money going in, and talent coming out', as he asks how we account for the upsurge of creativity in new writing in the mid 1990s: a time of financial hardship in the theatre industry.[19] Sierz weighs up the problems and possible benefits of limited funding, as he accepts that 'being poorly funded often means poor production values and tiny audiences' and that 'scarcity of funding can close theatres'. He also claims, however, that this scarcity 'can also help liberate creative energies', observing that although British theatre is now 'thoroughly commercialised', 'it may be that creative energy intensifies when people do things "improperly", unofficially'.[20]

Both Kershaw and Sierz acknowledge the increasing dominance of commercial values in British theatre, and yet still insist upon performance's potential to disrupt and critique our social and economic regimes. Kershaw argues that 'the commodity is always open to transformation into a weapon of radicalism', whilst Sierz concludes by quoting John Elsom:

> it's good to remember the sheer perversity of British theatre, its astonishing capacity to survive – whatever subsidies are granted or withheld, British theatre can perhaps still 'best be celebrated as a triumph of the human spirit over various schemes for its better organisation and improvement'.[21]

If nothing else, it seems our belief that theatre can prove resistant to commercial and political imperatives is extraordinarily resilient.

Besides, the belief that art should operate autonomously is not only held by reviewers, artists and scholars. The published proceedings of a large international symposium on 'Cultural Policy and Management in the United Kingdom', held at the University of Warwick in 1995, indicate that it has informed discussion and debate over corporate sponsorship amongst the business community. Speakers including Ugo Bacchella (President of Fondazione Fitzcarraldo, an Italian centre for cultural policy research) voiced concern over the increasing dependence of the arts upon industry and commerce, arguing that corporate sponsorship's tendency to favour large, established arts institutions was producing further imbalance in the dispersal of funding, whilst small companies could be inappropriately influenced by the priorities of their sponsors.[22] Bacchella's anxious exposition was challenged by spokesperson for the Association for Business Sponsorship of the Arts, Andrew McIlroy, who denied that corporate sponsors were trying to interfere in artistic decisions. He commented:

> We do not see significant evidence of sponsorship constraining artistic planning, and I think the main reason for this is that the business community in the UK would admit that they do not know much about it. In other words, the business community has tended to allow the arts to make the artistic decisions, while it makes the business decisions. A significant number of businesses have sponsored difficult or challenging works, and although I do not think we can expect that to become the normal situation in the UK, I do not think that the business community is particularly frightened of getting involved in controversial or innovative activities.[23]

On the page it is easy to read the cautious caveats contained in McIlroy's comments, and with hindsight his rebuttal of Bacchella's concerns seems over-confident: the years immediately following the conference provided evidence of censorious intervention by sponsors, as we shall see. But his insistence that business and the arts operate autonomously reflects a set of beliefs about the appropriate relationship between art and commerce that are widely shared.

Quite how widely these beliefs are held is illustrated by the controversy over the production of *Myra and Me* by Diane Dubois, which was originally programmed to appear at the Gilded Balloon, one of the main venues at the Edinburgh Festival Fringe. The actions of the venue's sponsors demonstrate the problems that can arise when businesses find themselves supporting controversial work, and the case provides further evidence of the paradoxical outcomes of some explicit acts of censorship, as well as showing the popular press playing the role of provocateur once again, encouraging and creating an act of censorship.

The press, the brewer, and *Myra and Me*

The tabloid press started a campaign against *Myra and Me* some three weeks before the Hull-based Northern Theatre Company were due to perform the play. The commentary quickly reached a hysterical pitch. *The Sun* referred to the play as 'twisted and sick', while the *Daily Mail* quoted Ann West (whose daughter was murdered by Hindley and Ian Brady) as saying that the theatre company would need police protection because of the large numbers of friends and supporters they had in Edinburgh.[24] The press coverage repeatedly returned to the idea that the play represented an unacceptable commercial exploitation of Hindley's crimes. In a report labelled 'Monster Hindley gets Star Billing at Fringe', the *Scottish Daily Record* made much of the company's decision to send a copy of the script to Hindley, along with a request to use her infamous police identity photograph, whilst an accompanying editorial fumed: 'Seeking her permission to use her notorious mug shot to publicise the sick spectacle shows how low they [the company] will stoop for cheap sensationalism.'[25]

The language of this polemic implies that the producers of the play are using Hindley's name in order to profit from its shock value: that they are 'only in it for the money'.[26] Protestors echoed this belief. A letter sent by Margaret Watson of the organisation Justice for Victims (Scotland) to the venue managers, quoted by the press, reflects the belief that the company is primarily motivated by financial gain, as it asked them to put the families of Hindley's innocent victims before greed.[27]

The company rejected these accusations of profiteering. The playwright, Diane Dubois, justified the play's use of Hindley's name, contending: 'I don't think this is tasteless or sensationalist and it isn't intended as a publicity device.' She claimed that she had found the play 'very troubling to write' and that she had no intention of causing 'any grief'.[28] Her insistence upon her sincerity and the play's serious intent went largely unheeded, however, perhaps because the actual content of the play was of no interest to the press. Condemnation of *Myra and Me* began long before its performance in Edinburgh, and none of its detractors had seen or read it. Had they done so, their objections would not, perhaps, have been based upon assertions that the play would

glamorise or glorify Hindley, or that it was an insensitive exploitation
of her crimes. Hindley's presence in the play is a distant one. Far from
being a biographical treatment of Hindley's life, the piece focuses upon
the intertwining stories of a group of five graduates and centres upon a
young woman who is attempting to write a television documentary on
Myra Hindley. Her moral qualms about the project frame an interrogation of our ability to deal with traumatic events, as the play asks how
we cope with the eruption of violence in everyday life.

Still, the media furore proved to be more than the sponsors of the
Gilded Balloon could bear. Calder's Cream Ale pressured Karen Koren,
the venue's artistic director, to drop the play from the venue's programme by threatening to withdraw their funding. Koren was critical
of the corporation's demands and yet had little choice but to comply.
The final outcome of this case indicates the unpredictable results of censorious intervention, however. The high profile press coverage the play
received provided invaluable pre-production publicity at a festival where
fringe productions often struggle to find audiences, and the company
managed to secure a last-minute slot at the Assembly Rooms: one of the
most popular theatre venues at the festival. The media coverage enabled
the play's transfer to a more prestigious venue, while Calder's were able
to report that they were 'comfortable with it being moved', rather than
having to fend off accusations of censorship.[29] Nonetheless, the sponsor's reaction to the controversy over *Myra and Me* presents a challenge
to Andrew McIlroy's firm rejection of the notion that commercial sponsors can operate as agents of artistic constraint. The actions of Calder's
Cream Ale show that business sponsors can – and do – wield censorious
powers.

Forced Upon Us: priorities and policy

The subsidy provided by the Arts Councils has often been thought
of as providing a space for artistic development and innovation, free
from immediate commercial constraints and resistant to the kind of
censorious pressures which were brought to bear upon the Gilded
Balloon. Comments made by Philip Howard in 2002, during his time
as artistic director of Edinburgh's Traverse Theatre, are representative
of this approach. He alludes to the 'arms length' principle – the commitment to a clear division between the artistic priorities of the Arts
Councils and the immediate political interests of the governing political party – as he describes public subsidy as 'a democratic antidote to the
marketplace, where the paymasters pull all the strings' and observes: 'It's

a mark of democracy for a culture to subsidise the artist even if the artist doesn't support the establishment.'[30]

Five years later, the notion that public subsidy provides a neutral ideological space, untouched by the values of the political establishment, seemed rather dated. Debate provoked by the announcement of funding cuts early in 2007 revealed that many artists believed that Arts Council policy was primarily driven by the delivery of the government's social agendas, as its emphasis upon education and outreach programmes reflected an increasingly utilitarian approach to the arts.[31] In fact, maintaining the fiction that the administration of public arts subsidy takes place in an ideological vacuum has always been a difficult, if not impossible, task. These difficulties were highlighted by the response to the decision taken by the ACNI to remove its funding from Dubbeljoint theatre company in the run up to their production of *Forced Upon Us* in July 1999.

Forced Upon Us was a joint production between Dubbeljoint and JustUs, a community drama group, and was planned for performance at the annual West Belfast festival, Féile an Phobáil. Written by Christine Poland and former IRA prisoner Brenda Murphy, the play presents a strongly republican portrait of the formation of the Northern Irish state, depicting a cover-up of a massacre of Catholics in 1922 by the Royal Ulster Constabulary, as well as earlier injustices. The play makes no attempt to be even-handed, and concentrates upon the injuries inflicted upon the Catholic community by the Unionists. Local reporter Malachi O'Docherty – who was critical of the Arts Council's actions – acknowledged: 'In it all Catholics are fine family folk, all Protestants either manipulative, cynical self-servers from the fringes of an arcane squirearchy or mad dog, cut-throat bigots, if not hunchback to boot.'[32]

Dubbeljoint were informed shortly before the play's production that the ACNI would be withholding their funding from the show. British and Irish playwrights (including John McGrath, Frank McGuinness and Trevor Griffiths) were quick to condemn the ACNI's actions and wrote to *The Guardian* to protest against the decision, denouncing it as unacceptable political interference with the freedom of artistic expression.[33] Controversy raged over whether or not the ACNI's decision had been taken on political grounds. Many had no doubt that this was the case. Sinn Fein leader Gerry Adams declaimed: 'It is not the responsibility of the Arts Council to act as "thought police" to decide what is and is not "acceptable" or "proper" drama.'[34] The ACNI maintained, however, that the decision to withdraw the funding – worth £18,000 – was taken on aesthetic grounds.

Philip Hammond, the Council's director of performing arts asserted that the ACNI's decision was not politically motivated:

> The Arts Council remains unconvinced that this script reaches the artistic standard expected from the professional theatre companies it supports. We are under an obligation to protect public funding. [...] The Arts Council isn't in the business of censorship. We only give out money on an artistic basis.[35]

Extracts from reports by a panel of anonymous ACNI assessors were leaked to the press, with the aim, presumably, of silencing further criticism. The reports attacked the play's characterisation and the quality of the writing, commenting that it was 'shockingly distasteful and exploitative' and a 'clumsy propagandist play [that] could only serve to deepen existing prejudices'. Pam Brighton, the play's director, seized upon these revelations, arguing that they demonstrated that the ACNI's decision was based upon political, rather than aesthetic grounds, and that they were embarrassed to be seen to be funding a production with an explicitly nationalist perspective. She asserted: 'This is an appalling situation. It is censorship. They are trying to destroy us by a process of financial attrition.'[36] This conflict reveals the fundamental paradox of Arts Council funding. The 'arm's length' principle explicitly asserts the autonomy of the funding institution – ensuring that ministers cannot intervene directly in individual funding decisions – but the completion of the tasks of distinguishing both between projects which are worth funding and those which are not, and establishing hierarchies of value – categorising, prioritising, selecting and rejecting – is only made possible by the existence of a set of shared values – values which are inevitably saturated with political ideology.

The Arts Council of England's 'National Policy for Theatre in England', published in 2000, provides a good example of the way in which the Labour government's wider policies on social inclusion have come to be reflected in the designation of funding priorities for the theatre. As might be expected, the policy retains an emphasis upon quality and the need to maintain the international reputation of British theatre, but it also foregrounds the need to extend access to the theatre, highlighting the importance of engaging with new and more diverse audiences. The connection to the government's wider policy on social inclusion is explicit: 'It must connect with people who have been excluded.' To this end, the work's 'relevance to its audience' is identified as a high priority. In addition, the policy states that the Arts Council will be seeking to 'encourage the unique local voice of theatre that combines quality with the edge that comes from making work in, and for, a particular community. Theatre companies and agencies should provide a meaningful contribution to the life of the community in which they exist.'[37] The difficulty of matching rhetoric to action when providing funding for community projects, however, is reflected in the controversy surrounding the ACNI's decision to withhold funding from *Forced Upon Us*.

Indeed, *Forced Upon Us* could be presented as a model of local, community-based work, and a strong line of argument in its defence focused upon its 'relevance to its audience'. The playwrights whose letter of protest to the press first brought news of the controversy to a broader public insisted that the play should be judged by its audiences, and Pam Brighton also sought to justify her production on these grounds, noting that they had been very positive about the play. Still, it is hardly surprising that *Forced Upon Us* was well received at the West Belfast festival; these supportive audiences were found during the play's performance in a venue just off the Falls Road, a well-known nationalist stronghold. Eoin O'Broin's review points out that the play provides this community with an interpretation of history which is in tune with its feelings and politics.[38]

Forced Upon Us could be celebrated as an excellent example of the kind of community-based project which the new British government appeared to be keen to promote. But the controversy over Dubbeljoint's politically committed, partisan work reveals the conflicting values inherent in such an approach to arts funding. The funding body will necessarily experience a split between responsibility to the audience that receives the end product and the wider community whose tax contributions pay for the grants; in other words, those who are seated in the auditorium may be delighted with the performance, but the wider community may not be prepared to accept such a use of public funds. The debate over *Forced Upon Us* failed to clarify which community subsidy is expected to serve.

This confusion reflects a wider lack of consensus over the primary aim of arts funding. On the one hand, those responsible for the administration of arts subsidy clearly retained their traditional commitment to supporting excellence, providing the country with flagships of artistic achievement, development and innovation. On the other, the 1997 Labour Party Manifesto made it clear that the arts should be instrumental in supporting public policy: 'The Arts are central to the task of recreating our sense of community, identity and civic pride that should define our country.'[39] The tension between the two approaches was reflected in off-the-cuff remarks by the Education Secretary, David Blunkett, who told a conference of head teachers in Birmingham in 1998 that Mark Ravenhill's acclaimed play, *Shopping and Fucking*, should not receive public funding. He attacked the play's use of strong language, and declaimed:

> Shakespeare didn't need that did he? [...] We don't want to shock all the time. We should be creating a society of civilised human beings by teaching democracy, citizenship and spiritual values. [...] I don't know how much the British Council is spending on supporting this tour. But if they are spending a penny on it, it is a penny too much [...] I don't think it is a good example of the best of British.[40]

Reporters were quick to point out that Chris Smith, the Culture Secretary, had praised the play, and made much of this ministerial 'Culture Clash'. Yet Blunkett's blunder is indicative of more than the difficulty of keeping MPs 'on-message'. It also indicates the lack of consensus at the governmental level over the function of public arts subsidy and reflects the truly *reactionary* nature of the highly publicised controversies explored above. In these cases, the actions of the institutions involved were obviously improvised and impromptu, resulting in an easily followed trail of adverse publicity. But when an institution's right to pick and choose becomes a matter of contractual right, it may become difficult, or even impossible, to detect the operation of censorious decision making. Here, the Jerwood Foundation's involvement in the Royal Court Theatre exemplifies the way in which the right of a sponsor to exercise influence over artistic content can be built into a theatre company's creative constitution.

Charitable prescriptions

The Jerwood Foundation was created in 1977 and has come to play a major role in providing sponsorship for a diverse range of prizes, exhibitions, one-off grants and commissions in the arts. The Foundation had already been supporting the Royal Court's programme of new writing for over two years when its relationship with the theatre became a matter of controversy in 1998. Allegations that the Foundation enjoyed an inappropriate level of control at the theatre developed following the Royal Court's inability to fulfil the terms of Lottery funding for an ambitious capital project – a new building in London's

Sloane Square. These terms state that the company receiving fund-ing must raise 25% of the finance from private sponsorship. In the Royal Court's case, this came to £7 million to match the Arts Council's donation of £25.8 million. In 1998, the Royal Court found them-selves well short of this target, with the board facing the prospect of being held personally liable for financial mismanagement. The Jer-wood Foundation stepped in with the £3 million required – a donation that formed part of a complex contract that would provide further financial backing to support the production of new work at the Royal Court.

Initially, disquiet centred upon proposals to call the theatre 'The Jerwood Royal Court'. This moniker attracted media disapproval for its usurpation of the theatre's traditional title and was finally vetoed by the Queen. A compromise was eventually reached and the name 'The Jerwood Theatres at the Royal Court Theatre' formally approved. This was not the end of the matter, however. Further controversy was gener-ated when the chairman of the Foundation, Alan Grieve, let it slip that he was accustomed to reading scripts for the new playwrights' season. *The Times* quoted him as saying: 'I see no reason why that should upset writers'. He added that it was just a matter of suggesting when 'more work is needed'.[41]

Ian Rickson, the Royal Court's new artistic director, was quick to dis-tance himself from this policy, which he characterised as a product of the personal relationship between his predecessor, Stephen Daldry, and Alan Grieve. He stated that there had been no artistic interference with the theatre in the past, and there would be none in the future, asserting: 'There will be a contractual clause ensuring this freedom, allowing our theatre to remain independent and pioneering.'[42]

A press statement from the Royal Court's chairman, the writer and barrister Sir John Mortimer, swiftly followed Rickson's pledge. He gave 'an absolute guarantee' that no sponsor would be allowed to intervene in the artistic work of the theatre, noting that this was 'written into the agreement'. Mortimer added that Alan Grieve had 'got slightly car-ried away' when giving his previous statement and had since retracted it. Grieve's subsequent press release was unequivocal, stating that the Jerwood Foundation's donation respected the theatre's 'artistic integrity' and that its 'artistic policy is a matter for the council and artistic director of the Royal Court alone.'[43]

This might have been the end of the matter, but when the deal came to be finalised in 1999, it emerged that the contract which formalised the Jerwood Foundation's five-year commitment to the sponsorship of new plays did not include a clause which would protect the theatre's artistic independence. Far from it. The Foundation had actually inserted several prescriptive criteria. These terms stated that in order to be eligible for sponsorship, the playwrights must be:

> British or Irish citizens
> Within ten years of the start of their career
> A major 'influencer' of contemporary playwrighting.[44]

The exclusions effected by this list were immediately obvious. Critics argued that the question of a writer's influence can only be assessed in retrospect and that the final clause would render any work from a genuinely new writer ineligible. Material from foreign writers would be inadmissible, as would new work from established contributors to the Royal Court repertoire, such as Caryl Churchill, Timberlake Wertenbaker and Harold Pinter. Further details revealed that Alan Grieve was to be given a seat on the theatre's board and that the Jerwood Foundation and the Royal Court were to reach mutual decisions over which plays were to receive sponsorship.

Following a well-publicised meeting of more than thirty concerned playwrights, a concession was reached over the issue of authorial citizenship. Eligibility was now to be gained by UK residence. Nevertheless, the final form of the contract explicitly contradicted Rickson's earlier conciliatory statements: the Jerwood Foundation's right to artistic intervention was written into the contract. Critics and commentators expressed anxiety over the precedent this was setting. Writing in *The Independent*, David Benedict observed that, by accepting the funding 'complete autonomy over programming has been relinquished,' and he speculated that given the Royal Court's tight finances, 'a new play by an esteemed playwright outside the Jerwood criteria is likely to be overlooked in favour of one within them.'[45]

The Jerwood Foundation's success in achieving this level of influence over the Royal Court's new writing programme indicates business sponsorship's potential to encroach on artistic decisions. Speaking in 1995 in Warwick, Andrew McIlroy sought to defend the role of business in arts sponsorship, arguing that maintaining a relatively low level of contribution from the private sector helps to safeguard the independent status of the arts organisation being sponsored. McIlroy suggests that as long as business only makes a 5–10% contribution to the overall budget,

It is still possible to say 'no, we do not want to do that programme, we do not want a relationship with you as a company'. When sponsorship reaches 40% or 50% of overall income, you are obviously in the same position as you are with a public funder. In other words, if you do not agree with them, there is not much you can do about it. The freedom that sponsorship gives you only exists if you actually restrain the impact of the sponsorship on the rest of your funding package. ABSA [The Association for Business Sponsorship of the Arts] has always said [...] that sponsorship should be a supplement to public funding, and not a substitute.[46]

The contractual terms of the Jerwood Foundation's relationship with the Royal Court refute McIlroy's hypothesis, revealing that corporate sponsors may intervene in artistic decisions, even if they are not providing the majority of the funding. Where there is a contractual link between public funding and the successful location of private funding, corporate sponsors or charitable foundations contributing a relatively low level of financial support may end up wielding a disproportionate measure of control.

It is important to remember that the publicity and public debate which surrounded the Jerwood Foundation's relationship with the Royal Court, and the controversies over *Myra and Me* and *Forced Upon Us*, is not the norm. Most negotiations between funders and theatre companies over artistic content will escape our purview; remaining a private affair, carried out in a spirit of informal consultation. It is also important to recognise that contemporaneity can produce greater obscurity, rather than clarity. As this study draws closer to the present day, tracing the operation of censorship becomes more challenging in some ways. Debates are still open, injustices more keenly felt; censors have greater reason to shield themselves from public scrutiny, and artists are understandably unwilling to go on record about problems they have had with institutions or organisations when they hope to maintain their financial support. Moreover, the removal of the Lord Chamberlain's responsibility for theatre licensing robs the researcher of a single centralised institution of censorship, which helpfully generates and preserves an archive of its operations. Records of the debates over artistic content that take place behind the scenes at businesses that sponsor the arts are unlikely to end up in the public domain, if they exist at all. And where the right to set parameters for exclusion and selection are the reason for the funder's existence – as in the case of the Arts Councils – or when an institution's right to select material is built into a contract it may become impossible to detect the operation of censorious decision-making.

Recognition of the significant power of constitutive forms of censorship does not, however, imply agreement with Langton's observation that 'if censorship is everywhere, it might as well be nowhere.' Instead, as Butler argues, it should encourage activists, artists and scholars to focus their attention upon the middle ground of the censorious continuum, where contingent forms of censorship – which all too often appear to be inexorable – may be contested.[47] Part of this project surely involves close examination of our own values. In this context, we could start by interrogating both our understanding of the function of public funding for the arts, the appropriate relationship between the arts and commerce and the broadly shared – but erroneous – belief that finance and the theatre operate autonomously.

8
Competing Fundamentalisms: *Behzti*, Freedom of Speech, Sacrilege and Silencing

When Gurpreet Kaur Bhatti's play *Behzti (Dishonour)* opened at the studio space at the Birmingham Repertory Theatre on 9 December 2004, it was accompanied by protests outside the theatre. These were organised by local Sikhs, who argued that the way in which the production placed acts of sexual abuse and murder within a Gurdwara – a Sikh temple – was nothing short of sacrilege. These protests grew in size during the run, and eventually became violent, culminating in rioting and an attack on the theatre on Saturday 18 December. Five policemen were injured, three people were arrested, and some 800 theatre-goers had to be evacuated, including a large number of children who were attending the theatre's main Christmas show. The riot resulted in thousands of pounds' worth of damage; glass windows and doors were smashed, and backstage equipment was destroyed when some of the demonstrators managed to get in. On Monday 20 December, following a meeting with the police and community leaders, the Rep's management took the decision to cancel the rest of the play's run on the grounds of health and safety. Plans for rehearsed readings of the play elsewhere were called off, apparently after the number of death threats to Bhatti, the playwright, increased. This extraordinary example of successful censorship precipitated a heated debate in the media over the competing rights of the artist and those who were offended in the Sikh community. Below, I examine some of the tensions, assumptions and contradictions inherent in the various positions adopted in this debate, placing these against an account of the development of the play in rehearsal.

Dirty linen: dishonourable exposure

No one could have anticipated the violence which greeted *Behzti*. The bold and light-hearted image which appeared on the poster and publicity materials for the production (which showed a woman, dressed in a red shalwar kameez, her face obscured by the enormous pair of white knickers held out in front of her) definitely did not do so. This photograph, selected long before controversy was associated with the play, seemed to suggest a humorous exposure of a private, domestic and very female world. The image, however, came to have other resonances, prefiguring, it seemed, the washing of a community's dirty linen in public.

There can be no doubt that Bhatti's script is written to shock. The elements of the play which attracted most comment and controversy were its inclusion of scenes of rape and murder within a Sikh Gurdwara, or temple; but the script also explores the unpleasant realities of caring for an incapacitated relative; the vicious, self-perpetuating cycles of domestic abuse; women's capacity for violence and for complicity in their own oppression. It also exposes the way in which hypocrisy and cant can displace genuine engagement with religion and ritual, as well as the potential for systematic abuse to find shelter within closed religious institutions.

Bhatti's script frequently gives these issues a visceral, physical reality. In the first moments of the play, we are introduced to the central relationship between foul-mouthed, bad-tempered Balbir and Min, her daughter and carer. The play exposes the indignities and unwanted intimacies inherent in such relationships. We first meet Balbir as she sits, naked, on a stool in the bath, and shouts a command to her daughter, voiced in ugly terms: 'No soap! [...] No bloddy soap, shitter!'[1] It quickly becomes apparent that their relationship has soured into a mutually manipulative mess of emotional and physical abuse, as both women are trapped by Balbir's incapacity. Balbir refuses to cooperate at every opportunity, clinging to the last vestiges of agency. She spits out food and remarks, having decided to piss in her commode after a long refusal to do so: 'I am exercising control you see. Omnipotence.' (p. 25) For her part, Min subjects her mother to petty cruelties, which are immediately followed by vigorous self-reproach. Having pulled her mother's hair, she then responds by doling out her own punishment:

Come on…don't be unhappy…I'll say I'm sorry…*MIN gaily and genuinely yanks one of her bunches.* Look I'm doing it to myself. Now you've got your own back.

(p. 28)

Despite her physical weaknesses, Balbir does indeed get her own back. She taunts her daughter with her virginity, her weight, her homely appearance, her lack of education and lack of friends: the very experiences and opportunities that her role as carer denies her. It is hard not to sympathise with Min, even as she tapes up her mother's mouth and wrists:

> *Almost in tears, MIN takes some sellotape out of a bag. She pulls some off and plasters it over BALBIR'S mouth. BALBIR struggles, but MIN suppresses her.*
>
> MIN: You're forcing me. I'm only doing this because you are forcing me. *She puts two more rounds of sellotape over BALBIR'S mouth and then ties her mother's wrists together.*

(p. 40)

It is to Bhatti's credit that we are able to sympathise with Min. The script succeeds in capturing the complexities of this claustrophobic relationship, as moments of emotional and physical violence are balanced with glimpses of affection and gentleness. At times, Balbir appears as a manipulative monster; at others she seems pathetic and vulnerable. Min manages to be both saintly and faintly sadistic.

Bhatti also succeeds in demonstrating that the violence of the exchanges between mother and daughter is part of a much wider problem, as the next scene shifts the action to the Gurdwara, where it remains for the rest of the play. Once out of the house, the conversations between Balbir's erstwhile friends, Polly and Teetee, are peppered with references to domestic violence. Teetee's response to the question 'Are you threatening me?' from Elvis, Balbir's part-time home help, emphasises the self-perpetuating misery of this form of abuse, and the effective autonomy of the Gurdwara:

> TEETEE: No rules in here boy. No police, no laws, no evidence, no witnesses, no nothing. […] Remember one thing boy. There is a man's soul in this woman's body. Our men are cruel to our women but we

get used to it and we follow the rules, letting each slap and tickle and bruise and headbutt go by. And at the end of this rubbish life, we write the rules. We find the beauty in our cruelty. My daughter-in-laws suffer just as I suffered. I make sure of it. Things happen. And no-one can do nothing. Because everything must stay the same.

(pp. 100–101)

These threats also materialise into actual violence. Teetee pushes Polly to the ground early on in the play, and Min is later brutally beaten by the two women following her rape by Mr Sandhu, a Gurdwara elder, as they assume that the blood on her dress is menstrual – a profound dishonour:

POLLY: Cursed girls and ladies do not come to God's house at that time of the month! […] So much Behzti. Nasty filthy dog! […] Look at your dishonourable daughter Bhanji.

TEETEE: Importing her dirty monthly blood into the Gurdwara.

(p. 117)

Throughout the play, the impulse to protect, promote and honour past ideals is shown as profoundly damaging. The older women's nostalgic attachment to their past glories prevents them from confronting the realities of their present circumstances, and Balbir's fantasies of an expensive and grandiose wedding for Min ultimately expose her daughter to the abusive attentions of Mr Sandhu. Mother and daughter end up paying a high price for what Balbir describes as 'A moment of perfection, captured and held, to be remembered and yearned for, forever.' (p. 42)

The contrast between a similar image of perfection – the good reputation of the Sikh community – and the imperfect reality is highlighted by the moment in the penultimate scene where we see Mr Sandhu reading out a letter he has written to the council, having raped Min three scenes earlier. He intones:

I would like to point out, since its arrival spanning the last forty years, the Sikh community has played an important role in the development and flourishing of our town. Our principles of hard work, humility, family values, coupled with our integrationist attitude […] have stood us in good stead.

(p. 131)

The play, however, celebrates other values. A sensual, sexual, desiring and profoundly hopeful energy bubbles out from beneath the weight of mundane routine and casual cruelty. Balbir, despite her age and incapacity, still relishes food and memories of other sensual pleasures. She tells Min, much to her daughter's disapproval, that 'the world is a big fat oyster, slimy and sticky in the hand. Always leaving some oyster optimism on the fingers' (p. 30). Elsewhere Bhatti uses dance – traditionally frowned upon by Sikh belief for its associations with Hinduism and thus prohibited in the Gurdwara – to give expression to this seemingly irrepressible energy. Min dances to 'Billie Jean' by Michael Jackson in excited anticipation of the visit to the Gurdwara; Polly and Teetee break into a gidha, a traditional folk dance; and Min dances with Elvis at the end of the play, as we catch a brief glimpse of a more positive future for her.

The play also explores the possibility of a revitalised commitment to religion. Min's enthusiasm for Sikhism, her interest in understanding the significance of its rituals, and her growing engagement with its fundamental principles are contrasted with the older generation's preoccupation with outward shows of piety. In the final moments of the play, Bhatti gives Min a long speech in which she rejects the institutionalised hypocrisy which she has found within the Gurdwara, but affirms her own faith in Sikhism and anticipates a more truthful relationship with the religion's spiritual leader:

> All you lot in here […] why do you always have to Say…and Show and Make it known what you are? How good you are…how kind and nice…rich and beautiful and worthy […] Seems to me like everyone's pretending the same as each other. […] my praising, it's nothing to do with this […] Next time…if I still manage to praise…I'll tell him about you lot, perhaps he'll help. See if he can…yes…If he can…I'll ask him…for all of us…
>
> (pp. 135–136)

Min's inheritance of the true spirit of Sikhism seems to be prefigured in a moment earlier in the play, when she dances with a ceremonial sword – a kirpan – as she waits for Mr Sandhu in his office. In theory, this is a moment of profound impropriety; both the dance, and her ignorance of the symbolic significance and sacredness of the kirpan, signal Min's transgression. We might imagine that the scene's title, 'Gurdwara – Gulthee (Mistake/Wrongdoing)' refers to her actions. But the stage directions make it plain that this is a moment of empowerment: '*She starts having a swordfight with an imaginary opponent. She moves around vigorously and becomes increasingly relaxed. [...] As the musical feelings rise inside her, she starts to dance with the kirpan, her movements are big and bold and fill the space.*' (p. 104) The actual transgression, it transpires, is the rape which occurs at the end of the scene.

The media debate: competing fundamentalisms

Behzti both celebrates female resilience and acknowledges women's complicity in systems of patriarchal repression. It delivers a powerful critique of institutionalised religion on the one hand, even as it points towards the possibilities of a renewed commitment to the foundations of Sikh belief. Perhaps unsurprisingly, the news coverage of the protests, and the play's closure, lacked engagement with these paradoxes. What the media debate lacked in subtlety, it made up for in heat and volume. In the days leading up to the Christmas holiday period, Government ministers, spokesmen from the Sikh community, Nicholas Hytner (the director of the National Theatre), author Salman Rushdie and Church leaders all passed judgement on the issue. The theatre's local paper, the *Birmingham Post*, received hundreds of phone calls and messages and published many of these. *The Guardian* ran an uncompromising open letter signed by over 300 members of the theatre world, whilst *The Independent* dedicated its entire front page to an extract from the play and an analysis of the circumstances of the production's closure.

Intriguingly, this debate was not characterised by a simple division between those people who thought that the silencing of the play was unfortunate, though for the best, and those who were appalled by its closure. Instead, those in the pro- and anti-censorship camps frequently used the same arguments. The right to freedom of expression and the right not to have one's religion insulted were both presented as non-negotiable, absolute and inalienable rights. Those setting out the case against the production argued that the play's setting and its use of phrases from Sikh scripture amounted to a violation of the sacred. This is well illustrated by comments made by Birmingham's Roman Catholic Archbishop, the Most Reverend Vincent Nichols, who voiced his support for those critical of the play in uncompromising terms, asserting that: 'Such a deliberate, even if fictional, violation of the sacred place of the Sikh religion demeans the sacred places of every religion. People of all faiths, therefore, will be offended by this presentation.'[2]

Commentators on the opposite side of the argument presented the right to freedom of expression as a similarly inflexible point of principle and began to adopt the language of religious belief in order to demonstrate the strength of their commitment to this concept. Journalists described freedom of speech as 'sacred'; the artist's right to freedom of expression as a 'question of honour'.[3] The fullest example of this heightened language occurred in writer Hanif Kureishi's interview on Radio 4. He asserted:

> I think the Sikh community should be ashamed of the fact that it is destroying theatres. Destroying a theatre is like destroying a temple: without our culture, we are nothing. Our culture is as crucial to the liberal community as temples are to the religious community and I think that the right to speak, the right to be heard is crucial to the lives of all of us in this country.[4]

Kureishi's language indicates how similar this stance is to the religious assertion of the right to protect the sacred. It is possible to think of these two positions as competing fundamentalisms. After all, as Susan Buck-Morss observes in *Thinking Past Terror*:

> There are as many types [of fundamentalism] as there are intolerances. The mark of fundamentalism is not religious belief but dogmatic belief that refuses to interrogate founding texts and excludes the possibility of critical dialogue, dividing humanity absolutely into pre-given categories of the chosen and the expendable, into 'us' and 'them'. And whether this is preached by a head of state, or in a place of worship, or at the IMF, no cultural practice is immune to fundamentalism's simplifying appeal.[5]

Still, neither side was keen to be associated with fundamentalist belief, whatever form it took. Instead, both sides of the debate also shared another rhetorical strategy; one which asserts that censorious intervention – or the decision to ignore such disapprobation – is not extreme, but is, instead, only reasonable. In contrast to the absolutist insistence upon the sacred, many contributors to the debate asserted that their position on the affair was reasonable and civilised, rather than radical. Spokesmen for the Sikh community stressed that their requests for changes to the play were moderate, not excessive. When Mohan Singh, President of a south Birmingham Gurdwara, was asked on Radio

4's 'Today' programme whether he was pleased that the play had been closed, he commented:

> I think we're more relieved than pleased that the play has come off. We never [...] requested the play to be taken off. We only requested with meetings with the Rep that certain elements of the play be deleted.[6]

Here, dissociating oneself from censorship – or, in this case, requests for the play to be taken off – goes hand in hand with assertions that a refusal to respond to a request to change an artwork is inflexible, inconsiderable and unreasonable; and that agreeing to changes would be sensible: the appropriate response in a civilised and polite society in which we seek to avoid causing unnecessary offence and wish to accommodate the needs of others. Another statement from Mohan Singh, made after the announcement of the play's closure, was indicative of this cast of mind, as he observed that it was a good thing the theatre had seen common sense.[7] But it is just as easy for those on the receiving end of censorship to claim that *their* position is the reasonable one: that it is those who wish to intervene who are behaving in an unacceptable way. Here witness commentary made in *The Express*, which acknowledged that although the protestors had the right to demonstrate outside the theatre, their protests inside the theatre were simply 'bad manners'. The editorial concluded that the protestors needed to be reminded of 'theatre etiquette, which is this: if you don't like what you're watching, clear off, causing the minimum amount of disturbance to other theatre-goers as you do so'.[8] This is not the only area in which those on both sides of the argument adopt the same strategy. Preoccupation with the character and motivation of the playwright can also be seen on both sides.[9]

Those critical of Bhatti suggested that she had mercenary motives for using such controversial material. A letter from a local Sikh to the *Birmingham Evening Mail* read:

> I fully agree with the fellow Sikh members of the community. The writer should have been aware of the controversy this play would cause. Maybe the play writer feels sensationalism is the ticket to furthering her career. Using a sacred place of worship to express opinion on homosexuality and crime is totally immoral and disgusting.[10]

In contrast, those supportive of the playwright highlighted her profes-sional credentials and experience as a writer for stage and television. Ex-colleagues bore witness to her other attributes – her warmth, compas-sion, sensitivity, sincerity, intelligence, excellent sense of humour and even her good looks.[11]

This commentary frequently made a direct link between the charac-ter of the author, and the perceived quality of the work. Snide remarks about Bhatti's mercenary motivation were often attended by assertions about the play's lack of literary merit. One critic suggested that *Behzti* was the product of 'a fatal attraction between third-rate talent and British libertarianism with a penchant for titillating tales of minor-ity voyeurism', concluding that the real dishonour behind the play belonged to 'an unsophisticated playwright and her grasping backers'.[12] In contrast, those supportive of Bhatti asserted the play's merit and the importance of its exploration of difficult issues. Thus, the quality of Bhatti's work is both grounds for its defence and for its suppression, depending upon your assessment of it.

No such thing as free speech?

Clearly, many commentators on either side of the debate occupied a lot of common ground. Both camps found themselves justifying their posi-tion on *Behzti* and its silencing by variously asserting that the values they hold are sacred; that their approach was only reasonable; or by delivering an assessment on the character of the playwright and the value of the play. There were some acknowledgements, however, that passing judgement on the play and its closure involved the negotia-tion of areas of ambiguity. Some of those who championed freedom of expression conceded that we must use this right responsibly, arguing that it is possible to be sensitive to the concerns of religious minorities whilst at the same time protecting the right to freedom of expression.

These concessions can be interpreted as being representative of a wider destabilisation of the traditional positions on censorship. Writing in *The Administration of Aesthetics* in 1994, Richard Burt observes that it has been accepted, until recently, that:

> Censorship clearly divides right and left: the right is for it, the left is against it; the right acts as an agent of censorship, the left is its victim; the right is for 'safe' or ornamental art without sexual content, the left accepts confrontational public art with graphic sexual images; the right is for artistic decency, the left is for artistic diversity.[13]

Burt goes on to state that debates over censorship – what he terms the 'new censorship' debates – reveal that it is no longer possible to link a particular political affiliation with a stance on censorship. He focuses upon calls for the regulation of hate speech and pornography that issued from race activists and feminists in North America during the 1990s, in order to demonstrate a breakdown in the traditional political alignments on censorship and suggests that it is becoming increasingly difficult to distinguish between progressive anti-censorship and reactionary pro-censorship lobbies, asserting that 'those on the left and the right occupy the same discursive terrain: both sides adopt the same rhetoric; both sides say they are against censorship and for diversity; each side accuses the other of trying to exercise censorship.'[14]

Burt is referring to a specifically North American context, but these are issues which have also become pressing in Britain, as the controversy over the government's incitement to religious hatred legislation demonstrated. The heat generated over the closure of *Behzti* surely indicates that we have to face up to the tension between the liberal ideals of freedom of expression and respect for cultural difference. Indeed, some commentators claimed that the response to the riots and the closure of the play was representative of a crisis in liberalism: a crisis that is a product of the shift towards recognition that mere tolerance of difference is not enough.

The Birmingham Rep certainly cannot be accused of being insensitive to the concerns of those within the Sikh community who were offended by the play. They made a serious effort to solicit feedback before the play opened, and to address the concerns raised: meetings were arranged with the city's inter-faith council and representatives from the community; members of the council were allowed to attend a dress rehearsal; and notes were included in the programme which described Sikhism in positive terms. Community leaders also produced a statement, which was distributed to every audience member, as well as being read out in the auditorium before each performance. Evidently, finding a balance between competing commitments to freedom of expression and respect for cultural difference is difficult to achieve.

Of course, we might wish to consider the possibility that one cannot remain equally committed to both these positions. Part of facing up to the tension between them must involve an assessment of the contingencies which surround freedom of expression: contingencies which are persuasively described by Stanley Fish in *There's No Such Thing as Free Speech*. In this monograph, Fish makes a strong case that 'all affirmations of freedom of expression are [...] dependent for their force on an exception that literally carves out the space in which expression can then emerge.'[15] This quote follows Fish's interrogation of John Milton's *Areopagitica*, an essay that is regularly cited in discussions of free speech as one of the first powerful arguments for toleration and unregulated publication.[16] He reveals that this essay includes just such an exclusion. Milton does not propose to extend the right to freedom of expression to Catholics, as he states: 'I mean not tolerated popery, and open superstition, which as it extirpates all religious and civil supremacies, so itself should be extirpate…'[17] Fish then goes on to contend that all institutions – whether they are governments, churches, universities or societies – are based upon a limited application of the right to say what you like. When speech threatens the underlying values of that institution, then the exceptional exclusion will be applied. In other words, no assertion of the right to freedom of speech is value-free.

The debate over *Behzti* indicates that the application of the abstract principle of freedom of expression is fraught with provisionality and conditioned by context. Ian Shuttleworth's discussion of the affair in *Theatre Record* provides a good example of this. Shuttleworth gives a lengthy description of the controversy and spends some time apportioning blame for the closure of the play, before discussing its content and the identities of the playwright and the protestors. Shuttleworth argues that it is unhelpful and inaccurate to think of the disagreement over the play 'in terms of a "them" refusing to accept the cultural norms of an "us"'. He insists that no such division can be applied in Birmingham, as Bhatti shares a British upbringing with many of those protesting against the play, but concludes: 'It's about freedom, pure and simple.' Nevertheless, he notes: 'I've been trying to avoid mentioning this, because in so many ways it isn't relevant, but as it happens, Bhatti is a British-born Sikh, her play involves sexual abuse and murder in a *gurdwara* (a Sikh temple), and the protestors were from the Sikh community.'[18]

Still, the central role this information played in all of the media coverage challenges Shuttleworth's judgement that the case was about 'freedom, pure and simple'.[19] The ubiquity of this information signals the values at work behind assertions about the right to freedom of speech, and provokes several telling questions. Would the silencing of *Behzti* have raised the same level of interest and concern if the play had been written by a member of the National Front or the British National Party (BNP)? Would there have been a greater expression of sympathy for the protestors? Would the critical consensus have been in favour of censorship? Our responses to these questions might well expose the contingency of our judgements and the mutability of the standards we use to measure controversial artworks like *Behzti*. Furthermore, these questions also indicate the problems inherent in thinking about freedom of speech or expression in abstract terms. The notion that a play critical of Sikhism which had been penned by a member of the BNP would acquire a venue, receive funding from within the theatre industry or find theatre professionals to work upon it is patently ridiculous, and its very impossibility serves as a useful reminder of the numerous explicit and implicit forms of constraint and control which affect the realisation of all staged performance.

Restraint, cuts and compromises

Analysis of the changes *Behzti* underwent in rehearsal also reminds us that every artwork is the product of a complex series of negotiations. In contrast to the media's insistence upon the importance of unfettered freedom of expression, Janet Steel, the director of Kali Theatre, recalled the many practical considerations and contingencies that informed the development of the piece. Although she insisted the changes between the published script and the version the company performed were not the result of external intervention, her discussion of the rehearsal process reveals a reality of cuts and compromises.

Some of these cuts were governed by the usual concerns over the plausibility of character development and the piece's overall length.[20] Other changes were the result of the negotiations that inform every collaborative artistic venture. Steel reflected upon the input of the playwright, Bhatti, who was in rehearsals every day; the contribution of the set designer, Matthew Wright; and needs of the cast. For example, the actress playing Balbir was not prepared to appear naked, and in deference to her wishes Steel placed the action in the first moments of the play behind a shower curtain, rather than using the bath that appears in the script. Other cuts were governed by Steel's sense of how the show would best succeed as a piece of powerful and affecting theatre. Whilst she acknowledged that certain elements of *Behzti* were likely to shock, she asserted that, in order to work, the play had to be 'about engaging an audience, taking them on this journey, [...] showing them things'. She highlighted the importance of 'choosing the moments to hit hard on'. To this end, the majority of the swearing in the script was removed. She explained that much of the bad language seemed superfluous and unnecessarily provocative: 'it just didn't add anything. It [the play] was so powerful as it was, it [...] took away from the power of it [...as] in the Asian community swearing is a really bad thing to do, still.' She averred that in order to affect an audience, it was better to use 'the drama of the piece to do that for you, rather than having people say shocking things'.

Steel's discussion of her direction of the violence within the play revealed that her approach was informed by an aesthetic of suggestion and subtlety, rather than graphic exposure and display. Her staging did not show the rape at all, and the murder of Mr Sandhu was dealt with by a series of distancing devices. She explained: 'you don't really know what happens [...] it's left to your imagination.'[21] The one violent episode which her production did deal with explicitly – the women's attack on Min following her rape – was made less brutal than its initial realisation in rehearsal. Finally, Steel reiterated that Bhatti's play was not an attack upon Sikhism per se but upon the behaviour of individuals, and her directorial choices had sought to bring this out. She reflected upon her own respect for the tenets of the religion and noted that the minimal aesthetic of the set design and the decision not to place symbolic objects on stage (such as the sacred book, the Guru Granth Sahib) were informed by the need to avoid being unnecessarily provocative. Steel was absolutely clear that the show had not been altered as a direct result of the interventions of the Sikh community's representatives; but it is equally apparent that she had sought to be sensitive to her audiences' levels of tolerance and the delicate balance between affect and transgression.

After analysis of the complex system of exclusions which informed the critical defence of *Behzti* – and the cuts, compromises and restraint which attended its development for production – comments in the media which celebrated freedom of expression as a long established British tradition appear less than convincing; whilst those which asserted that the history of British theatre has been characterised by unfettered artistic exploration seem simply erroneous.[22] Here it seems apposite to recall that freedom of expression in Britain was merely a 'legal leftover' – what remained after the application of the laws which cover libel, obscenity, privacy and official secrets – until the 1998 Human Rights Act became domestic law in 2000. Similarly, the way in which individuals and the media have come up against the limitations of the Government's 2004 Freedom of Information Act provides an excellent example of how far we are from the unrestricted circulation of information in Britain. So, assertions that the silencing of *Behzti* marked the erosion of a long-standing British tradition of freedom of speech might best be understood as wishful thinking or rather convenient forgetting – a rewriting of history in which Britain has always been libertarian and tolerant, rather than being the kind of place that has a long history of religious persecution, repression and silencing.[23] At times these assertions also appear to reflect the influence of North American culture and politics, where freedom of speech is a constitutional right, enshrined in the First Amendment. There were undoubtedly moments in the debate when commentators failed to differentiate between the British and American traditions. Jonathan Sentamu, then Anglican Bishop of Birmingham, chose to end his interview on Radio 4 with the following quotation from Mark Twain, confidently amalgamating the United Kingdom and the United States of America: 'It is by the goodness of God that in our country we have those three unspeakable precious things: freedom of speech, freedom of conscience, and the prudence never to practice either of them.'[24]

The unsatisfying reductiveness of Sentamu's choice of quotation serves as a useful reminder that the protection of the right to free speech is not something trans-historical, or universal, but that it is always the product of a set of societal values which are context bound and value-driven. This is the point made by Sarita Malik, writer, researcher and lecturer on the representation of blacks and Asians in British TV and film, in a letter to *The Guardian* about *Behzti*. In it, she observes:

> Liberalism, and its core value of freedom of speech, is not anti-racist. The freedom of speech principle which claims to be democratic is, in fact, deeply racially coded. And so it is important that we recognise those individuals and communities who have taken issue with the play, even if their argument sits outside the 'western' ideal of what is legitimate or civilised 'freedom of speech'. 'Sensitivities' are very context-bound and any serious debate needs to acknowledge this.[25]

Ostensibly, the source of offence within *Behzti* does indeed lie outside Western tradition, and it is unquestionably essential to engage with Sikh religious belief in order to understand the response to the play. For Sikhs, their sacred book, the Guru Granth Sahib, is not merely a textual record or copy. It is thought of as the living embodiment of the Guru, the spiritual head of the religion. The text retains this status at all times, and the Gurdwara is sanctified by its presence. Sikhs argue that this is what distinguishes a Gurdwara from other religions' places of worship.[26]

Truth vs. fiction or the perception of performative influence

We might imagine that these beliefs can expect to find little sympathy in a predominantly secular society. But I would suggest, on the contrary, that cultural beliefs which allow us to conflate the real and the representational, or to distinguish between the two, are at the heart of the conflict over *Behzti*. The majority of anti-censorship commentators acknowledged that the protestors had every right to demonstrate and then concluded that they sacrificed this right when their protests became violent. Within this ethical framework, the protests were sanctioned provided they remained symbolic: they were acceptable as long as they did not actually affect the play or its continued presentation.

The Rep's defence of the play seems to be based upon a similar sense of the proper division between the fictional and the real. The theatre issued a statement that pointed out that the production was a work of fiction:

> Although the setting of Behzti [is in] a Sikh Temple, neither the writer nor the theatre is making comment on Sikhism as a faith or the temple as an entity. Equally, the characters in the play are not intended to be representative of the Sikh community. They are works of fiction characterising the fallibility of human nature.[27]

So, here the play is legitimised by its fictional nature – its containment within the realm of the imagination. This defence obviously resonated with many local people, as versions of it were voiced by the local correspondents who wrote into the *Birmingham Evening Mail*. For these correspondents, the protestors' objections to the piece indicated a basic failure to understand the nature of the theatrical medium. Their comments included the observations that 'A play is not intended to be a mirror of facts'; 'It's made up for goodness sake'; '… the western tradition of questioning via the arts must be respected […]. This includes not taking a play as a literal truth. After all, do we take the works of Shakespeare to be historically accurate?'[28]

Nonetheless, you do not have to delve very deeply into the play to realise that this line of defence is rather weak. Bhatti's foreword anticipates the controversy that the play will cause, as well as noting that it is specific to the Sikh community and that it is written to confront dubious practices. The foreword makes it quite plain that she is not interested in hiding behind platitudes about theatre's fictional status and that the play contains her perception of the truth about the situation she portrays:

> Truth is everything in Sikhism, the truth of action, the truth of an individual, God's truth. [...] Clearly the fallibility of human nature means that the simple Sikh principles of equality, compassion and modesty are sometimes discarded in favour of outward appearance, wealth and the quest for power. I feel that distortion in practice must be confronted and our great ideals must be restored. [...] I believe that drama should be provocative and relevant. I wrote Behzti because I passionately oppose injustice and hypocrisy. [...] The writers I admire are courageous. [...] Such writers sometimes cause offence. But perhaps those who are affronted by the menace of dialogue and discussion need to be offended.
>
> (pp. 17–18)

Comments from Sikh spokesmen indicated that some within the Sikh community were also preoccupied with the 'truth' of Bhatti's play. The chairman of the Council of Birmingham's Gurdwaras, Sewa Singh Mandla, noted that Bhatti's play was not based on actual events:

> In a Sikh temple, sexual abuse does not take place, singing and dancing does not take place, rape does not take place, homosexual activities does not take place, murders does not take place. Now, I am seventy-seven years of age now and most of my life I have been connected with the institution of Gurdwaras and I have in my life never ever heard of such kind of incidents taking place in a Gurdwara.[29]

From this perspective, the Rep's insistence upon the fictional status of the play undermined their case, rather than supporting it.

The tension between these positions – the Rep's assertion of the play's innocuous, fictional nature; Bhatti's unequivocal commitment to provocation; and the belief that the play represented an unsubstantiated and therefore unjustified attack – was not lost on Singh Mandla. He told reporters:

> On the one hand she [Bhatti] agreed with me when I said these things did not happen in gurdwaras, but said that it was fiction so should go ahead. On the other hand [the fact that she] said she wished to expose hypocrisy implies it was based on fact. Such protests against

a play have rarely, if ever, happened. Doesn't that suggest this really hurt people and that they protested for a good reason?[30]

Others took this point further, contending that the content of the play constituted actual harm. A letter to *The Daily Telegraph* from a Sikh from Coventry stated: 'the use of Sikh symbols and a Sikh temple in the play causes not just offence but alarm and physical distress.'[31]

In contrast to the Rep's attempt to draw a definite line between fact and fiction, both protestors and playwright – censors and censored – seemed to be convinced that theatre possessed the power to blur the distinction between the two. The response of prominent figures in the theatre industry suggests that investment in this form of influence is more widely shared, as leading artistic directors celebrated theatre's role in unsettling and challenging its audiences in the days after the closure of *Behzti*. Nicholas Hytner, director of the National Theatre, who was outspoken in his condemnation of the play's closure, declared that the theatre was supposed to provoke powerful emotions.[32] Ian Rickson, director of the Royal Court theatre, observed that the controversy 'reminds us of the potency of live theatre', stating: 'It can be more impactful than any other form.'[33] These commentators were attempting to position Bhatti's play as part of a long tradition of political performance which seeks to effect change and to disturb and provoke, rather than simply divert.

Minorities within minorities

These statements exemplify the strength of the continuing belief in theatre's performative influence, which informed the response to *Behzti*, but they do not deliver significant insight into the specific conditions in Birmingham which generated the protests and led to its closure. However, retrospective assessment, such as Amardeep Bassey's documentary for Radio 4, *The Birmingham Rep Riot: Behind the Scenes*, reveals that casual media references to 'the Sikh community' erroneously present British Sikhs as a homogeneous group, and give spokesmen – who appear to speak for that community – a problematic authority.[34] Bassey claims that these generalising references elide the differences and disputes between particular factions amongst British Sikhs.

When asked to explain why the protests had become violent, there was a notable lack of consensus amongst the religious leaders who had been involved in consultation with the Rep and the organisation of the campaign against the play: a lack of consensus which makes the differences which Bassey alludes to very apparent. Sewa Singh Mandla attributed the disorder outside the Rep to militant groups attracted by the growing media coverage of the protest, specifically the Sikh Federation, noting that they are 'a group of militant people who just want to stir up problems'. He described his experiences on the Saturday night: 'I was pushed and jostled by people. They called me a cissy and told me to resign.' He even went so far as to claim that some of the protestors who broke into the theatre 'did not seem to be Sikhs'.[35] On the other hand, journalists reported that Mohan Singh (President of Guru Nanak Gurdwara) did not recognise this version of events. He stated: 'I didn't see extremists [...] the play was put on to provoke the deepest feelings in a community and peace-loving people were up in arms.'[36]

Bassey argues that the protests were caused by competing groups – such as the Sikh Federation and the Council of Sikh Gurdwaras – attempting to take control of the protests and mobilise support for their cause. He also contends that this was a situation partly created by the Rep's failure to take the importance of the traditional Sikh emphasis upon honour and pride into account and their failure to anticipate that the very act of appearing to consult representatives of some groups, but not others, would be problematic. In the event, it seems that those who *were* invited to attend meetings with the Rep felt publicly humiliated, because the theatre had refused to make the changes they had requested, and those who *were not* consulted were also angered because they felt that they had been ignored.

Other commentary on the controversy reveals further division along generational and gender lines. Discussion on the 'Asians in Media' web-site indicated that some younger Sikhs had been dismayed not so much by the play but by the behaviour of the Sikh spokesmen and elders who had placed themselves in the full glare of the media spotlight. Sunny Hundal noted that their contributions to the debate had done more harm than good:

> When the media circus started, there seemed no cohesive strategy for damage limitation. Most condemned the violence but didn't seem too disappointed by it. [...] Meanwhile, all manner of rent-a-quote representatives vyed to get on TV and into the press, with conflicting messages and some without even a good grasp of English.[37]

Hundal's critique of the group of older men who dominate the leadership of Gurdwaras was clearly grounded in his sense of the injustice of the play's silencing. In an earlier article, written in response to the closure of the play, he conjectured:

> People are objecting to the play not because of its content [...] but because it raises issues they'd rather not discuss. Especially in front of white people, in a major venue, and at such a 'sensitive' time. The play [...] also questions the supposedly unquestionable authority of religious leaders. Not surprisingly the most vociferous opponents of the play are the very same people. [...] They don't want to debate because it might bring out skeletons from their closets. The whole saga stinks of hypocrisy, a point Gupreet Kaur Bhatti is making in her own play. Pity it is playing out in real life so close to home.[38]

An assessment of the affair written by a Sikh Professor of inter-religious relations at Birmingham University, Gurharpal Singh, is more specific about the skeletons which Hundal alludes to. He observed that the play could not simply be dismissed as an aberration but that it reflected profound tensions within the Sikh community itself: 'There are generational differences, differences within orthodoxy [...] it's a response to the patriarchy, male dominance and abuse that affect a society that has a peasant, rural background.'[39] Elsewhere, he acknowledged:

> Marginal groups, like the Southall Black Sisters, have long complained of physical abuse within minority ethnic communities; only last week a Sikh father was sentenced for plotting to kill his daughter who, according to him, had brought disgrace on the family by marrying a Jew. [...] There is an increasing number of third and fourth generation British Sikhs who are seriously disaffected from a tradition that remains obstinately rooted to the politics of homeland while being ambivalent or unresponsive to the challenges of British society. Community leadership appears incapable of addressing their concerns. The choice before it is stark: relapse into a narrow agitational Sikhism or recognise the need to accommodate young British Sikhs' voices.[40]

It seems as though we should consider the possibility that the protests represented the silencing of a dissident voice, and the assertion of the homogeneity and respectability of a community that is jealous of its reputation for tolerance, equality and industry, as well as being a response to a very real sense of sacrilege.

The future for *Behzti*, and the wider repercussions of its closure at the Rep, still remain undecided. Perhaps the play will eventually be produced again elsewhere; perhaps it will not. It is difficult to say whether the case has resulted in greater self-censorship by emerging artists from minority communities, or from regional theatre companies such as the Rep, as some have suggested it might. The affair does indicate, however, that theatre can still find itself successfully silenced by overt forms of censorship. In fact, debates over censorship seem more pressing than ever, as those who seek to justify acts of intervention – and those who defend the rights of the artist – continue to fight it out over the much-contested boundary between the representational and the real. As this debate continues, I would propose that we should be more honest with ourselves about the British traditions of censorship and silencing. We should avoid hiding behind platitudes about freedom of speech, attend to the particular context of controversy and confrontation, admit when our values are in conflict and acknowledge our investment in the performative potency of theatrical expression.

Conclusion

Theatre is the most temporal of arts. It is realised in a moment of transient performance, constructed around the performance conventions of its period and often addresses issues which are of most concern to a contemporary audience. Academic engagement with censored theatre is inevitably complicated by these qualities, and it is difficult, if not impossible, to assess the full impact of censorship upon the development of the British theatre tradition. But these case studies do, I hope, provide an illustration of the various outcomes of censorious intervention and offer an opportunity to consider what generates the desire to silence and suppress performance.

Still, the latter task is complicated by the fact that many denunciations of challenging performance assume that the nature of their offensiveness is self-evident: assertions that a play is 'disgusting', 'repugnant', 'sick' or 'unacceptable' are often made without any explanation of what, exactly, is so offensive about it. Yet where objections are clearly articulated, it seems that performance's potential to have a physical impact upon those who witness it is a central concern, and the case studies show that extraordinary claims have been made about performance's effect. Mary Whitehouse, for example, argued that exposure to the violent, simulated rape in *The Romans in Britain* would arouse and excite its audience to the extent that men would be 'so stimulated by the play that they will commit attacks on young boys'.[1] The notion that the content of a performance can have a corporeal impact also surfaces in the case of *Behzti*, where objections to the play were based not only on the belief that it presented an unsubstantiated, inaccurate and distorted image of the institutions of Sikh religion but also on the argument that it 'really hurt people', causing 'not just offence but alarm and physical distress'.[2] These responses presume that theatre can create an active, visceral response, mysteriously bypassing intellectual engagement.

The censorious anxieties expressed in the case studies return again and again to theatre's realisation as a specifically corporeal art form, as the threatening volatility of theatre is frequently established through unflattering comparison with the decorous stability of text. Stopes's case for the respectability of her work was based upon her insistence that the body was self-effacing and subdued in her plays and that they privileged speech and verbal reasoning. Suspicion of physical display was evident in the hostile critical commentary which greeted *The Romans in Britain*. Reviewers took particular exception to the play's portrayal of the brutal physical realities of life under Roman rule, and damned it for lacking thoughtful exposition and reasoned argument. Even in 2006, the reviewers' judgements on director Sam West's treatment of the infamous rape scene indicate an enduring critical preference for tasteful veiling, rather than 'vulgar' or explicit demonstration. Similarly, many commentators concluded that Rolf Hochhuth's historical arguments belonged on the page, rather than on the stage. Concern that *Soldiers* might mislead its audiences rested on the notion that belief is assumed when watching theatre, whereas reading a text encourages a critical intellectual engagement. The conclusion of the 1909 Joint Select Committee on Censorship and Licensing epitomises this discrimination between stage and page:

> Ideas or situations which on a printed page may work little mischief, when represented through the human personality of actors may have a more deleterious effect. The existence of an audience, moved by the same emotions, its members conscious of one another's presence, intensifies the influence of what is done and spoken on stage [...] The performance, day after day, in the presence of numbers of people, of plays containing [indecency, libel, blasphemy] would have cumulative effects to which the conveyance of similar ideas by print offers no analogy.[3]

Some censors go so far as to describe these 'cumulative effects' in terms of disease, suggesting that enacted behaviour can pass from performer to audience member, and then out into the world at large like a virus. The Lord Chamberlain prohibited the dramatic portrayal of lesbianism in 1934 with the assertion that he had no intention of seeing 'the germ' of homosexuality 'fostered on the British stage', and Section 28 was based upon a similar rationale.[4] The solipsistic logic of this piece of back-bench bigotry presented 'abnormal' sexual preference as a disease which could be caught, citing representation as the carrier. These metaphorical connections between mimesis and contagion work to provide a rationale for censorship: if the censored object is diseased, then it requires quarantine; if the unsuspecting audience is vulnerable to infection, then they need protection; if the spread of 'undesirable' ideas or imagery amounts to an epidemic, then it demands authoritarian intervention.

Concern about theatre's impact upon its audiences has created a market for rhetoric which sets up a conceptual division between those types of theatre which are promoted as proper and respectable, and those which are not. This is well illustrated by the Birmingham Rep's claims that *Behzti*, and the characters in it, were simply 'works of fiction', contained within the realm of the imagination; that the play was effectively 'non-serious', *pace* Austin.[5] But the notion that performance should be protected whilst it remains within an autonomous, fictional world of 'just pretend' is employed just as often by those who wish to attack the theatre as by those who want to defend it; the Lord Chamberlain received several letters begging him to ban Stopes's plays on the grounds that they were not just theatre, but 'deadly propaganda', or an 'advertisement' for her cause, and allegations that shocking subject matter was being exploited for financial gain were levelled at the producers of the London Grand Guignol, *Myra and Me*, and *Behzti*. These accusations are based on the idea that the artistic autonomy of these plays has been compromised by their engagement with politics or the market.

Judgements about whether a show is acceptable or not are often generated by the context in which it appears, rather than content alone. Many of the decisions taken by the Lord Chamberlain and his staff illustrate this point. Their actions were significantly informed by their relationship to the Monarchy; as their authority was secured by royal prerogative, granting a licence signalled royal approval. Without appreciation of this concern, some of their pronouncements can seem to have been generated by an almost inexplicable set of sensitivities.[6] By the same token, the generous public subsidy received by the National Theatre – together with its official title, the Royal National Theatre – places particular pressure upon its artistic director. Here it is worth recalling that the felicity of Austin's performatives is governed by context: words only have performative force when they are delivered in circumstances in which their authority is recognised.

Of course, suspicion that performance can transform those who witness it is not a recent phenomenon. It has made recurring appearances in different historical guises since Plato planned the exclusion of poets and theatre from his ideal city-state, the Republic.[7] Whilst commenting on the controversy and debate surrounding the Lord Chamberlain's function in 1967, Jonathan Miller highlighted its longevity:

> [Theatrical] censorship then is a taboo on certain sorts of public mimicry. It has something in common, therefore, with the ancient ban upon mimesis in general. [...] in modern censorship, most of whose bans involve very sophisticated rationalisations, there are still remains of this fear of mimicry as a thing in itself.[8]

Criticism of actor John Colicos's convincing impersonation of Churchill in the 1968 British premiere of *Soldiers* certainly seemed to be based on the irrational fear that theatrical mimesis effects a subtle disruption or usurpation of identity; both of the subject being copied and of those who witness the performance.

The case studies covered in this book suggest that the representation of corporeal experiences which blur the boundaries between bodies provokes a particularly strong brand of squeamish censoriousness. Looking back on the advent of Aids, the decision to attempt to proscribe the 'promotion' of homosexuality appears as part of a wider anxiety about the permeability of personal and national boundaries, whilst the censorious energies directed towards the depiction of rape, and the display – or indeed the mere discussion – of the female reproductive body on stage signal a deep disturbance about experiences which trouble the body's margins. These fears can be attributed to our ambivalent relationship to the abject – in Julia Kristeva's words, that which 'disturbs identity, system, order. What does not respect borders, positions, rules. The in-between, the ambiguous, the composite'.[9]

Here it seems worth reminding ourselves that psychoanalysts claim that identity formation is generated through processes of exclusion; Freudian thought proposes that sexual identity is formed through the taboo against incest, and Butler's development of Freud's theories focuses upon the melancholia inherent in the work of repression required for the maintenance of a stable sexual and gender identity. It also seems significant that these are figured as ongoing processes which require constant reiteration. For example, Freud states:

> the process of repression is not to be regarded as an event which takes place once, the results of which are permanent [...] repression demands a constant expenditure of force, and if this were to cease the success of the repression would be jeopardised, so that a fresh act of repression would be necessary.[10]

This ongoing project of repression might well explain the effort we can see being made to protect the heterosexual norm in several of the case studies. It also suggests that the maintenance of national, corporate, institutional and, latterly, racial or religious identities requires a 'constant expenditure of force'.

Bearing this in mind, it is telling that the *imagined* content of a production can be enough to generate outrage. The number of shows that are subject to censure or more concerted attempts at silencing when the complainant has not seen the performance suggests that indignation over the *actual* content of a production is not always the primary motivation in a censorious attack. Occasionally it can appear that a controversial production simply represents a convenient focus for a campaign which produces publicity for a political or religious cause. It sometimes seems that attacks upon theatrical productions occur because they present an easily identifiable target, a tangible common enemy, or can be figured as a symptom of a broader set of social problems or perceived inequities. Calls for censorship enable the public reassertion of beliefs, values and identity.

The outcomes of censorship can seem much easier to assess than the sources of censorious anxiety. Many of the case studies covered in this book generated a high level of publicity and confirm Butler's observation that explicit censorship can be remarkably self-defeating. The furore over *Soldiers* provoked questions at Westminster, the broadcast of two television talk shows and finally resulted in a well-publicised court case; *The Romans in Britain* played to full houses following Mary Whitehouse's intervention; and the introduction of Section 28 provoked an increase in very visible activism in the gay community. In fact, scandals over censorship can be considered performances in their own right, with distinct protagonists, crises and denouements. And, as Aleks Sierz points out, these secondary dramas can provide an opportunity for valuable debate over the rights and wrongs of theatrical representation.[11] Nevertheless, it is important to recognise that such controversies are not always welcomed by those at the centre of the furore and that association with a censorship scandal can have an enduring and deleterious effect on the reputation and reception of a play.

In addition, we should not underestimate the chilling effect of explicit regulation. It seems that the most pernicious effect of the licensing system may have been its encouragement of self-censorship, as the publicity which often attended the Lord Chamberlain's more draconian interventions would have had the effect of establishing the boundaries beyond which he would not countenance a licence; discouraging managers and playwrights from investing time and energy in projects which explored similar issues or used a comparable style. Naturally, we cannot expect to find comprehensive records of this form of censorship, though traces of it can be detected. John Osborne told Kenneth Tynan in the early 1960s:

> I know playwrights who almost seem to be *living* with the Lord Chamberlain – it's like an affair. There's a virgin period when you aren't aware of him, but eventually you can't avoid thinking of him while you're writing. He sits on your shoulder, like a terrible nanny.[12]

Osborne's confession confirms the conditioning power wielded by the Lord Chamberlain, but the impact of this form of censorship will remain incalculable. In his examination of the depiction of revolution on the British stage during the 1920s, Steve Nicholson cites the playwright Hubert Griffith, who referred to the 'unborn children – the plays that a generation of intelligent young dramatists might have liked to have written but had been warned that they must not write.'[13] Elsewhere Nicholson suggests that many scripts were abandoned, or never even started, due to the author's prior knowledge that they would not pass the licensing procedure, and that, when undertaking research in this area, 'one has the sense of touching the tip of an iceberg; the rest of that iceberg can never be seen, for it consists of plays that were never submitted for licence, and probably never written.'[14] It is important to remember that the object of totally successful censorship will escape our examination completely. Consideration of what Judith Butler describes as the 'foreclosure' produced by self-silencing – where controversial utterance is stifled before it reaches expression or consciousness – serves as a useful reminder that the only censorship we become aware of is fundamentally unsuccessful.[15]

Yet it seems that overt censorship can also be an inadvertent spur to creativity. Michael Levine addresses the question of the artistic response to censorship in his monograph, *Writing Through Repression*, foregrounding the way in which an awareness of censorship simultaneously inhibits and provokes the writer. He infers that work which anticipates or negotiates censorship begins to take on a style which addresses these limitations, commenting that censorship can be figured both 'as a debilitating impediment and [...] as an impetus to stylistic innovation'.[16] These creative responses to censorship can produce sophisticated and complicit audiences in their turn, capable of decoding the dual structure of a censored text. For these audiences, comprehension of the simultaneous existence of manifest and latent levels of meaning opens the censored performance to an entirely new mode of reception: they become accustomed to listening for the hidden significances which lurk between the lines.

Overt censorship also tends to generate resistance. The decisions, methods, and even the very existence of the British system of licensing were sources of frustration and anger for many playwrights and producers, and during the 1960s, it became increasingly apparent that some theatre practitioners were no longer prepared to participate in games of textual hide and seek with the Lord Chamberlain's examiners. Instead of looking for ways to evade censorship, growing numbers of playwrights and performers sought to do away with pre-licensing altogether. Kenneth Tynan's determined antagonism towards all forms of censorship, and his point-blank refusal to countenance the establishment's rejection of *Soldiers*, was indicative of this growing resistance. Moreover, the barbed comments contained within Tynan's vitriolic anti-censorship essay, 'The Royal Smut-Hound', written in 1965, hit home. Not only did the Lord Chamberlain appear to inhabit 'a limbo aloof from democracy, answerable only to his hunches', but the 'insane bargaining' that producer and playwright were obliged to enter into with his staff began to appear increasingly absurd.[17] By the middle of the 1960s, there was no disguising the fact that the system was an embarrassing – and profoundly non-democratic – anachronism.

The internal contradictions and paradoxes inherent in this system also made it particularly vulnerable. Its dependence upon the examination of a script tied the Lord Chamberlain and his examiners to the figure of the author. Without a script, or playwright to attribute it to, the censorship would have had nothing to tie its proscriptions and prescriptions to. This logocentrism resulted in the criminalisation of improvisation: Theatre Workshop were prosecuted and fined in 1958 for an improvised departure from their approved and licensed script.[18] Evidence from the St James's censorship office, given at the 1967 inquiry, reveals the insurmountable problems posed by improvisation to their procedures:

A few attempts have been made in recent years to revive this branch of the Actor's art, and the Lord Chamberlain has been anxious to find a way of allowing it. After an extensive review of the question, no way was found of bringing improvisation within the existing law, nor indeed of making it compatible with the existence of censorship.[19]

The Lord Chamberlain's inability to deal with the concept of improvisation betrays theatrical censorship's greatest weakness. An unreliable, unpredictable relationship between the author's script and the resulting performance is inherent in all theatrical productions. All theatre negotiates the gap between the text and the spoken word or physical gesture. This rupture is present in all theatrical productions, not just those performances which draw attention to their break with this textual dependency. Script or no script, every performance will differ from the last, in a compelling demonstration of its basic lack of ontological fixity. The Lord Chamberlain's correspondence files show that his examiners were well aware of this problem. Acknowledgement that a scriptural reference was indistinct – or open to interpretation – was frequently accompanied by the admonition that performance could bring these vague outlines into sharp focus: the Lord Chamberlain was fighting a losing battle as he attempted to capture the corporeal art of theatre through textual regulation.

This issue is not particular to this doomed attempt to police performance. The potential for any text to produce an unstoppable proliferation of interpretation poses problems for all systems of censorship. Michael Holquist suggests that censors are haunted by a 'monologic terror of indeterminacy'; that they are motivated by a desire to fix meaning, expunge ambiguity and to fill the vacuum into which interpretation rushes. Holquist uncovers the fundamental productivity at the foundations of the censorial edifice, proposing that, in attempting to cement interpretation,

> Censors intend to construct rather than prohibit. What they wish to make is a certain kind of text, one that can be read in only one way: its grammatical (or logical) form will be seamlessly coterminous with all its rhetorical (or semiotic) implications.[20]

This desire for absolute textual fixity is destined to remain unsatisfied, however. The iterability of text means that it constantly releases new meaning as it circulates in new contexts and amongst new audiences, whilst the impossibility of exact, or enduring, definitions of obscenity, propriety or sexual identity reveals the chinks in the censor's self-justificatory armour.

The correspondence files show that questions of interpretation and moral relativism dogged the Lord Chamberlain's examiners, as they struggled to negotiate the radical social transformations of the twentieth century. They also reveal that they sometimes dealt with these difficulties by shifting their attention towards the intention and identity of the playwright. Our contemporary preoccupation with the legitimating authority of authentic, lived experience means that this tactic is perhaps even more prevalent today, as cultural commentators ask companies and artists who include controversial or shocking material in their work to explain themselves, questioning whether they are sincere or acting in good faith.[21] But this approach generates as many problems as it solves. It overlooks the complex relationship between a script and its writer, ignoring the possibility that its characters may not be espousing points of view that the writer shares: an observation which David Edgar made in a public letter of protest against Section 28.[22] And, as Butler's *Excitable Speech* reminds us, the meaning of even the most offensive term of abuse is never entirely under the speaker's control. Whilst the performative power of hate speech is secured through a history of reiteration, this reiteration also offers a space of agency and the possibility of progressive political change.[23]

Finally, the controversy over *Behzti* presents a valuable corrective to the comfortable conviction that histories of censorship are inevitably characterised by progress towards increasing tolerance. Plays such as Hochhuth's *Soldiers* and Dubois's *Myra and Me* provoked threats and hate mail, but the success of the overt and sustained campaign of intimidation that greeted *Behzti* was a new departure. Indeed, the contemporaneity of the final case studies indicates that censorship remains a live issue, requiring the attention of all those with an investment in the development of theatre in Britain today.

Notes

Introduction

1. I witnessed the demonstrations against Terrence McNally's play, *Corpus Christi*, in 1999 at Edinburgh's Bedlam Theatre, the home of the University's student theatre company. But these protests were not taken seriously by anyone I knew: acknowledged as a nuisance, certainly, but also judged to be very good for publicity in the competitive Festival fringe.
2. At 'How Was it for You? British Theatre Under Blair', a conference held in London on 9 December 2007, the presentations of directors Nicholas Hytner, Emma Rice and Katie Mitchell, writers Mark Lawson, Kwame Kwei-Armah, Tanika Gupta and Mark Ravenhill, and actor and Equity Rep Malcolm Sinclair all included reflection upon issues of censorship, the policing of performance or indirect forms of constraint upon content. Ex-Culture Minister Tessa Jowell's opening presentation also discussed censorship and the closure of *Behzti*.
3. Andrew Anthony, 'Amsterdammed', *The Observer*, 5 December 2004; Alastair Smart, 'Where Angels Fear to Tread', *The Sunday Telegraph,* 10 December 2006.
4. Christian Voice went on to organise protests at the theatre production's West End venue and then throughout the country on a national tour. 'Springer protests pour in to BBC', *BBC News*, 6 January 2005, http://news.bbc.co.uk/1/hi/entertainment/tv_and_radio/4152433.stm [accessed 1 August 2007].
5. Angelique Chrisafis, 'Loyalist Paramilitaries Drive Playwright from His Home', *The Guardian*, 21 December 2005.
6. 'Tate "Misunderstood" Banned Work', *BBC News*, 26 September 2005, http://news.bbc.co.uk/1/entertainment/arts/4281958.stm [accessed 1 August 2007]; for discussion of the Bristol Old Vic's decision, see Ian Shuttleworth, 'Prompt Corner', *Theatre Record*, 25.23, 6 December 2005, pp. 1479–1480.
7. See David Edgar, 'Shouting Fire: Art, Religion and the Right to be Offended', *Race & Class* 48.2 (2006), 61–76 (p. 70); Steven Winn, 'As Germans Cancel Mozart Opera, Arts World Shudders', *The San Francisco Chronicle*, 30 September 2006; Nick Cohen, 'Yet Again We Cave Into Religious Bigots. And This Time They're Hindus', *The Observer*, 28 May 2006; Anjum Katyal, 'Summer of Discontent: Religion, Censorship and the Politics of Offence', *Index on Censorship* 35.4 (2006), 157–161.
8. These powers were granted in the 2001 Anti-Terrorism, Crime and Security Act, the 2003 UK–US Extradition Treaty and the 2005 Prevention of Terrorism Act, respectively. See Patrick Wintour and Alan Travis, 'Brown Sets Out Sweeping but Risky Terror and Security Reforms', *The Guardian*, 26 July 2007.
9. See Henry Porter and Tony Blair, 'Britain's Liberties: The Great Debate', *The Observer*, 23 April 2006; 'Britain is "Surveillance Society"', *BBC News*, 2 November 2006, http://news.bbc.co.uk/1/hi/uk/6108496.stm [accessed

2 August 2007]; K. Ball, S. Graham, D. Lyon, C. Norris and C. Raab, *A Report on the Surveillance Society*, ed. by David Murakami Wood (Wilmslow, UK: Office of the Information Commissioner, 2006).

10. Mark Wallinger's exhibition, *State Britain*, mounted at the Tate Britain in 2007, recreated anti-war protestor Brian Haw's banners which were lined up in Parliament Square until they were confiscated by police in the middle of the night in May 2006. A line across the gallery's floors highlighted the limits of the 'exclusion zone' around Parliament.

11. George Monbiot, 'Protest is Criminalised and the Huffers and Puffers Say Nothing', *The Guardian*, 4 October 2005.

12. 'Muslim Cartoon Row Timeline', *BBC News*, 19 February 2006, http://news.bbc.co.uk/1/hi/world/middle_east/4688602.stm [accessed 1 August 2007].

13. Timothy Garton Ash, 'The Struggle to Defend Free Expression is Defining Our Age', *The Guardian*, 5 October 2006.

14. Salman Rushdie, 'Coming After Us', in *Free Expression is No Offence*, ed. by Lisa Appignanesi (London: Penguin, 2005), pp. 21–26 (p. 24).

15. Frederick Schauer, 'The Ontology of Censorship', in *Censorship and Silencing: Practices of Cultural Regulation*, ed. by Robert C. Post (Los Angeles: Getty Research Institute for the History of Art and the Humanities, 1998), pp. 147–168 (p. 147); Timothy Murray, *Drama Trauma: Specters of Race and Sexuality in Performance, Video and Art* (London and New York: Routledge, 1997), p. 219.

16. Richard Findlater, *Banned! A Review of Theatrical Censorship in Britain* (London: McGibbon & Kee, 1967); Nicholas de Jongh, *Politics, Prudery and Perversions: The Censoring of the English Stage 1901–1968* (London: Methuen, 2000), p. viii; Steve Nicholson, *The Censorship of British Drama 1900–1968: 1900–1932*, Vol. 1 (Exeter: University of Exeter Press, 2003). John Johnston's book, *The Lord Chamberlain's Blue Pencil* (London: Hodder & Stoughton, 1990) is the exception to this rule, whilst Nicholson's approach is, in fact, more complex than his dedication would suggest. His engagement with the detail of the Lord Chamberlain's licensing system occasionally leads him to view its decisions and judgements sympathetically (see pp. iv, 187, 215). For further discussion of Johnston's work, see Helen Freshwater, 'The Allure of the Archive', *Poetics Today* 24.4 (Winter 2003), 729–758.

17. Nicholas Harrison, *Circles of Censorship: Censorship and Its Metaphors in French History, Literature and Theory* (Oxford: Oxford University Press, 1995), p. 210.

18. See Yasmin Alibhai-Brown, 'No Religion is Immune from Criticism', *The Independent*, 20 December 2004.

19. Rowan Atkinson, 'The Opposition's Case', in *Free Expression is No Offence*, ed. by Lisa Appignanesi (London: Penguin, 2005), pp. 59–63 (p. 60).

20. It must be noted, however, that Dworkin did continue to assert that this statement should not be 'taken as an endorsement of the widely held opinion that freedom of speech has limits'. Ronald Dworkin, 'Even Bigots and Holocaust Deniers Must Have Their Say', *The Guardian*, 14 February 2006.

21. *Schenck v. United States*, 249 U.S. 47 (1919), 52, cited in John Durham Peters, *Courting the Abyss: Free Speech and the Liberal Tradition* (Chicago: University of Chicago Press, 2005), p. 149.

22. See, for example, David Edgar, 'Rules of Engagement', *The Guardian*, 22 October 2005; Frank Fisher, 'Take that article down. In *Index*

it's disgraceful', *Index on Censorship*, 22 November 2004, http://www.
indexonline.org.uk/news/20041122_netherlands.shtml [accessed 26 October
2006]. John Durham Peters demonstrates that this form of reductive reference is common in many of today's debates over freedom of speech, where
single phrases regularly stand in for longer tracts. See, for example, 'Let Truth
and Falsehood Grapple' (John Milton); 'Sunlight is the Best Disinfectant'
(Louis Dembitz Brandeis); and last but not least, 'I Detest What You Say,
but I Will Defend to the Death Your Right to Say It' (E. Beatrice Hall, usually wrongly attributed to Voltaire). John Durham Peters, *Courting the Abyss*,
pp. 144–145, 156–157.

23. J.L. Austin, *How to Do Things with Words* (Oxford: Clarendon Press, 1962),
p. 22.
24. Critical assessments of this declaration have pointed to the anti-theatricality
contained within Austin's assertion. Eve Kosofsky Sedgwick, for example,
cites the dictionary meaning of 'etiolation', as she notes: 'the pervasive-
ness with which the excluded theatrical is hereby linked to the perverted,
the artificial, the unnatural, the abnormal, the decadent, the effete, the diseased [...] inseparable from a normatively homophobic thematics of the
"peculiar", anomalous, exceptional, non-serious.' Eve Kosofsky Sedgwick
and Alan Parker, eds., *Performativity and Performance* (London and New York:
Routledge, 1995), pp. 4–5.
25. Janelle Reinelt, 'The Limits of Censorship', *Theatre Research International* 32.1
(2007), 3–15 (p. 3).
26. See Michel Foucault, 'Two Lectures', *Power/Knowledge: Selected Interviews and
Other Writings 1972–1977*, ed. by Colin Gordon (London: Harvester, 1980),
pp. 92–108.
27. See Michel Foucault, *Discipline and Punish: The Birth of the Prison*
(Harmondsworth: Penguin, 1991).
28. Ibid., pp. 202–203.
29. See Judith Butler, 'Ruled Out: Vocabularies of the Censor', in *Censorship and
Silencing: Practices of Cultural Regulation*, ed. by Robert C. Post (Los Angeles:
Getty Research Institute for the History of Art and the Humanities, 1998),
pp. 247–259 (p. 258).
30. Annette Kuhn, *Cinema, Censorship and Sexuality, 1909–1925* (London and
New York: Routledge, 1988), p. 127.
31. Judith Butler, 'Ruled Out', pp. 248, 251–252. As Butler acknowledges,
this understanding of censorship as productive, rather than straightfor-
wardly repressive is informed by Michel Foucault's work on the relationship between power and knowledge and, specifically, his critique
of the 'repressive hypothesis', which he set out in *The History of
Sexuality*.
32. See Rae Langton, 'Subordination, Silence, and Pornography's Authority',
in *Censorship and Silencing: Practices of Cultural Regulation*, ed. by Robert
C. Post (Los Angeles: Getty Research Institute for the History of Art and the
Humanities, 1998), pp. 261–284 (p. 261).
33. See Robert C. Post, ed., *Censorship and Silencing: Practices of Cultural Regulation* (Los Angeles: Getty Research Institute for the History of Art and the
Humanities, 1998), p. 4.
34. Judith Butler, 'Ruled Out', p. 249.

35. Marie Stopes, *A Banned Play and a Preface on Censorship* (London: John Bale, Sons and Danielsson, Ltd, 1926) and Pam Brighton, quoted in Amelia Gentleman, 'Dubble Trouble', *The Guardian*, 5 August 1999.
36. John Johnston provides an explanation of the historical background to this system in *The Lord Chamberlain's Blue Pencil*.
37. See Nicholas de Jongh, *Politics, Prudery and Perversions*, pp. 136–137.
38. Steve Nicholson also shows that the Lord Chamberlain approached Prime Minister Ramsay Macdonald directly in 1924. See *The Censorship of British Drama*, Vol. 1, p. 255. The Advisory Board was set up following the 1909 Parliamentary inquiry into theatre censorship, and its members were all establishment figures. Some had a particular interest in the theatre, but many had no such qualification. They included Professor Allardyce Nicoll, Lord Buckmaster (Asquith's Lord Chancellor), Squire Bancroft and Lady Violet Bonham-Carter.
39. Although plays written before the 1737 Censorship Act did not technically require a licence, in practice new translations of ancient Greek plays were submitted for licensing, and Restoration plays were usually bowdlerised. See Steve Nicholson, *The Censorship of British Drama*, Vol. 1, pp. 6–7. For discussion of the inconsistent treatment received by music halls in the nineteenth century, and private clubs during the twentieth century, see Dominic Shellard and Steve Nicholson with Miriam Handley, *The Lord Chamberlain Regrets... A History of British Theatre Censorship* (London: The British Library, 2004), pp. 48–50, 124, 155, 168–169.
40. *Report from the Joint Select Committee of the House of Lords and the House of Commons on the Stage Plays (Censorship) together with the Proceedings of the Committee, Minutes and Appendices* (London: Government Publications, 1909).
41. Judith Butler, *The Psychic Life of Power* (Stanford: Stanford University Press, 1997), pp. 18–19.
42. Judith Butler, 'Ruled Out', p. 257. Butler's emphasis.

1 London's Grand Guignol: sex, violence and the negotiation of the limit

1. For discussion of the deleterious effects of 1950s pulp fiction, see Richard Hoggart, *The Uses of Literacy* (London: Chatto and Windus, 1957). On the development of a new 'torture porn' subgenre in horror film, see Kira Cochrane, 'For your entertainment', *The Guardian*, 1 May 2007.
2. Martin Barker reveals that the story that the children who killed James Bulger were influenced by the film *Child's Play III* was a press fabrication: neither boy had seen the film. See *Ill Effects: The Media/Violence Debate*, ed. by M. Barker and J. Petley (London and New York: Routledge, 1996). For further analysis of the controversy over the impact and possible influence of representations of violence, see Mark Kermode, 'Horror: On the Edge of Taste', *Index on Censorship*, 24.6 (1995), 59–68; and Joseph Grixti, *Terrors of Uncertainty: The Cultural Contexts of Horror Fiction* (London and New York: Routledge, 1989). For media discussion of the connections between the massacres at Columbine High School and Virginia Tech and film and computer

games, see Mark Ward, 'Columbine Families Sue Computer Games Makers', *BBC News*, 1 May 2001, http://news.bbc.co.uk/1/hi/sci/tech/1295920.stm [accessed 22 August 2007], and Devin Gordon, 'A Killer's Movie Connection', *Newsweek*, 19 April 2007, http://www.msnbc.msn.com/id/18207904/site/newsweek/?from=rss [accessed 22 August 2007].

3. The BBFC oversees the age limit for computer games as well as films. For discussion of their decision to ban *Manhunt 2*, see Bobbie Johnson, 'Escape Asylum, Stab Nurse, Kill Prostitutes. Not Here You Won't, Say British Censors', *The Guardian*, 20 June 2007, http://www.guardian.co.uk/technology/2007/jun/20/games.news [accessed 22 August 2008].

4. Jon McKenzie, *Perform or Else* (London and New York: Routledge, 2002), pp. 30–33.

5. The London Grand Guignol alternated comedy sketches with short horror plays, following the Parisian pattern of the '*douche écossaise*' (hot and cold showers). It also included translations of French plays by André de Lorde, as well as pieces by English writers such as Eliot Crawshay-Williams. Richard J. Hand and Michael Wilson's *London's Grand Guignol and the Theatre of Horror* (Exeter: Exeter University Press, 2007) is the first publication to focus exclusively on the London Grand Guignol.

6. Michel Foucault, 'A Preface to Transgression', in *Bataille: A Critical Reader*, ed. by Fred Botting and Scott Wilson (Oxford: Blackwell, 1998), pp. 24–40 (p. 27).

7. 'The Little – London's Grand Guignol', *The Stage*, 9 September 1920, p. 16.

8. George Street, Report, LCP Corr., *Blind Man's Buff*, LR 1921, 22 May 1928. References to material consulted in the Lord Chamberlain's Plays and Correspondence Archive at the British Library appear in the form in which one orders material in the Manuscript Room.

9. Lord Buckmaster, Letter, LCP Corr., *Blind Man's Buff*, LR 1921, 25 February 1921.

10. For a discussion of Grand Guignol's relationship to melodrama, see Odile Krakovitch, 'Avant le Grand-Guignol', *Europe-Revue Litteraire Mensuelle*, 836 (1998), 123–137 and Richard J. Hand and Michael Wilson, *Grand-Guignol: The French Theatre of Horror* (Exeter: Exeter University Press, 2002), pp. 8, 27.

11. St John Ervine, 'At the Play', *The Observer*, 5 September 1920, p. 9.

12. See LCP Corr., *Dr Goudron's System*, LR 1922, 4 May 1922, and LCP Corr., *Blind Man's Buff*, LR 1921, 22 February 1921, respectively.

13. 'More Grand Guignol', *Sunday Times*, 3 July 1921, p. 6.

14. Serge, 'A London Grand Guignol', *The Spectator*, 25 September 1920, pp. 402–403.

15. 'New Grand Guignol Series: Tragedy to Comedy', *The Times*, 26 January 1922, p. 8.

16. See Mel Gordon, *Grand Guignol: Theatre of Fear and Terror* (New York: Amok Press, 1988); John M. Callaghan, 'The Ultimate in Theatre Violence', and Victor Emeljanow, 'Grand Guignol and the Orchestration of Violence', in *Violence in Drama*, ed. by James Redmond (Cambridge and New York: Cambridge University Press, 1991), pp. 165–176, 151–164; Agnès Pierron, ed. *Le Grand Guignol: Le Theatre des Peurs de la Belle Epoque* (Paris: Robert Laffont, 1995); Agnès Pierron, 'Avorter, Vomir ou S'évanouir', *Europe-Revue Litteraire Mensuelle*, 836 (1998), 101–107; Richard J. Hand and Michael Wilson, 'The

Grand-Guignol: Aspects of Theory and Practice', *Theatre Research International*, 25.3 (2000), 266–275.
17. Mel Gordon, *Grand Guignol*, p. 2.
18. Richard J. Hand and Michael Wilson, *Grand Guignol*, p. 52.
19. Ibid., p. 49.
20. Léon Métayer, 'Le Grand-Guignol? Une Bonne Affaire!' *Europe-Revue Litteraire Mensuelle*, 836 (1998), 184–193 (p. 191).
21. 'Grand Guignol in the Strand', *The Era*, 8 September 1920, p. 12.
22. José Levy, 'Foreword', in *The Grand Guignol Annual Review*, ed. by Mervyn McPherson (London: Little Theatre, 1921), p. 9.
23. John Casson, *Lewis & Sybil: A Memoir* (London: Collins, 1972), p. 70.
24. George Street, Report, LCP Corr., *The Old Women*, 1921/3534, 29 April 1921.
25. George Street, Report LCP Corr., *Euthanasia*, LR 1921, 27 October 1921.
26. See Steve Nicholson, *The Censorship of British Drama 1900–1968: 1900–1932*, Vol. 1 (Exeter: University of Exeter Press, 2003), pp. 180–181.
27. José Levy, letter to H. Trendall, LCP Corr., *The Old Women*, 1921/3534, 7 July 1921.
28. Léon Métayer, *Europe-Revue Litteraire Mensuelle*, p. 189.
29. John Casson, *Lewis & Sybil*, p. 72.
30. Richard J. Hand and Michael Wilson, *Grand-Guignol*, p. 76.
31. Critics have pointed out that Foucault's concept of the disciplinary society leaves no room for resistance at all, and is unable to explain social change, unlike his theorisation of the operation of power and knowledge in *The History of Sexuality*. See Sara Mills, *Michel Foucault* (London and New York: Routledge, 2003), pp. 46–47.
32. *Histoire de l'oeil* was first published in 1928, under the pseudonym Lord Auch.
33. Judith Still, 'Horror in Kristeva and Bataille: Sex and Violence', *Paragraph*, 20.3 (1997), 221–239 (p. 231).
34. Michel Foucault, 'A Preface to Transgression', p. 35.
35. John Casson, *Lewis & Sybil*, p. 70.
36. See Linda Badley, *Film, Horror, and the Body Fantastic* (Westport, CT and London: Greenwood Press, 1995), p. 11.
37. George Street, Memo, LCP Corr., *The Old Women*, 1921/3534, 4 July 1921.
38. Agnès Pierron, 'Avorter, Vomir ou S'évanouir', p. 102.
39. *Clive Barker's A–Z of Horror*, BBC A&E Network Productions, broadcast 25 October 1997. One actor, Bernard Charlan, recalled: 'You could see these boxes from the stage and once I shouted "You enjoy yourselves in there!" '
40. See Léon Métayer, 'Le Grand-Guignol? Une Bonne Affaire!', pp. 188–189, and Agnès Pierron, *Le Grand Guignol*, p. lxii.
41. Fredric Jameson, *Signatures of the Visible* (London and New York: Routledge, 1992), p. 1.
42. Quoted in Elizabeth Sprigge, *Sybil Thorndike Casson* (London: Victor Gollancz Ltd, 1971), p. 140.
43. 'New Plays at the Little', *The Era*, 22 October 1920, p. 10.
44. Simon Shepherd and Peter Womack, *English Drama: A Cultural History* (Oxford: Blackwell, 1996), p. 247.
45. Sybil Thorndike, quoted in Elizabeth Sprigge, *Sybil Thorndike Casson*, p. 142.
46. Russell Thorndike, *Sybil Thorndike* (London: Thornton Butterworth Ltd, 1929), p. 278.

47. Simon Shepherd and Peter Womack, *English Drama*, p. 222.
48. The French Grand Guignol's fall from favour has been attributed to several changes in the broader cultural context. See Richard J. Hand and Michael Wilson, *Grand Guignol*, pp. 24–25.
49. 'The Little – Grand Guignol: Eighth Series', *The Stage*, 8 June 1922, p. 16.
50. Harold Conway, 'Non-Stop Horrors – But Audience Refuses to be Thrilled', undated and unattributed clipping, Theatre Museum file, Duke of York's Theatre, Grand Guignol season, 1932.
51. Henry Game, report, LCP Corr., *Coals of Fire*, LR 1922, 7 April 1945.

2   The representation of reproduction: Marie Stopes and the female body

1. See Office of National Statistics, 'Under-18 and Under-16 Conception Statistics 1998–2005 – England' (February 2007), http://www.everychildmatters. gov.uk/resources/IG00200/ [accessed 23 August 2007]; John Carvel, 'Sex Education Demand After Rise in Teenage Pregnancies', *The Guardian*, 27 May 2005.
2. The charity provides sexual and reproductive health services and information worldwide. See Marie Stopes International website, http:// www.mariestopes.org.uk/uk/advocacy-current-uk-campaigns.htm [accessed 23 August 2007].
3. Marie Stopes, quoted in introduction to *Married Love* (London: Victor Gollancz, 1995), p. 11.
4. Squire Bancroft wrote: 'This play should not be licensed: it makes me think the time has come for me to leave the Advisory Board: I no longer understand things.' Squire Bancroft, Report, LCP Corr., *Vectia*, LR 1924, 29 December 1924.
5. During the production of the much-edited *Our Ostriches* at the Royal Court Theatre in 1923, the critics concluded that this was not theatre but propaganda. See O.S., 'At the Play: Our Ostriches (Court)', *Punch*, 21 November 1923; I.B., 'Dr Marie Stopes's Play', *The Manchester Guardian*, 15 November 1923.
6. In his report on *Vectia*, George Street concedes that 'the author's intention is probably good' but comes to the conclusion: 'I do not think this theme is possible on the English stage. [...] the subject is outside of what can be discussed before a mixed audience in this country.' George Street, Report, LCP Corr., *Vectia*, LR 1924, 19 December 1924.
7. C. Saville, letter, LCP Corr., *Our Ostriches*, LR 1923, 3 November 1923.
8. W.P. Mara, letter, LCP Corr., *Our Ostriches*, LR 1923, 6 December 1923.
9. See Linda Gordon, 'The Struggle for Reproductive Freedom: Three Stages of Feminism', in *Capitalist Patriarchy and the Case for Socialist Feminism*, ed. by Zillah Eisenstein (London and New York: Monthly Review Press, 1979), pp. 107–135 (p. 112).
10. More than one million copies of *Married Love* had been sold by the outbreak of the Second World War, and it was to be translated into more than a dozen languages.

11. Preserved amongst them is a letter from the publishers, which notes that they are enclosing 1400 letters that had been received in just three days. They complain that they have had to hire the services of two clerks in order to cope with what they describe as this 'never-ending and unprofitable' deluge of correspondence. See introduction to *Married Love*, p. 13.

12. Unattributed note, LCP Corr., *Vectia*, LR 1924, 9 January 1925.

13. Comments such as 'I am not sure it is silly enough to excuse the theme' (examiner's report, LCP Corr., *The Cure*, LR 1935) were commonplace in examiners' reports. Charlotte Francis's *Lysistrata to Date* provoked the following dismissive critique: 'I am afraid I still feel dubious about the wisdom of granting it a licence – not that I think it will do anybody any harm, but that I regard all these comedies, which are built up around the sexual act, as in questionable taste, *only to be excused if sufficiently witty*.' (Henry Game, memo, LCP Corr., *Lysistrata to Date*, LR 1942, 23 April 1942, my emphasis).

14. Marie Stopes, *A Banned Play and a Preface on Censorship* (London: John Bale, Sons and Danielsson, Ltd, 1926), p. 9.

15. Ibid., p. 8.

16. Sir Douglas Dawson, Report, LCP Corr., *Our Ostriches*, LR 1923, 22 October 1923.

17. George Street, Report, LCP Corr., *Cleansing Circles*, LR 1926, 16 February 1926.

18. Janet Price and Margrit Shildrick, eds., *Feminist Theory and the Body: A Reader* (Edinburgh: Edinburgh University Press, 1999), p. 3.

19. Kristeva points out in *Revolution in Poetic Language* that it is specifically the reproductive element of femininity that produces this involuntary aversion. See Julia Kristeva, *La Révolution du Langue Poétique* (Paris: Seuil, 1974), p. 453. Trans. in Victor Burgin, 'Geometry and Abjection', in *Abjection, Melancholia and Love: The Work of Julia Kristeva*, ed. by John Fletcher and Andrew Benjamin (London and New York: Routledge, 1990), pp. 104–123.

20. Julia Kristeva, *Powers of Horror: An Essay on Abjection*, trans. by Leon S. Roudiez (New York: Columbia University Press, 1982), p. 4.

21. Ibid., pp. 4, 9.

22. See Elizabeth Grosz, 'The Body of Signification', in *Abjection, Melancholia and Love: The Work of Julia Kristeva*, ed. by John Fletcher and Andrew Benjamin (London and New York: Routledge, 1990), pp. 80–103 (p. 89).

23. Nicholas Harrison, *Circles of Censorship: Censorship and its Metaphors in French History, Literature and Theory* (Oxford: Oxford University Press, 1995), p. 206.

24. Ibid.

25. Marie Stopes, *Wise Parenthood*, 23rd edn (London: Putnam and Co. Ltd, 1940 [1918]), p. 13.

26. Marie Stopes, *A Banned Play and a Preface on Censorship*, p. 1.

27. Marie Stopes, *Our Ostriches*, Unlicensed LCP List 1, 1923/7, pp. 63, 71.

28. Marie Stopes, *Our Ostriches*, p. 69.

29. See O.S., 'At the Play: Our Ostriches (Court)'.

30. Marie Stopes, *Wise Parenthood*, p. 27.

31. Ibid., pp. 3–4.

32. See Richard Soloway, *Birth Control and the Population Question in England 1877–1930* (Chapel Hill, London: University of North Carolina Press, 1982).

33. See Soloway, *Birth Control...*, p. xi.

34. See Marie Stopes, *Our Ostriches*, pp. 66, 68.
35. Marie Stopes, *Cleansing Circles*, Unlicensed LCP List 1, 1926/10, pp. 25, 30 respectively.
36. See Marie Stopes, *Our Ostriches*, p. 63 and *Wise Parenthood*, p. 27, respectively.
37. Marie Stopes, *A Banned Play and a Preface on Censorship*, p. 3.

3 Suppressed desire: dramatic inscriptions of lesbianism

1. See Patrick Wintour, 'Lords Back Gay Adoption Rights', *The Guardian*, 6 November 2002. Channel 4 dedicated a whole season of programmes to the celebration of 40 years anniversary of the decriminalisation of homosexuality in July 2007.
2. See Reina Lewis, 'The Death of the Author and the Resurrection of the Dyke', in *New Lesbian Criticism: Literary and Cultural Readings*, ed. by Sally Munt (New York and London: Harvester Wheatsheaf, 1992), pp. 17–32.
3. Jill Davis, ed., *Lesbian Plays* (London: Methuen, 1987), p. 9.
4. Cited in David Tribe, *Questions of Censorship* (London: George Allen & Unwin Ltd, 1973), p. 36.
5. Cited by Jeffrey Weeks, *Sex, Politics and Society: The Regulation of Sexuality Since 1800* (London: Longman, 1981), p. 105.
6. St John Ervine, cited by Richard Findlater, *Banned! A Review of Theatrical Censorship in Britain* (London: MacGibbon and Kee, 1967), p. 141.
7. See Richard Dyer, *Now You See It: Studies on Lesbian and Gay Film* (London and New York: Routledge, 1990), p. 29.
8. George Street, Report, LCP Corr., *Children in Uniform*, 1932/11437, 19 May 1932. Street's judgement has attracted a lot of critical commentary. Nicholas de Jongh attributes his attitude towards the representation of homosexuality to wilful ignorance, whilst John Deeney suggests that the censorship system's emphasis upon text, rather than performance, can explain this apparent oversight. Steve Nicholson assesses both of these analyses and proffers another explanation for Street's approach. He proposes that during this period the system of censorship was motivated by a need to 'prevent public outcry rather than to repress for its own sake' and argues that the examiner's occasional decision 'not to notice something can be seen as a highly plausible strategy for avoiding confrontations and arguments'. (See Nicholas de Jongh, *Politics, Prudery and Perversions: The Censoring of the English Stage 1901–1968* (London: Methuen, 2000), pp. 92–97; John F. Deeney, 'Censoring the Uncensored: The Case of "Children in Uniform"'. *New Theatre Quarterly*, 16.3 (2000), 219–226; Steve Nicholson, *The Censorship of British Drama 1900–1968: 1900–1932*, Vol. 1 (Exeter: University of Exeter Press, 2003), pp. 219, 221).
9. See Havelock Ellis, 'Appendix B: The School-Friendships of Girls', in *Studies in the Psychology of Sex*, Vol. 2 (New York: Random House, 1936), pp. 368–384 (pp. 374–375).
10. Martha Vicinus, 'Distance and Desire: English Boarding School Friendships ' in *The Lesbian Issue: Essays from Signs*, ed. by Estelle Freedman et al. (Chicago and London: University of Chicago Press, 1985), pp. 43–66.

11. See Maggie B. Gale, *West End Women: Women and the London Stage, 1918–1962* (London and New York: Routledge, 1996), pp. 198–237.
12. Aimée Stuart, Letter, LCP Corr., *Love of Women*, LR 1934, 4 June 1935.
13. This difficulty is reflected in the many contradictory statements in the examiner's report. First, he declaims 'Homosexuality between two women is much of the theme', only to add the proviso: 'it does not exist but it is talked about.' He then appears to contradict himself: 'Lesbianism is never mentioned [...] The girl['s...] advance is Lesbian, but that could easily be cut out.' He brushes past these apparent inconsistencies (lesbianism is 'never mentioned', but 'it is talked about' – 'it does not exist', but the girl's 'advance is Lesbian') to draw the conclusion that the Lord Chamberlain should not license the play due to its 'atmosphere'. (George Street, Report, LCP Corr., *Love of Women*, LR 1934, 27 October 1934.) Steve Nicholson provides a useful discussion of these inconsistencies in *The Censorship of British Drama*, Vol. 2, pp. 117–118.
14. W.A. Darlington, 'Marriage or a Career: Old Conflict in a New Play', *The Daily Telegraph*, 2 June 1935. The play ran for three performances from 2 June 1935 at the Phoenix Theatre, London, where the Repertory Players were directed by Margaret Webster.
15. 'Love of Women', *Variety*, 15 December 1937.
16. Richard Lockridge, 'The New Play', *New York Sun*, 14 December 1937.
17. See Lillian Faderman, 'Love Between Women in 1928: Why Progressivism is Not Always Progress', in *Historical, Literary and Erotic Aspects of Lesbianism*, ed. by Monika Kehoe (New York and London: Harrington Park Press, 1986), pp. 23–42 (p. 28).
18. Gardner notes that her literary debut in 1894 was greeted with some hostility. See Viv Gardner, in *The New Woman and her Sisters: Feminism and Theatre 1850–1914* ed. by Viv Gardner and Susan Rutherford (London and New York: Harvester Wheatsheaf, 1992), pp. 3–4.
19. As George Chauncey observes, this 'resexualisation' of women effectively tied women to 'heterosexual institutions such as marriage'. See George Chauncey, Jnr., 'From Sexual Inversion to Homosexuality: Medicine and the Changing Conceptualisation of Female Deviance', *Salmagundi*, 58–59 (1982–1983), 114–146 (p. 144).
20. See Jill Davis, 'The New Woman and the New Life', in *The New Woman and her Sisters: Feminism and Theatre 1850–1914*, ed. by Viv Gardner and Susan Rutherford (London and New York: Harvester Wheatsheaf, 1992), pp. 17–36.
21. The critical emphasis of women's studies in the seventies would have encouraged the reading of Vere and Brigit's relationship as 'woman-identification'. For example, Adrienne Rich's influential essay, 'Compulsory Heterosexuality and Lesbian Existence' advocated a broader definition of lesbianism, and a revalorisation of female friendship and comradeship, introducing the idea of the 'lesbian continuum'. But some critics, such as Eve Kosofsky Sedgwick, were unhappy with a definition of lesbianism that appeared to obscure the importance of physical expression and sexual practice. What this debate reveals is the importance of acknowledging the reader's cultural context. Vere and Brigit could have been interpreted as New Women at the turn of the century, radical lesbian separatists during the 1970s or as sexually repressed and self-deluding today. (See Adrienne Rich, 'Compulsory Heterosexuality

and Lesbian Existence', in *Blood, Bread and Poetry: Selected Prose 1979–1985* (London: Virago, 1986), pp. 23–75 (pp. 51–52); Eve Kosofsky Sedgwick, *The Epistemology of the Closet* (New York and London: Harvester Wheatsheaf, 1991), p. 37).

22. For example, report which condemned Richard Griffith's *The House of Death* (a dramatisation of the background to the Christie murders, written in 1953) included the observation: 'the author seems to have been so fired by his subject that, in spite of being a theatrical impresario, he enjoys himself describing stage directions that even he must realise could never be carried out [...] poisonous and degenerate.' (Charles Heriot, Report, LCP Corr., *The House of Death*, LR 1953, 27 August 1953). Similarly, the examiner of John Osborne's *A Patriot For Me* seems to be more concerned with the character of the author than that of the play: 'Mr Osborne's overweening conceit and blatant anti-authoritarianism causes him to write in a deliberately provocative way. He almost never misses a chance to be offensive.' (Charles Heriot, Report, LCP Corr., LR 1965, 30 August 1964).

23. Lillian Hellman interviewed by Harry Gilroy of the *New York Times*, on 14 December 1952, reprinted in Lillian Hellman, *The Children's Hour* (New York: The Dramatists Play Service Inc, 1981), p. 4.

24. See Mary Titus, 'Murdering the Lesbian: Lillian Hellman's The Children's Hour', *Tulsa Studies in Women's Literature*, 10.2 (1991), 215–232.

25. Earl of Cromer, Memo, LCP Corr., *The Children's Hour*, LR 1935, 14 May 1953. File contents enclosed in file for licensing, 1964/4458. The decision to refuse a licence was to be reiterated many times. The play was finally licensed in 1964, having been refused a licence eleven times in the interim: once in 1936, 1939, 1942, 1945 and 1946, and twice in 1950, 1955 and 1956.

26. See Roland Barthes, 'The Death of the Author', *Image-Music-Text* (London: Fontana, 1977).

27. Reina Lewis, 'The Death of the Author and the Resurrection of the Dyke', p. 19.

28. Ibid., p. 25.

29. Marie Stopes's use of several pseudonyms (including George Dalton and Clifford Cooper) illustrates this problem. See correspondence files for *Married Love* and *Cleansing Circles*, LR 1923 and LR 1926, respectively.

30. Lynda Hart, 'Canonising Lesbians?' in *Modern American Drama: The Female Canon*, ed. by June Schlueter (London and Toronto: Associated University Presses, 1990), pp. 275–292 (p. 291n).

31. Reina Lewis, 'The Death of the Author and the Resurrection of the Dyke', p. 26.

32. Alan Sinfield, *Out on Stage* (London and New York: Routledge, 1999), p. 3.

33. Patricia Juliana Smith, *Lesbian Panic: Homoeroticism in Modern British Women's Fiction* (New York: Columbia University Press, 1997), pp. 2–3.

34. Judith Butler, *The Psychic Life of Power* (Stanford: Stanford University Press, 1997), pp. 18–19.

35. Judith Butler, *Subjects of Desire: Hegelian Reflections in Twentieth-Century France* (New York: Columbia Universiry Press, 1987), p. 187.

36. Judith Butler, *The Psychic Life of Power*, pp. 135–136.

37. The reception and treatment of *The Well of Loneliness* has been well documented – see Jeffrey Weeks, *Coming Out: Homosexual Politics in Britain*

from the Nineteenth Century to the Present, rev. edn (London and New York: Quartet Books, 1990); Vera Brittain, *Radclyffe Hall: A Case of Obscenity?* (London: [n.pub], 1968); Alan Travis, *Bound and Gagged: A Secret History of Obscenity in Britain* (London: Profile Books, 2000).

38. George Street, Report, LCP Corr., *Alone*, LR 1930, 13 December 1930.
39. See Diane Hamer, 'I Am a Woman: Ann Bannon and the Writing of Lesbian Identity in the 1950s', in *Lesbian and Gay Writing: An Anthology of Critical Essays*, ed. by Mark Lilly (London: Macmillan, 1990), pp. 47–75.
40. The value judgements inherent in these models are clear in Krafft-Ebing's description of what he viewed as the 'extremes' of female homosexuality. See Richard von Krafft-Ebing, *Psychopathia Sexualis*, trans. by Franklin S. Klaf (New York: Bell Publishing Co., 1965), pp. 262–264.
41. See Esther Newton, 'The Mythic Mannish Lesbian: Radclyffe Hall and the New Woman', in *The Lesbian Issue: Essays from Signs*, ed. by Estelle Freedman et al. (Chicago and London: University of Chicago Press, 1985), pp. 7–26.
42. Alan Sinfield, *Out on Stage*, p. 143.
43. Michel Foucault, *History of Sexuality: Volume 1*, trans. by Robert Hurley (London: Penguin, 1998 [1976]), p. 18.
44. Alan Sinfield, *Out on Stage*, pp. 72–73.
45. Alan Sinfield, 'Private Lives/Public Theatre: Noël Coward and the Politics of Homosexual Representation', *Representations*, 36 (1991), 43–63 (pp. 45, 53).
46. Henry Broadwater, *Riviera*, Unlicensed LCP List 1, 1935/23, Act III, Sc I, p. 25.
47. Earl of Cromer (Lord Chamberlain), Note on Report, LCP Corr., *Riviera*, LR 1935, 17 July 1935.
48. C.L. Gordon, Memo, LCP Corr., *Riviera*, LR 1935, 16 July 1935.
49. Earl of Cromer (Lord Chamberlain), Note on Report, LCP Corr., *Lady of the Sky*, LR 1934, 23 February 1935.

4 *Soldiers*: playing with history

1. John Peter, 'Play About Churchill Rejected: Vote of No Confidence in Sir Laurence Olivier', *The Times*, 25 April 1967.
2. Terry Coleman, 'National Theatre Rejects Play on Churchill', *The Guardian*, 25 April 1967.
3. Jacques Derrida, *Archive Fever: A Freudian Impression*, trans. by Eric Prenowitz (Chicago and London: University of Chicago Press, 1995), p. 91.
4. See Kenneth Tynan, Letter to Rolf Hochhuth, 11 January 1967, Kenneth Tynan Papers.
5. *Report from the Joint Select Committee of the House of Lords and the House of Commons on the Stage Plays (Censorship) together with the Proceedings of the Committee, Minutes and Appendices* (London: Government Publications, 1909).
6. Steve Nicholson provides effective exemplification of the difficulties that the Lord Chamberlain's close association with the crown produced and the influence of the reigning monarch upon the operation of censorship in *The Censorship of British Drama*, Vol. 2 (Exeter: University of Exeter Press, 2005), pp. 9–54, 146–161.
7. Ronald Hill, Note, LCP Corr., *Soldiers*, WB 1967, 11 January 1967.

8. Lord Cobbold (Lord Chamberlain), Letter, LCP Corr., *Soldiers*, WB 1967, 12 January 1967.
9. A scribbled addendum addressed to Sir Robert Saundby (Deputy Chief of Bomber Command under Sir Arthur Harris, who had vetted the text) on a letter of 13 January from Lord Chandos to Tynan indicates Tynan's concerns: 'He asked whether it was usual for the Lord Chamberlain to consult in such a way before reading a play, who had suggested the meeting, and if Olivier knew about it.' Kenneth Tynan, Note, 13 January 1967, Kenneth Tynan Papers.
10. John Johnston, Letter, LCP Corr., *Soldiers*, WB 1967, 6 April 1967.
11. Academia was represented by Sir Kenneth Clark and the principal of London University, Douglas Logan. Commercial interests were upheld by Hugh (Binkie) Beaumont, who at the time was the managing director of HM Tennant, the production company. Aesthetic considerations were no doubt deemed to be covered by the inclusion of the sculptor Henry Moore and the former director of the Birmingham Repertory Theatre, Miss Nancy Burman, while the Arts Council was represented by Hugh Willat, chairman of the Arts Council Drama Panel. The Board also included Sir Maurice Pariser, a merchant banker and Manchester alderman who was connected with the Arts Council and Sadler's Wells and Victor Mischon, who was a solicitor and former member of the Greater London Council.
12. See John Peter, 'Play About Churchill Rejected'.
13. 'Did Churchill Connive at Murder?', *Daily Mail*, 26 April 1967.
14. John Peter, 'Play About Churchill Rejected'.
15. The *Evening Standard* even ran a 'picture probe', asking people in the street what they thought of the National Theatre Board's decision. 'Picture Probe', *Evening Standard*, 26 April 1967.
16. See Sean Day-Lewis, 'Green Room', *Plays and Players*, February 1969.
17. 'BBC 2 To Show Extract From Banned Play', *Daily Telegraph*, 4 October 1967.
18. David Frost, talk show, ITV, 19 October 1967. See Carlos Thompson, *The Assassination of Winston Churchill* (Gerards Cross: Colin Smythe, 1969), p. 215.
19. 'Commons Query on Play Row', unattributed article, Kenneth Tynan Papers: 'Mr Ben Whittaker (Lab. Hampstead) is to ask Mr Crosland, Minister of Education, on Friday, whether he will take steps to make it a condition of a public subsidy to any artistic concern, including the National Theatre, that the artistic directors have complete freedom in choice and presentation of their works.'
20. The power of the conglomerate system – whereby one management team ran several theatres – meant that an individual could choose to bar the show from a number of theatres. In this case, Bernard Delfont's refusal to take the play at any of his theatres was influential. Delfont's brother, Lew Grade, was sympathetic to his decision. As managing director of ATV, Grade controlled programming at the Apollo, the Globe, Her Majesty's, the Lyric, the Palladium, Queen's, the Victoria Palace and the Theatre Royal, Drury Lane. The main alternatives were the Palace and the Cambridge Theatres, owned by the Littler group; the Aldwych, the Duchess and the Fortune, run by the Garrick group; and the Wyndhams, the New Theatre, the Criterion and the Piccadilly, managed by the Donald Albery group. Initially, none were prepared

to take the play. For an account of this impasse, see Michael White, *Empty Seats* (London: Hamish Hamilton, 1984), p. 109.

21. White's comments appear in 'Soldiering On', *Evening Standard* (early edition), 7 November 1968. Tynan is quoted in 'Private Censorship', *Evening Standard*, 4 November 1968.
22. Editorial, 'Still in Chains', *Evening Standard*, 5 November 1968.
23. Michael White, *Empty Seats*, p. 109.
24. Philip Toynbee, 'Playing with History', *The Observer*, 1 December 1968.
25. Lord Chandos, 'Poison Ivy', *The Spectator*, 9 May 1969, p. 620.
26. Irving Wardle, 'Hochhuth as Europe's Conscience', *The Times*, 14 December 1968.
27. Dominic Shellard, *Kenneth Tynan: A Life* (London and New Haven: Yale University Press, 2003), p. 314.
28. Michael White, *Empty Seats*, p. 110.
29. See Rhoda Koenig, *Evening Standard,* 2 August 2004; Aleks Sierz, *Whats On,* 4 August 2004; Michael Billington, *The Guardian,* 3 August 2004; Sam Marlowe, *The Times,* 11 August 2004; Robert Hewison, *Sunday Times,* 8 August 2004.
30. Stephen Bottoms, 'Putting the Document into Documentary: An Unwelcome Corrective?', *TDR* 50.3 (Fall 2006), 56–68 (pp. 57–60).
31. Ibid., p. 61.
32. See interview with Judy Stone in Eric Bentley, *The Storm Over the Deputy* (New York: Grove Press, 1964), p. 50.
33. This tome is divided into white and yellow pages, the latter not intended for performance but to present Hochhuth's argument in greater detail and provide more information about the historical background to the play. The dialogue also contains footnotes directing the reader to further reading. See Rolf Hochhuth, *Soldiers*, Unlicensed LCP List 2, 1967/29.
34. Rolf Hochhuth, *Soldiers: An Obituary for Geneva*, trans. by Robert David MacDonald (London: Andre Deutsch with Penguin Books, 1968).
35. See Martin Esslin, 'Truth and Documentation: A Conversation with Rolf Hochhuth', *Brief Chronicles: Essays on Modern Theatre* (London: Temple Smith, 1970), p. 145.
36. Rolf Hochhuth, quoted in 'Truth and Documentation: A Conversation with Rolf Hochhuth', in Martin Esslin's *Brief Chronicles: Essays on Modern Theatre* (London: Temple Smith, 1970), p. 143.
37. Rolf Hochhuth, *Soldiers,* p. 14.
38. Ibid., p. 120.
39. Irving Wardle, 'Soldiers Adds to Churchill Legend, Without Offending', [n. pub.], *Soldiers* V&A Theatre Collections production file, New Theatre 1968, 13 December 1968.
40. Rolf Hochhuth, Letter to Kenneth Tynan, translation in Tynan's papers, 2 February 1967, KTP.
41. David Pyrce-Jones, 'The Imposition of Guilt', *The Sunday Times*, 15 October 1967.
42. Bernard Miles, Letter to Kenneth Tynan, 1 November 1967, KTP.
43. Eric Bentley, *The Theatre of War* (New York: The Viking Press, 1972), p. 368.
44. Leopold von Ranke, quoted in Keith Jenkins, *Why History? Ethics and Postmodernity* (London and New York: Routledge, 1999), p. 106.

45. See Georg G. Iggers and James M. Powell, *Leopold von Ranke and the Shaping of the Historical Discipline* (Syracuse, NY: Syracuse University Press, 1990); Bonnie Smith, *The Gender of History: Men, Women and Historical Practice* (Cambridge, MA: Harvard University Press, 1998), pp. 116–120; and Joyce Appleby, Lynn Hunt and Margaret Jacob, *Telling the Truth about History* (London: Norton, 1994), pp. 73–76.
46. Jacques Lacan, *The Seminar of Jacques Lacan. Book 1: Freud's Papers on Technique, 1953–1954*, ed. by Jacques-Alain Miller, trans. by John Forrester (Cambridge: Cambridge University Press, 1988), p. 14. For more on this, see Helen Freshwater, 'The Allure of the Archive', *Poetics Today* 24.4 (Winter 2003), 729–758.
47. Hayden White, *Tropics of Discourse: Essays in Cultural Criticism* (Baltimore: Johns Hopkins University Press, 1978), p. 2.
48. See Michel Foucault, 'Nietzsche, Genealogy, History', in P. Rabinow (ed.), *The Foucault Reader* (Harmondsworth: Peregrine, 1986), pp. 75–100.
49. See Hayden White, *The Content of Form: Narrative Discourse and Historical Representation* (Baltimore and London: Johns Hopkins University Press, 1987).
50. Michael Shanks in Mike Pearson and Michael Shanks, *Theatre/Archaeology* (London and New York: Routledge, 2001), p. 11.
51. Jacques Derrida, *Archive Fever*, p. 90.
52. The Hon. Mr Justice Gray, www.hmcourts-service.gov.uk/judgmentsfiles/j22/queen_irving.htm [accessed 8 August 2007]. Irving was released in December 2006, with the remaining 23 months of sentence to be served on probation. Luke Harding, 'Holocaust Denier Irving Freed Early From Prison', *The Guardian*, 21 December 2006.
53. See 'Truth and Documentation: A Conversation with Rolf Hochhuth' in Martin Esslin's *Brief Chronicles: Essays on Modern Theatre*, Programme notes, *Soldiers* V&A Theatre Collections production file, New Theatre 1968, [n.d.]; David Irving, *Accident: The Death of General Sikorski* (London: William Kimber, 1967).
54. See David Shears' 'Hostile Questions as "The Soldiers" Opens', *Daily Telegraph*, 10 October 1967. Producer Michael White described Irving's persistent contributions to the media debate (in which he championed Hochhuth's 'more dubious contentions') as 'distinctly unhelpful', *Empty Seats*, p. 110.
55. For two differing arguments over Irving's jailing in the context of the broader debate over freedom of speech, see Ronald Dworkin's 'Even Bigots and Holocaust Deniers Must Have Their Say', *The Guardian*, 14 February 2006; Marcel Berlin, 'Drawing the Line', *The Guardian*, 22 February 2006.
56. Janelle Reinelt, 'Towards a Poetics of Theatre and Public Events', *TDR* 50.3 (Fall 2006), 69–87 (pp. 81–82).

5   Mary Whitehouse, *The Romans in Britain*, and 'The Rape of Our Senses'

1. Judith Butler, *Excitable Speech: A politics of the performative* (London and New York: Routledge, 1997), pp. 129–130.
2. Howard Brenton, 'Look Back in Anger', *The Guardian*, 28 January 2006.

3. The voluminous contemporary coverage of the case is indicated by the size of the relevant folder held by the Theatre Museum. Critical commentary and descriptions of the events between the show's opening in October 1980 and the end of Bogdanov's trial can be found in Philip Roberts' 'The Trials of The Romans in Britain', in *Howard Brenton: A Casebook*, ed. by Ann Wilson (London and New York: Garland Publishing Inc, 1992), pp. 59–70; Keith D. Peacock, *Thatcher's Theatre: British Theatre and Drama in the Eighties* (London and Westport: Greenwood Press, 1999), pp. 69–71. 2005 saw the broadcast of a BBC Radio 4 drama documentary on the subject by Mark Lawson, *The Third Soldier Holds His Thighs*, on 18 February. Consequently, this chapter only includes a brief outline of these elements of the case.

4. Mary Whitehouse, quoted in Nicholas de Jongh, 'Sir Peter Refuses to Fall on his Sword', *The Guardian*, 18 October 1980.

5. The poor wording of the 1968 Theatres Act did not make it clear that proceedings could not be brought under statute law without the Attorney General's consent.

6. See 'Peter Hall Defends Sex Scene in Romans Play', *The Daily Telegraph*, 30 June 1981.

7. Mary Whitehouse, *A Most Dangerous Woman?* (Tring: Lion Publishing, 1982), p. 248.

8. This was because of a legal precedent set by a police prosecution in 1964 of Raymond's Revue Bar over a stripper, who performed with a snake. The Court of Appeal ruled that the jury could not see the girl's act as there was no guarantee that the snake would exactly repeat its original performance. See Philip Knightely, 'Roman Debut at the Old Bailey', *Sunday Times*, 14 March 1982.

9. Geoffrey Robertson QC, *The Justice Game* (London: Chatto & Windus, 1998), pp. 177–178.

10. Mary Whitehouse, quoted in Stephen Fay, ' "The Lord Will Provide" for Cost of Romans Trial', *Sunday Times*, 21 March 1982. In a further confusion between art, life, theatre and the court, the Oxford Playhouse Company staged a reading of first day's proceedings at the trial on 15 March 1982.

11. See Peter Hall, *Making an Exhibition of Myself* (London: Sinclair Stevenson, 1993), p. 307; Richard Boon, *Brenton: The Playwright* (New York and London: Methuen, 1991), p. 177. Boon notes that the majority of Whitehouse's costs were paid by an anonymous well-wisher.

12. See Howard Brenton et al., *Lay by* (London: Calder and Boyars, 1972).

13. Howard Brenton, *The Romans in Britain* (London: Methuen, 1982), Part 2, Sc. 7, p. 97.

14. Fredric Jameson, *The Political Unconscious: Narrative as a Socially Symbolic Act* (London: Methuen, 1981), p. 102.

15. Mary Whitehouse, quoted in Richard Evans, 'I Did It for Britain, Mrs Whitehouse Says', *The Times*, 22 March 1982.

16. Mary Whitehouse, *A Most Dangerous Woman?*, p. 239.

17. John Southam, Letter, *The Times*, 25 October 1980.

18. Mark Lawson, 'Passion Play', *The Guardian*, 28 October 2005.

19. See Nicholas de Jongh, 'Havers Leaves Doubts on Theatre Prosecution Risk', *The Guardian*, 23 March 1982.

20. Philip Hensher, 'Good Dramas Need Protection', *The Guardian*, 9 January 2006.
21. Richard Boon cites abandoned productions of the play at Swansea and Warwick universities. See Richard Boon, *Brenton*, p. 178.
22. See Louise Jury, ' "Romans in Britain" Ready to Revive Old Hatreds', *The Independent*, 2 February 2006. John Beyer quoted in Chris Hastings and Beth Jones, 'Epic, Funny and Beautiful', *The Sunday Telegraph*, 18 September 2005.
23. The anal rape in Sarah Kane's *Blasted*, for example, attracted critical opprobrium and notoriety when it opened at the Royal Court in 1995, but no prosecution. See Graham Saunders, *Love Me or Kill Me: Sarah Kane and the Theatre of Extremes* (Manchester: Manchester University Press, 2002), p. 9.
24. Louise Jury, ' "Romans in Britain" Ready to Revive Old Hatreds'.
25. Steve Nicholson, *The Censorship of British Drama 1900–1968: 1900–1932*, Vol. 1 (Exeter: University of Exeter Press, 2003), p. 2.
26. Howard Brenton, 'Look Back in Anger'.
27. This issue has recently been highlighted by a group of playwrights, calling themselves the Monsterists, who argue that new writing has come to be dominated by small-scale domestic dramas and extended monologues due to the limitations imposed by black box studio spaces and the financial management of theatres, who are adverse to the risk presented by a new play. A survey commissioned by the group demonstrated that the average cast size for a new play was 4.3. See Chris Wilkinson, 'Monsterism: An End to the Tyranny of the Tiny', *Financial Times*, 6 January 2006.
28. Samuel West, quoted in Christopher Hart, 'Like a Hole in the Head', *Sunday Times*, 12 February 2006.
29. See Paul Taylor, 'The Romans in Britain', *The Independent*, 10 February 1006.
30. Peter Hall, *Making an Exhibition of Myself*, p. 307.
31. 'Peter Hall Defends Sex Scene in Romans Play', *The Daily Telegraph*, 30 June 1981.
32. Sir Horace Cutler, quoted in *The Evening Standard*, 17 October 1980.
33. See Richard Boon, *Brenton*, p. 173.
34. See Philip Roberts' 'The Trials of The Romans in Britain', p. 61. Peter Hall recalls that they shouted: 'Get poofs off the stage.' *Making an Exhibition of Myself*, p. 307.
35. Sir Horace Cutler, quoted in Richard Boon, *Brenton*, p. 173.
36. Mark Lawson, 'Passion Play'.
37. Michael Billington, 'Hollow Epic', *The Guardian*, 17 October 1980.
38. Sheridan Morley, *Punch*, 29 October 1980.
39. Ned Chaillet, 'The Romans in Britain', *The Times*, 17 October 1980.
40. John Barber, 'Rape of the Senses', *The Daily Telegraph*, 18 October 1980.
41. Ian Stewart, 'The Curse of Empire', *Country Life*, 13 November 1980.
42. Michael Billington, 'Imperialism's Filth Without the Fury: The Romans in Britain', *The Guardian*, 10 February 2006.
43. Paul Taylor, 'The Romans in Britain'.
44. See Georgina Browns' 'Chop Down This Creeper', *Mail on Sunday*, 12 February 2006; Susannah Clapp, 'What the Romans Did for Sheffield', *The Observer*, 12 February 2006.
45. Paul Taylor, 'The Romans in Britain'.

46. Samuel West, quoted in Dominic Cavendish, 'Less Nudity, Fewer Dogs', *The Daily Telegraph*, 6 February 2006.
47. Benedict Nightingale, 'The Romans in Britain', *The Times*, 10 February 2006.
48. Howard Brenton, 'Look Back in Anger'.
49. Samuel West, quoted in Lynne Walker, 'Shock Tactics', *The Independent*, 26 January 2006.
50. Quentin Letts, 'Romans? It's Still No Holiday', *Daily Mail*, 10 February 2006.
51. Thomas Sutcliffe, 'Violence, Savagery and Entertainment', *The Independent*, 14 February 2006; Susan Irvine, 'The Romans in Britain', *The Daily Telegraph*, 12 February 2005.
52. The Lord Chamberlain's office was always keen to disassociate itself from explicit political intervention, but its decisions were permeated by politics. (See Dominic Shellard and Steve Nicholson with Miriam Handley, *The Lord Chamberlain Regrets...*, pp. 116–117, 172.) In 1965, Lord Cobbold gave a comprehensive interview to *The Sunday Times* in which he foregrounded the censor's political impartiality and sought to stress the censor's role in maintaining an inoffensive discourse on sex and religion. He asserted that the subject of sex had given him the most trouble as censor. (See J.W. Lambert, 'The Censorship', *The Sunday Times*, 11 April 1965, p. 11.) Of course, not all were prepared to accept this whitewash. Michael Foot used a review of Richard Findlater's book, *Banned!* to refute Lord Cobbold's characterisation of the censorship as the nation's moral custodian and to argue that the role was profoundly political. (See ' "The Politicians" Long, Long Love Affair with the Censor', *Evening Standard*, 14 March 1967.)

6 Section 28: contagion, control and protest

1. Clause 28, cited in *Index on Censorship*, 39 (September 1988). Section 28 was variously referred to as Clause 27, 28 and 29 before it became law. In the interests of clarity, I refer to it as Clause 28 before it became law and as Section 28 after its introduction.
2. Subsection 1(b) of Section 28 was redundant, as an earlier Act had already removed responsibility for decisions about the content of school sex education from local authorities and had placed it in the hands of school governing bodies. No local authorities have been prosecuted under the Act. However, it is impossible to tell how many times it has been invoked in order to veto a project or directive.
3. Jeffrey Weeks, *Coming Out: Homosexual Politics in Britain from the Nineteenth Century to the Present*, rev. edn (London and New York: Quartet Books, 1990), p. 242.
4. Ibid., p. 239.
5. See Rachel Thomson, 'Moral Rhetoric and Public Health Pragmatism – the Recent Politics of Sex Education', *Feminist Review*, 48 (1994), 40–60; Jeffrey Weeks, *Coming Out*, pp. 237–248.
6. See Patrick Wintour and James Naughtie, 'Lords Alliance Forms to Fight Gay Curb Clause', 2 February 1988, p. 8.
7. See Nicholas de Jongh, 'Homosexual Clause "Threatens" Arts', *The Guardian*, 23 January 1988, p. 5.

8. Channel Four's groundbreaking gay television programme, 'Out on Tuesday', ran a satirical item 'Ads for Ourselves' which featured an advertising campaign 'promoting' homosexuality supposedly designed by Saatchi and Saatchi. See Kevin Jackson, 'Clause for Concern', *The Independent*, 15 February 1989, p. 13.

9. See, for example, N. Abercrombie and B. Longhurst, *Audiences: A Sociological Theory of Performance and Imagination* (London: Sage, 1998); David Gauntlett, 'Ten Things Wrong with the "Effects Model" ', *Approaches to Audiences: A Reader*, ed. by R. Dickinson, R. Harindranath and O. Linné (London: Arnold, 1998); Will Brooker and Deborah Jermyn, eds., *The Audience Studies Reader* (London and New York: Routledge, 2003).

10. Judith Butler, *Excitable Speech*, pp. 110, 114.

11. Sigmund Freud, *Totem and Taboo*, trans. by James Strachey (New York: Norton, 1950), p. 32, cited by Judith Butler, *Excitable Speech*, p. 115.

12. See Susan Sontag, *Illness as Metaphor and AIDS and its Metaphors* (London: Penguin, 1991), p. 59.

13. Ibid., p. 42.

14. Michel Foucault, *Discipline and Punish*, trans. by Alan Sheridan (London: Penguin, 1977), pp. 195–203.

15. One William F. Buckley proposed that all AIDS sufferers should be tattooed on the arm and the buttocks. See W.F. Buckley, 'Identify all the Carriers', *New York Times*, 18 March 1986, A27. Unsurprisingly, civil and gay rights groups vigorously contested the introduction of these practices.

16. Ronald Reagan asked the American College of Physicians: 'When it comes to preventing AIDS, don't medicine and morality teach the same lessons?' cited in Douglas Crimp, ed., *AIDS: Cultural Analysis/Cultural Activism* (Cambridge, MA: MIT Press, 1987), p. 27.

17. Noel Grieg, *The Guardian*, 15 December 1987, p. 12.

18. David Edgar, *The Guardian*, 28 January 1988, p. 14.

19. See Patrick Wintour and James Naughtie, 'Lords Alliance Forms to Fight Gay Curb Clause'.

20. The Bristol-based Avon Touring Company experienced the effects of anxiety about the applicability of the new legislation. Keynsham Broadlands School refused to book its production of *Trapped in Time*, a historical pageant that questioned the exclusion of minorities from official versions of history. Glyndebourne Touring Opera also had to abandon a planned production of Benjamin Britten's *Death in Venice* at the Kent and Sussex Schools Festival, following the Kent education authority's decision that the opera was not suitable for the 11–15 age group. Jill Davis, ed., See *Lesbian Plays II* (London: Methuen, 1989), p. ii; and David Lister, 'Arts Council Monitors Effects of Clause 28', *The Independent*, 21 January 1989, p. 6.

21. 'Revise Section 28 Plea', *The Stage*, 3 July 1997, p. 4.

22. Leader column, *The Stage*, 3 July 1997, p. 8.

23. See Philip Osment, ed., *Gay Sweatshop: Four Plays and a Company* (London: Methuen Drama, 1989).

24. Ibid., p. lxvii.

25. David Benedict, quoted in David Lister, 'Cash Cuts Force Closure of Gay Theatre Company', *The Independent*, 5 December 1990, p. 5. Benedict gave the example of Newcastle's Gulbenkian theatre, which had been keen to

stage the company's work but had had difficulties with securing funding from the city council, who believed the play 'contravened Section 28'.

26. Judith Butler, *Excitable Speech*, p. 130.

27. Ibid.

28. Judith Butler, *The Psychic Life of Power* (Stanford: Stanford University Press, 1997), p. 99.

29. Michel Foucault, quoted in Philip Barker, *Michel Foucault: Subversions of the Subject* (London and New York: Harvester Wheatsheaf, 1993), p. 78.

30. Patrick Wintour, 'Labour in Two Minds over Ban on Teaching about Homosexuality', *The Guardian*, 15 December 1987, p. 6.

31. See Nicholas de Jongh, 'Thousands Join Protest Against Section 28 Curb on Gay Rights', *The Guardian*, 2 May 1988, p. 4. 50,000 is the organiser's estimate. The police estimated 20,000. The demo was led by Chris Smith (then Labour MP for Islington South) and Michael Cashman, star of 'Eastenders'. The theatrical world was represented by banners announcing the presence of Theatre Royal, Stratford East, Avon Touring and Gay Sweatshop.

32. See Alan Travis, 'Rope Trick Ladies Drop in on the Lords', *The Guardian*, 3 February 1988, p. 1; also Jeffrey Weeks, *Coming Out*, p. 242.

33. See Maev Kennedy, 'News Team Repels Invaders', *The Guardian*, 24 May 1988, p. 1.

34. Simon Garfield, *End of Innocence: Britain in the Time of AIDS* (London and Boston: Faber and Faber, 1994), p. 183.

35. Visual elements have included a life-size model of a sheep, an oversize model of a syringe and a camp Statue of Liberty. See Ian Lucas, *Impertinent Decorum* (London: Cassell, 1994), pp. 72–78.

36. See Simon Garfield, *End of Innocence*, p. 181.

37. Queer Wedding Vows, 12 June 1991. The 'I do' of marriage is proposed as an exemplary instance of the performative statement in J.L. Austin's seminal work *How to Do Things with Words*. For Austin, the agency of the statement is assured by its reiteration in a context sanctioned by society. The performance of queer wedding vows in a public space both draws attention to their lack of conventional force and brings those who utter them closer to the institutional recognition and inclusive legislation they seek.

38. Tatchell's statistics suggested that sexual acts between consenting men aged 16 and over resulted in 3,500 prosecutions, 2,700 convictions, 380 cautions and over 40 prison sentences during 1989. See Simon Garfield, 'The Age of Consent', *Independent on Sunday*, 10 November 1991, p. 3.

39. Judith Butler, *The Psychic Life of Power*, p. 100.

40. Judith Butler, *Excitable Speech*, p. 140.

41. As Sara Salih notes, though 'nigger' may provide Butler with an excellent example of the resignification of a potent and distressing term of abuse, she 'shies away from' its analysis in *Excitable Speech* (see Sara Salih, *Judith Butler* (London and New York: Routledge, 2004), p. 109). Butler's discussion of her difficult experiences teaching this material may explain her decision not to use this term in her argument: 'There is no way to invoke examples of racist speech, for instance, in a classroom without invoking the sensibility of racism, the trauma, and, for some, the excitement.' *Excitable Speech*, p. 37. Perhaps more significantly, Butler's belated discussion of race, which only appears in *Bodies that Matter*, may reflect the fact that the

construction of racial identity raises different issues than gender or sexual
identities.

42. Judith Butler, *The Psychic Life of Power*, p. 93.
43. Alex Spillius, 'Lesbian With a Vengeance: "Hello, We're Lesbians, We Can
    Spot Your Homophobia"', *The Independent*, 2 July 1995.
44. Jeffrey Weeks discusses this impasse and refers to the two positions 'cit-
    izenship' and 'transgression'. See Jeffrey Weeks, *Making Sexual History*
    (Cambridge: Polity Press, 2000), p. 190.
45. Phelan's argument is also concerned with the interaction of capitalism
    and visibility. She states that visibility politics are 'additive rather than
    transformational (to say nothing of revolutionary)' and that contemporary
    preoccupation with obtaining a public platform for the display of identity
    can simply lead to mindless 'me-ism'. She proposes that the unquestioning
    adoption of 'visibility as empowerment' as a maxim amounts to little more
    than buying into the productive ideology of Western capitalism wholesale.
    Peggy Phelan, *Unmarked: The Politics of Performance* (London and New York:
    Routledge, 1993), p. 11.
46. In some cases, the tabloids were more interested in the activities of the
    protestors than the quality press. For example, when a group of lesbians
    dressed as suffragettes chained themselves to the railings at Buckingham
    Palace on 8 March 1988, their protest was only reported in *The Sun*. See
    Helen Chappell, 'The Gender Trap', *The Guardian*, 30 March 1988, p. 16.
47. Peggy Phelan, *Unmarked*, p. 140.
48. Ibid., p. 5. Foucault's description of the principles of the Panopticon in
    Discipline and Punish also reminds us that the law has had a long rela-
    tionship with the operation of surveillance and that visibility has often
    been utilised as a means of control. This insight is seconded by psy-
    choanalysis. Lacan emphatically observed: 'In this matter of the visible,
    everything is a trap', Jacques Lacan, *Four Fundamental Concepts of Psycho-
    analysis*, ed. by Jacques-Alain Miller, trans. by Alan Sheridan (New York:
    Norton, 1978), p. 93.
49. Peggy Phelan, *Unmarked*, p. 6.
50. McKellen went on to found the first organised professional lobbying group
    for gay rights, Stonewall, which continues to push for equality in the work-
    place, in the age of consent and in welfare provision. On 9 January 1991
    eighteen actors, playwrights and directors made public statements about
    their homosexuality, including the playwrights Nicholas Wright, Bryony
    Lavery, David Lan and Martin Sherman; directors John Schlesinger, Nancy
    Diuguid, Tim Luscombe and Philip Hedley; musicals producer Cameron
    Mackintosh; comedians Stephen Fry and Simon Fanshawe; actors Antony
    Sher, Simon Callow, Pam St Clement, Alec McCowen and Michael Cashman.
    See David Lister, 'Celebrities "Come Out"', *The Independent*, 10 January 1991.
51. Philip Osment, ed., *Gay Sweatshop* (London: Methuen Drama, 1989),
    p. lxvi.
52. See Kathy Marks, 'Two Cheers for Section 28', *The Independent*, 3 December
    1998, p. 9.
53. See 'Plans to Outlaw Inciting Gay Hate', *BBC News*, 8 October 2007,
    http://news.bbc.co.uk/1/hi/uk_politics/7034649.stm [accessed 3 January
    2008].

54. See Elizabeth Wilson, 'Is Transgression Transgressive?' in *Activating Theory: Lesbian, Gay, Bisexual Politics*, ed. by Joseph Bristow and Angelia R. Wilson (London: Lawrence and Wishart, 1993), pp. 107–117 (p. 117). Stonewall's 1996 report on attacks on gay men revealed disturbing levels of violence and intimidation. For details of this report, and others, see Angela Mason and Anya Palmer, 'Queer Bashing: A National Survey of Hate Crimes Against Lesbians and Gay Men' (London: Stonewall, 1996), 18 June 2002, http://www.stonewall.org.uk/template.asp?Level1=2& Level2=23&Level3=214&UserType=6.
55. Martha Buckley, 'Gay Man's Killing "Tip of the Iceberg" ', *BBC News*, 16 June 2006, http://news.bbc.co.uk/1/hi/uk/5080164.stm [accessed 22 December 2007].

7 Capital constraint: the right to choose?

1. See Lyn Gardner, 'This Arts Council Cut Will Devastate Theatre', *The Guardian Unlimited*, 30 March 2007, http://blogs.guardian.co.uk/theatre/ 2007/03/this_arts_council_cut_will_dev.html [accessed 17 September 2007].
2. Tracy C. Davis, *The Economics of the British Stage* (Cambridge: Cambridge University Press, 2000), p. 2.
3. Howard Barker, 'The Olympics Killed My Theatre Company', *The Guardian Unlimited*, 5 June 2007, http://blogs.guardian.co.uk/theatre/2007/ 06/the_olympics_killed_my_theatre.html [accessed 17 September 2007].
4. Rae Langton, 'Subordination, Silence, and Pornography's Authority', in *Censorship and Silencing: Practices of Cultural Regulation*, ed. by Robert C. Post (Los Angeles: Getty Research Institute for the History of Art and the Humanities, 1998), p. 261.
5. Judith Butler, 'Ruled Out: Vocabularies of the Censor', in *Censorship and Silencing: Practices of Cultural Regulation*, ed. by Robert C. Post (Los Angeles: Getty Research Institute for the History of Art and the Humanities, 1998), p. 250.
6. See Dan Glaister, 'Guinness Makes Comic Beer', *The Guardian*, 17 February 1998.
7. Frederick Schauer, 'The Ontology of Censorship', in *Censorship and Silencing: Practices of Cultural Regulation*, ed. by Robert C. Post (Los Angeles: Getty Research Institute for the History of Art and the Humanities, 1998), pp. 147–169.
8. Norman St John Stevas, cited in Andrew Sinclair, *Arts and Cultures: The History of Fifty Years of the Arts Council of Great Britain* (London: Sinclair-Stevenson, 1995), p. 248.
9. Sponsorship was making a substantial contribution to theatre budgets in the 1990s: according to the Arts Council of England's annual report for 1994–1995, the theatre companies supported by the Arts Council had attracted business sponsorship amounting to 5% of their income. Institutions such as the Royal Court Theatre and the RSC were particularly successful in attracting sponsorship: the Royal Court received £1.2 million of financial backing from Barclays Bank for their 'New Stages' project in 1992; and the RSC took £2.1 million in sponsorship from the Royal Insurance Company during

the same year. See Dan Glaister, 'Guinness Makes Comic Beer', and the Arts and Business Survey, www.AandB.org [accessed 14 July 2001]; David Hutchison, 'Economics, Culture and Playwrighting', in *Scottish Theatre Since the Seventies*, ed. by Randall Stevenson and Gavin Wallace (Edinburgh: Edinburgh University Press, 1996), pp. 206–214 (p. 206); John Bull, *Stage Right* (London: Macmillan, 1994), p. 26.

10. Jennifer Edwards, Esther Kuperji and Eleanor Simmons, *Theatre in Crisis. The Plight of Regional Theatre: A National Campaign for the Arts Briefing* (London: National Campaign for the Arts, July 1998), pp. 1–3.
11. The Boyden report of 2000 stated that under-funding was a major constraint for producing theatres. It concluded that theatre boards felt exposed to personal liability, and consequently programmes tended towards greater conservatism, whilst innovation was discouraged. See Fiachra Gibbons, 'Curtains for Debt-Laden Theatres?', *The Guardian*, 28 January 2000.
12. John Bull, *Stage Right*, p. 14; John McGrath, *The Bone Won't Break: On Theatre and Hope in Hard Times* (London: Methuen Drama, 1990), p. viii.
13. Sir Richard Eyre, cited in Oliver Bennett, ed., *Cultural Policy and Management in the United Kingdom: Proceedings of an International Symposium* (Warwick: Centre for the Study of Cultural Policy, 1995), p. 15.
14. John Carey provides an entertaining and provocative interrogation of these beliefs in *What Good are the Arts?* (London: Faber and Faber, 2005).
15. Michael Billington, 'The Arts in the Eighties', *The Guardian*, 28 December 1985.
16. John Bull, *Stage Right*, p. 26.
17. Lyn Gardner outlines director Chris Goode's commission from the Pizza Express restaurant chain, Vicky Featherstone's work with fashion house Prada, and the relationship between drinks company Southern Comfort and Gideon Reeling, the sister company of performance group Punchdrunk. Lyn Gardner, 'An Offer They Can't Refuse', *The Guardian Unlimited*, 20 June 2006, http://blogs.guardian.co.uk/theatre/2006/06/an_offer_they_can't_refuse.html [accessed 21 June 2006].
18. Baz Kershaw, 'Discouraging Democracy: British Theatre and Economics, 1979–1999', *Theatre Journal*, 51.3 (1999), 267–283 (p. 283).
19. Aleks Sierz, 'Art Flourishes in Times of Struggle': Creativity, Funding and New Writing', *Contemporary Theatre Review* 13.1 (2003), 33–45 (p. 34).
20. Ibid., p. 38.
21. Baz Kershaw, 'Discouraging Democracy', p. 270. Aleks Sierz, 'Art Flourishes in Times of Struggle', p. 45. Quotation from John Elsom, 'United Kingdom', in *The World Encyclopaedia of Contemporary Theatre Vol. 1 Europe*, ed. by Don Rubin (London and New York: Routledge, 1994), p. 906.
22. Ugo Bacchella, cited in Oliver Bennett, ed., *Cultural Policy and Management in the United Kingdom*, pp. 35, 37.
23. Andrew McIlroy, cited in Oliver Bennett, ed., *Cultural Policy and Management in the United Kingdom*, p. 43.
24. See Ann West, quoted in Michael Booker, 'Protest from Mother of Victim Over Hindley Play', *Daily Mail*, 16 July 1998.
25. 'Monster Hindley Gets Star Billing at Fringe', *Scottish Daily Record*, 16 July 1998; Editorial, 'A Sick Act: Record View', *Scottish Daily Record*, 16 July 1998.

26. See David Edgar, 'Rules of Engagement', *The Guardian*, 22 October 2005, for a critique of this attitude.
27. Dan Glaister, 'Hindley Play Forced to Quit by Sponsor's Objection', *The Guardian*, 11 August 1998.
28. 'Monster Hindley Gets Star Billing at Fringe', *Scottish Daily Record*.
29. The self-reflexive nature of Dubois' play adds an extra level of irony to the development of these events. The play uses Hindley as a vehicle for discussion of the problem of addressing emotive or controversial material. Interviewed immediately after Calder's decision to eject *Myra and Me* from the Gilded Balloon, Dubois was quoted as saying that the company knew that Calder's were unhappy and that 'they were threatening to withdraw their funding'. She continued, 'It's ironic because this is what the play is about – censorship and artistic freedom.' Her comments appeared in the *Scottish Daily Record*, the paper that had originally started the controversy. See 'Myra Play is Ditched after Just One Show', *Scottish Daily Record*, 10 August 1998.
30. Philip Howard, interviewed by Aleks Sierz, cited in 'Art Flourishes in Times of Struggle', p. 42.
31. Howard Barker, 'The Olympics Killed My Theatre Company'.
32. Malachi O'Docherty, 'The Arts Council are Wrong', *Fortnight*, Issue 380, September 1999. See www.fortnight.org/current/CULTURE.HTM [accessed 17 July 2001].
33. John McGrath, Frank McGuinness, and Trevor Griffiths et al., *The Guardian*, 31 July 1999.
34. Gerry Adams, quoted in Malachi O'Docherty, 'The Arts Council are Wrong'.
35. Quoted in Amelia Gentleman, 'Dubble Trouble', *The Guardian*, 5 August 1999.
36. Pam Brighton, quoted in Amelia Gentleman, 'Dubble Trouble'.
37. Arts Council of England, 'National Policy for Theatre in England' (2000), pp. 4–6. See www.artscouncil.org.uk/publications/publication_detail.php?sid=15&id=138 [accessed 15 July 2001].
38. See Eoin O'Broin, 'A Clear Case of Political Censorship' in Dubble Trouble, *Fortnight*, Issue 380, September 1999. See www.fortnight.org/current/CULTURE.HTM [accessed 17 July 2001].
39. 'New Labour Because Britain Deserves Better', 1997 Labour Party Manifesto, cited in Andrew Brighton, 'Towards a Command Culture: New Labour's Cultural Policy and Soviet Socialist Realism', *Critical Quarterly*, 41.3 (October 1999), 24–34 (p. 25).
40. Stephen Bates, 'Ministers in Culture Clash as Drama Upsets Blunkett', *The Guardian*, 24 March 1998.
41. Dalya Alberge, 'Theatre's 3 Million Sponsor Checks Writer's Scripts', *The Times*, 3 December 1998. Grieve gave the example of being reassured that the teenage gang rape included in Rebecca Pritchard's *Fair Game* would occur off stage. He was obviously aware that this statement might prove provocative, and he was careful to state that when he did have concerns about a script, he had not taken matters further than a discussion with the theatre's artistic director and the board.
42. Dalya Alberge, 'Theatre's 3 Million Sponsor Checks Writer's Scripts'.

43. Dalya Alberge, 'Royal Court's Backers Pledge No Interference', *The Times*, 5 December 1998, p. 5a.
44. David Benedict, 'Shopping and Funding', *The Independent*, 19 May 1999, p. 11.
45. David Benedict, 'Shopping and Funding'.
46. Andrew McIlroy, *Cultural Policy and Management in the United Kingdom*, p. 42.
47. Judith Butler, 'Ruled Out', p. 257.

8   Competing fundamentalisms: *Behzti*, freedom of speech, sacrilege and silencing

1. Gurpreet Kaur Bhatti, *Behzti (Dishonour)* (London: Oberon Books, 2004), p. 21. All further references will appear in the text.
2. Quoted in Matthew Brown, 'MP Urges Theatres Not to Give in to Violence', *Western Mail*, 20 December 2004.
3. 'Lights Down', *The Times*, 21 December 2004; Ash Kotak, 'Not in Our Gurdwaras', *The Guardian*, 21 December 2004.
4. Hanif Kureishi, interviewed on 'Today', BBC Radio 4, 21 December 2004.
5. Susan Buck-Morss, *Thinking Past Terror* (London and New York: Verso, 2003), p. 93.
6. Mohan Singh, President of the Guru Nanak Gurdwara in south Birmingham, interviewed on 'Today', BBC Radio 4, 21 December 2004.
7. See Terry Kirby, 'Sikh Play Controversy', *The Independent*, 21 December 2004.
8. Rod Liddle, 'Meddling Zealots are Threatening Our Free Speech', *The Express*, 21 December 2004.
9. The Lord Chamberlain's examiners also demonstrated an interest in the character and motivation of the playwright from time to time. See my 'Anti-Theatrical Prejudice and the Persistence of Performance: The Lord Chamberlain's Plays and Correspondence Archive', *Performance Research*, 7.4 (December 2002), 50–58 (p. 57).
10. Kulvinder Singh Sura, Solihull, 'Sikh Play Fury: A Matter of Respect', *Birmingham Evening Mail*, 21 December 2004.
11. Louise Jury, 'Sikh Play Controversy: A Warm, Sensitive Writer Who Did Not Set Out to Offend', *The Independent*, 21 December 2004.
12. Gurharpal Singh, 'Sikhs are the Real Losers from Behzti', *The Guardian*, 24 December 2004.
13. Richard Burt, ed., *The Administration of Aesthetics: Censorship, Political Criticism and the Public Sphere* (Minneapolis: University of Minnesota Press, 1994), p. xii.
14. Ibid., p. xv.
15. Stanley Fish, *There's No Such Thing as Free Speech* (Oxford: Oxford University Press, 1994), p. 103.
16. Milton's essay made an appearance in the coverage of the controversy in the leader writer's column for *The Daily Telegraph* which argued that government ministers were pandering to intolerance in order to secure the vote of religious minority communities. The writer asserted that these minority communities should be taught to celebrate the centrality of the principle of

the right to freedom of speech in the British tradition by reading Milton's *Areopagitica*. See 'Running Scared', *The Daily Telegraph*, 22 December 2004.

17. John Milton, *Areopagicita* (1644) quoted in Stanley Fish, *There's No Such Thing as Free Speech*, p. 103.

18. Ian Shuttleworth, 'Prompt Corner', *Theatre Record*, xxiv (2004), p. 1659.

19. Here the enormous gulf between the tropes of academic analysis – where Barthes' 'death of the author' theory is now common currency – and the popular understanding of the link between a writer and their work is particularly stark. But then 'death of the author' theories never seem less convincing than when the author in question has received death threats.

20. For example, Steel recalled that Min's large speeches in the final scene were cut down as it appeared that she had become 'too knowledgeable too quickly.' Janet Steel, interview with the author, 15 June 2005. All further quotes from Steel are from this interview.

21. Steel explained that she had decided to place the actor playing Mr Sandhu upstage, with his back to the auditorium, and to distract the audience from the action by foregrounding a downstage image of the Gurdwara's priest. A scream from Polly, upstage of Mr Sandhu, and a sudden drop in the light level signalled the moment of his murder.

22. For example, see comments made by Home Office Minister for Race Equality, Community Policy and Civil Renewal, Fiona Mactaggart, on the Today programme: 'I think that when people are moved, by theatre, to protest, in a way that's a sign of the free speech that is so much part of the British tradition.' Interviewed on 'Today', BBC Radio 4, 21 December 2004. Writing on *Behzti*, Jaswant Guzdar celebrated British theatre's history of addressing controversial material in 'Behzti: Dishonour in Birmingham', *alt.theatre: cultural diversity and the stage*, 3.3 (December 2004), 4–5.

23. The vocal support for the protestors provided by the Roman Catholic Church seems both infelicitous, given ongoing revelations about instances of institutionalised sexual abuse within the Church, and curious, when one considers the longer history of prejudice, persecution and silencing experienced by Roman Catholics in Britain.

24. Jonathan Sentamu, interviewed on 'Today', BBC Radio 4, 21 December 2004.

25. Sarita Malik, Letter, *The Guardian*, 18 January 2005.

26. Jasdev Singh Rai, 'Behind Behzti: Colonial Attitudes Linger, Finding Their Most Xenophobic Expression Among Liberal Defenders of Free Speech', *The Guardian*, 17 January 2005.

27. Statement by the Birmingham Rep, quoted in Tania Branigan, 'Tale of Rape at the Temple Sparks Riot at Theatre', *The Guardian*, 20 December 2004.

28. Dr Henry Warson (of Solihull), A. Lloyd (of Kingstanding), and Mr A. Donovan. Letters printed in the *Birmingham Evening Mail*, 21 December 2004.

29. Sewa Singh Mandla, interviewed on 'Today', BBC Radio 4, 21 December 2004.

30. Quoted in Anushka Asthana, 'Art vs Religion: Tempest of Rage Shakes Sikh Temple', *The Observer*, 26 December 2004.

31. Ranbir Singh Lakhpuri, Letter, *The Daily Telegraph*, 22 December 2004.

32. Nicholas Hytner, interviewed on 'Today', BBC Radio 4, 20 December 2004.

33. Ian Rickson, quoted in 'Theatre Community Defends "Courageous" Birmingham Rep', *The Guardian*, 21 December 2004.
34. 'The Birmingham Rep Riot: Behind the Scenes', BBC Radio 4, 23 August 2004.
35. Sean O'Neill and Nicola Woolcock, 'Extremists Hijacked Play Protest', *The Times*, 22 December 2004.
36. See Torcuil Crichton, 'Cancelled Due to Lack of Tolerance', *Sunday Herald*, 26 December 2004.
37. Sunny Hundal, 'Sikh Leaders are Not Without Blame for Behzti Controversy', 4 January 2005, www.asiansinmedia.org/news/article.php/theatre/763 [accessed 15 February 2005].
38. Sunny Hundal, 'The Violent Reaction to Behzti is Despicable and Hypocritical', 20 December 2004, www.asiansinmedia.org/news/article.php/theatre/746 [accessed 15 February 2005].
39. Gurharpal Singh, quoted in Torcuil Crichton, 'Cancelled Due to Lack of Tolerance'.
40. Gurharpal Singh, 'Sikhs are the Real Losers from Behzti'.

Conclusion

1. Mary Whitehouse, quoted in Nicholas de Jongh, 'Sir Peter Refuses to Fall on his Sword', *The Guardian*, 18 October 1980.
2. Quoted in Anushka Asthana, 'Art vs Religion: Tempest of Rage Shakes Sikh Temple', *The Observer*, 26 December 2004; Ranbir Singh Lakhpuri, Letter, *The Daily Telegraph*, 22 December 2004.
3. *Report from the Joint Select Committee of the House of Lords and the House of Commons on the Stage Plays (Censorship) Together with the Proceedings of the Committee, Minutes and Appendices* (London: Government Publications, 1909).
4. Earl of Cromer (Lord Chamberlain), Note on Report, LCP Corr., *Lady of the Sky*, LR 1934, 23 February 1935.
5. Statement by the Birmingham Rep, quoted in Tania Branigan, 'Tale of Rape at the Temple Sparks Riot at Theatre', *The Guardian*, 20 December 2004.
6. See Steve Nicholson, *The Censorship of British Drama 1900–1968: 1933–1952*, Vol. 2 (Exeter: University of Exeter Press, 2005), pp. 34–39.
7. See Plato, *The Republic*, ed. by G.R.F. Ferrari, trans. by Tom Griffith (Cambridge: Cambridge University Press, 2000).
8. Jonathan Miller, 'Censorship', *The Guardian*, 16 October 1967.
9. Julia Kristeva, *Powers of Horror: An Essay on Abjection*, trans. by Leon S. Roudiez (New York: Columbia University Press, 1982), p. 4.
10. Sigmund Freud, 'Repression', in *The Freud Reader*, ed. by Peter Gay (London: Vintage, 1995), pp. 568–572 (p. 572).
11. Aleks Sierz, ' "The Element That Most Outrages": Morality, Censorship and Sarah Kane's *Blasted*', *European Studies* 17 (2001), 225–239 (p. 226).
12. John Osborne, quoted in Kenneth Tynan, *A View of the English Stage 1944–1965* (London: Methuen, 1975), p. 374.
13. Cited in Dorothy Knowles, *The Censor, The Drama and the Film* (London: George Allen & Unwin Ltd, 1934), p. 4, in Steve Nicholson, 'Censoring

Revolution: The Lord Chamberlain and the Soviet Union', *New Theatre Quarterly*, 8.32 (1992), 305–312 (p. 311).

14. Steve Nicholson, *The Censorship of British Drama*, Vol. 1, pp. 1–2.

15. See Judith Butler, *Excitable Speech: A Politics of the Performative* (London and New York: Routledge, 1997), pp. 127–140.

16. Michael Levine, *Writing Through Repression* (Baltimore: Johns Hopkins University Press, 1995), p. 2.

17. See Kenneth Tynan, 'The Royal Smut-Hound', in *Post-War British Drama: Looking Back in Gender*, ed. by Michelene Wandor (London and New York: Routledge, 2001), pp. 98–111, 379.

18. This was over *You Won't Always Be on Top*, at the Theatre Royal, Stratford East. See Paul O'Higgins, *Censorship in Britain* (London: Nelson, 1972), p. 95. Jen Harvie provides an insightful discussion of the influence of anti-theatrical prejudice and the British investment in dramatic literature in *Staging the UK* (Manchester and New York: Manchester University Press, 2005), pp. 115–118.

19. Cited in John Florance, 'Theatrical Censorship in Britain 1901–1968', unpublished thesis (Cardiff: University of Wales, 1980), p. 292.

20. Michael Holquist, 'Corrupt Originals: The Paradox of Censorship', *Publications of the Modern Language Association of America*, 109.1 (1994), 14–25 (p. 22).

21. See Janelle Reinelt, 'The Limits of Censorship', *Theatre Research International* 32.1 (2007), 3–15.

22. David Edgar, *The Guardian*, 28 January 1988, p. 14.

23. Judith Butler, *Excitable Speech*, p. 140.

Bibliography

Primary Sources

Lord Chamberlain's Plays

Hellem, Charles and Pol d'Estoc, *Blind Man's Buff*, Unlicensed LCP List 1, 1921/6.
Berton, René, *Euthanasia*, Unlicensed LCP List 1, 1921/6.
Holland, Christopher, *The Old Women*, LC Play 1921/10, Add. MSS. 66280.
De Lorde, André, *Dr Goudron's System*, Unlicensed LCP List 1, 1922/7.
Witney, Frederick, *Coals of Fire*, Unlicensed LCP List 1, 1922/7.
Stopes, Marie, *Our Ostriches*, Unlicensed LCP List 1, 1923/7.
Stopes, Marie (Clifford Cooper) *Cleansing Circles*, Unlicensed LCP List 1, 1926/10.
Norris, Marion, *Alone*, Unlicensed LCP List 1, 1930/18.
Winsloe, Christa, *Children in Uniform*, LC Play 1932/26, Add. MSS. 66818.
Stuart, Aimée and Philip, *Love of Women*, Unlicensed LCP List 1, 1934/21.
Wakefield, Gilbert, *Lady of the Sky*, Unlicensed LCP List 1, 1934/21.
Broadwater, Henry, *Riviera*, Unlicensed LCP List 1, 1935/23.
Hochhuth, Rolf, *Soldiers*, Unlicensed LCP List 2, 1967/29.

Lord Chamberlain's correspondence files

Blind Man's Buff, LR 1921.
Euthanasia, LR 1921.
The Old Women, 1921/3534.
Dr Goudron's System, LR 1922.
Coals of Fire, LR 1922.
Our Ostriches, LR 1923.
Vectia, LR 1924.
Cradle Snatchers, LR 1925.
Cleansing Circles, LR 1926.
The Vortex Damned, LR 1930.
Alone, LR 1930.
Children in Uniform, 1932/11437.
Who Made the Iron Grow, LR 1933.
Love of Women, LR 1934.
Lady of the Sky, LR 1934.
Children's Hour, LR 1935.
Riviera, LR 1935.
The Cure, LR 1935.
Lysistrata to Date, LR 1942.
Soldiers, WB 1967.

Gabrielle Enthoven collection at the V&A theatre collection

Production file: Grand Guignol Series, Little Theatre, 1920–1922.
Production file: Our Ostriches, Royal Court Theatre, 1923.

Production file: Continuous Grand Guignol, Duke of Yorks, 1932.
Production file: Love of Women, Phoenix Theatre, 1935.
Production file: Soldiers, New Theatre, 1968.
Censorship files.
Kenneth Tynan biography files.

Mander and Mitchenson collection
Little Theatre file, 1920–1922.

Kenneth Tynan papers
At the time of consultation these were uncatalogued.

Secondary sources

Newspapers and periodicals
Birmingham Evening Mail.
Country Life.
The Daily Telegraph.
Daily Mail.
The Era.
Evening Standard.
Evening News.
Fortnight.
The Express.
The Guardian.
The Illustrated London News.
The Independent.
The Independent on Sunday.
The Irish Times.
The Manchester Guardian.
New York Herald Tribune.
New York Sun.
New York Times.
The Observer.
Plays and Players.
Punch.
Scottish Daily Record.
The Spectator.
The Stage.
Sunday Herald.
Sunday Times.
Theatre Record.
The Times.
Variety.
Western Mail.

Contemporary or published sources

Abercrombie, N. and B. Longhurst, *Audiences: A Sociological Theory of Performance and Imagination* (London: Sage, 1998).

Althusser, Louis, *For Marx*, trans. by Ben Brewster (London: Verso, 1986).

Appignanesi, Lisa, ed., *Free Expression is No Offence* (London: Penguin, 2005).

Appleby, Joyce, Lynn Hunt and Margaret Jacob, *Telling the Truth about History* (London: Norton, 1994).

Austin, J.L., *How to Do Things with Words* (Oxford: The Clarendon Press, 1962).

Badley, Linda, *Film, Horror, and the Body Fantastic* (Westport, Connecticut and London: Greenwood Press, 1995).

Barish, Jonas, *The Anti-Theatrical Prejudice* (Berkeley: University of California, 1981).

Barker, M. and J. Petley, eds., *Ill Effects: The Media/Violence Debate* (London and New York: Routledge, 1996).

Barker, Philip, *Michel Foucault: Subversions of the Subject* (London and New York: Harvester Wheatsheaf, 1993).

Barthes, Roland, *Image-Music-Text* (London: Fontana, 1977).

——, 'The Metaphor of the Eye', in Georges Bataille, *The Story of the Eye*, trans. by J.A. Underwood (London: Marion Boyars Publishers Ltd, 1979), pp. 119–127.

Bataille, Georges, *Literature and Evil*, trans. by Alistair Hamilton (London: Calder and Boyars, 1973).

——, *The Story of the Eye* (London: Marion Boyars Publishers Ltd, 1979).

——, *The Accursed Share*, trans. by Robert Hurley (New York: Zone, 1991).

——, *Eroticism*, trans. by Mary Dalwood (London: Penguin, 2001).

Bennett, Oliver, ed., *Cultural Policy and Management in the United Kingdom: Proceedings of an International Symposium* (Warwick: Centre for the Study of Cultural Policy, 1995).

Bhatti, Gurpreet Kaur, *Behzti (Dishonour)* (London: Oberon Books, 2004).

Boon, Richard, *Brenton: The Playwright* (New York and London: Methuen, 1991).

Bottoms, Stephen, 'Putting the Document into Documentary: An Unwelcome Corrective?', *TDR* 50.3 (Fall 2006), 56–68.

Brenton, Howard, *The Romans in Britain* (London: Methuen, 1982).

Brenton, Howard, et al., *Lay by* (London: Calder and Boyars, 1972).

Brighton, Andrew, 'Towards a Command Culture: New Labour's Cultural Policy and Soviet Socialist Realism', *Critical Quarterly*, 41.3 (October 1999), 24–34.

Brittain,Vera, *Radclyffe Hall: A Case of Obscenity?* (London: Femina, 1968).

Brooker, Will and Deborah Jermyn, eds., *The Audience Studies Reader* (London and New York: Routledge, 2003).

Buck-Morss, Susan, *Thinking Past Terror* (London and New York: Verso, 2003).

Bull, John, *Stage Right* (London: Macmillan, 1994).

Burgin, Victor, 'Geometry and Abjection', in *Abjection, Melancholia and Love: The Work of Julia Kristeva*, ed. by John Fletcher and Andrew Benjamin (London and New York: Routledge, 1990), pp. 104–123.

Burt, Richard, ed., *The Administration of Aesthetics: Censorship, Political Criticism and the Public Sphere* (Minneapolis: University of Minnesota Press, 1994).

Butler, Judith, 'Imitation and Gender Insubordination', in *Inside/Out: Lesbian Theories, Gay Theories*, ed. by Diana Fuss (London and New York: Routledge, 1991), pp. 13–31.

——, *Excitable Speech: A Politics of the Performative* (London and New York: Routledge, 1997).

——, *The Psychic Life of Power* (Stanford: Stanford University Press, 1997).

——, 'Ruled Out: Vocabularies of the Censor', in *Censorship and Silencing: Practices of Cultural Regulation*, ed. by Robert C. Post (Los Angeles: Getty Research Institute for the History of Art and the Humanities, 1998), pp. 247–259.

Callaghan, John M., 'The Ultimate in Theatre Violence', in *Violence in Drama*, ed. by James Redmond (Cambridge and New York: Cambridge University Press, 1991), pp. 165–176.

Carey, John, *What Good are the Arts?* (London: Faber & Faber, 2005).

Casson, John, *Lewis & Sybil: A Memoir* (London: Collins, 1972).

Chauncey, George, Jr., 'From Sexual Inversion to Homosexuality: Medicine and the Changing Conceptualisation of Female Deviance', *Salmagundi*, 58–59 (1982–1983), 114–146.

Collecott, Diana, 'What is Not Said: A Study in Textual Inversion', in *Sexual Sameness: Textual Differences in Lesbian and Gay Writing*, ed. by Joseph Bristow (London and New York: Routledge, 1992), pp. 91–110.

Crawshay-Williams, Eliot, *Five Grand Guignol Plays* (London and New York: Samuel French, 1924).

Crimp, Douglas, ed., *AIDS: Cultural Analysis/Cultural Activism* (Cambridge, MA: MIT Press, 1987).

Davis, Jill, ed., *Lesbian Plays* (London: Methuen, 1987).

——, ed., *Lesbian Plays II* (London: Methuen, 1989).

——, 'The New Woman and the New Life', in *The New Woman and Her Sisters: Feminism and Theatre 1850–1914*, ed. by Viv Gardner and Susan Rutherford (London and New York: Harvester Wheatsheaf, 1992), pp. 17–36.

Davis, Tracy C., *The Economics of the British Stage* (Cambridge: Cambridge University Press, 2000).

Davis-Brown, Beth and Richard Harvey-Brown, 'The Making of Memory: The Politics of Archives, Libraries and Museums in the Construction of the National Consciousness', *History of the Human Sciences*, 11.4 (1998), 17–32.

Deak, Frantisek, 'Theatre du Grand Guignol', *TDR*, 18.1 (1974), 34–43.

Deeney, John F. 'Censoring the Uncensored: The Case of "Children in Uniform" ', *New Theatre Quarterly*, 16.3 (2000), 219–226.

de Jongh, Nicholas, *Not in Front of the Audience* (London and New York: Routledge, 1992).

——, *Politics, Prudery & Perversions: The Censoring of the English Stage 1901–1968* (London: Methuen, 2000).

Derrida, Jacques, *Archive Fever: A Freudian Impression,* trans. by Eric Prenowitz (Chicago and London: University of Chicago Press, 1995).

Dickinson, R., R. Harindranath and O. Linné, eds., *Approaches to Audiences: A Reader* (London: Arnold, 1998).

Douglas, Mary, *Purity and Danger: An Analysis of the Concepts of Pollution and Taboo* (London: Ark, 1984).

Dowling, William C., *Jameson, Althusser, Marx: An Introduction to The Political Unconscious* (London: Methuen, 1984).

Durham Peters, John, *Courting the Abyss: Free Speech and the Liberal Tradition* (Chicago: University of Chicago Press, 2005).

Dyer, Richard, *Now You See It: Studies on Lesbian and Gay Film* (London and New York: Routledge, 1990).

Edgar, David, 'Shouting Fire: Art, Religion and the Right to be Offended', *Race & Class*, 48.2 (2006), 61–76.

Edwards, Jennifer, Esther Kuperji and Eleanor Simmons, *Theatre in Crisis: The Plight of Regional Theatre. A National Campaign for the Arts Briefing* (London: National Campaign for the Arts, July 1998).

Ellenberger, Harriet, 'The Dream is the Bridge: In Search of Lesbian Theatre', *Trivia*, 5 (Fall 1984), 17–59.

Ellis, Havelock, 'Sexual Inversion in Women', in *Studies in Psychology of Sex*, Vol. 2 (New York: Random House, 1936a), pp. 195–263.

——, 'Appendix B: The School-Friendships of Girls', in *Studies in the Psychology of Sex*, Vol. 2 (New York: Random House, 1936b), pp. 368–384.

Emeljanow, Victor, 'Grand Guignol and the Orchestration of Violence', in *Violence in Drama*, ed. by James Redmond (Cambridge and New York: Cambridge University Press, 1991), pp. 151–164.

Esslin, Martin, *Brief Chronicles: Essays on Modern Theatre* (London: Temple Smith, 1970).

Faderman, Lillian, *Surpassing the Love of Men: Romantic Friendship and Love between Women from the Renaissance to the Present* (London: The Women's Press, 1981).

——, 'Love Between Women in 1928: Why Progressivism is Not Always Progress', in *Historical, Literary and Erotic Aspects of Lesbianism*, ed. by Monika Kehoe (New York and London: Harrington Park Press, 1986), pp. 23–42.

Findlater, Richard, *Banned! A Review of Theatrical Censorship in Britain* (London: McGibbon & Kee, 1967).

Fish, Stanley, *There's No Such Thing as Free Speech* (Oxford: Oxford University Press, 1994).

Foucault, Michel, *Discipline and Punish*, trans. by Alan Sheridan (London: Penguin, 1977).

——, *Power/Knowledge: Selected Interviews and Other Writings 1972–1977*, ed. by Colin Gordon (London: Harvester, 1980).

——, *History of Sexuality: Volume 1*, trans. by Robert Hurley (London: Penguin Books, 1998 [1976]).

——, 'A Preface to Transgression', in *Bataille: A Critical Reader*, ed. by Fred Botting and Scott Wilson (Oxford: Blackwell, 1998), pp. 24–40.

Freshwater, Helen, 'Anti-Theatrical Prejudice and the Persistence of Performance: The Lord Chamberlain's Plays and Correspondence Archive', *Performance Research*, 7.4 (December 2002), 50–58.

——, 'The Allure of the Archive', *Poetics Today*, 24.4 (Winter 2003), 729–758.

——, 'Towards a Redefinition of Censorship', in *Censorship and Cultural Regulation in the Modern Age*, ed. by Beate Müller, Critical Studies 22 (Amsterdam and New York: Rodopi, 2004), pp. 225–245.

Gale, Maggie B., *West End Women: Women and the London Stage, 1918–1962* (London and New York: Routledge, 1996).

Gardner, Viv and Susan Rutherford, eds., *The New Woman and her Sisters: Feminism and Theatre 1850–1914* (London and New York: Harvester Wheatsheaf, 1992).

Garfield, Simon, *End of Innocence: Britain in the Time of AIDS* (London and Boston: Faber and Faber, 1994).

Gordon, Linda, 'The Struggle for Reproductive Freedom: Three Stages of Feminism', in *Capitalist Patriarchy and the Case for Socialist Feminism*, ed. by Zillah Eisenstein (London and New York: Monthly Review Press, 1979), pp. 107–135.

Gordon, Mel, *Grand Guignol: Theatre of Fear and Terror* (New York: Amok Press, 1988).

Grixti, Joseph, *Terrors of Uncertainty: The Cultural Contexts of Horror Fiction* (London and New York: Routledge, 1989).

Grosz, Elizabeth, 'The Body of Signification', in *Abjection, Melancholia and Love: The Work of Julia Kristeva*, ed. by John Fletcher and Andrew Benjamin (London and New York: Routledge 1990), pp. 80–103.

Guzdar, Jaswant, 'Behzti: Dishonour in Birmingham', *alt.theatre: Cultural Diversity and the Stage*, 3.3 (December 2004), 4–5.

Hall, Peter, *Making an Exhibition of Myself* (London: Sinclair Stevenson, 1993).

Hamer, Diane, 'I Am a Woman: Ann Bannon and the Writing of Lesbian Identity in the 1950s', in *Lesbian and Gay Writing: An Anthology of Critical Essays*, ed. by Mark Lilly (London: Macmillan, 1990), pp. 47–75.

Hand, Richard J. and Michael Wilson, 'The Grand-Guignol: Aspects of Theory and Practice', *Theatre Research International*, 25.3 (2000), 266–275.

——, *Grand-Guignol: The French Theatre of Horror* (Exeter: Exeter University Press, 2002).

——, *London's Grand Guignol and the Theatre of Horror* (Exeter: Exeter University Press, 2007).

Harrison, Nicholas, *Circles of Censorship: Censorship and its Metaphors in French History, Literature and Theory* (Oxford: Oxford University Press, 1995).

Hart, Lynda, 'Canonising Lesbians?', in *Modern American Drama: The Female Canon*, ed. by June Schlueter (London and Toronto: Associated University Presses, 1990), pp. 275–292.

Harvie, Jen, *Staging the UK* (Manchester and New York: Manchester University Press, 2005).

Hellman, Lillian, *The Children's Hour* (New York: The Dramatists Play Service Inc, 1981).

Hochhuth, Rolf, *Soldiers: An Obituary for Geneva*, trans. by Robert David MacDonald (London: Andre Deutsch with Penguin Books, 1968).

Hoggart, Richard, *The Uses of Literacy* (London: Chatto and Windus, 1957).

Holquist, Michael, 'Corrupt Originals: The Paradox of Censorship', *Publications of the Modern Language Association of America*, 109.1 (1994), 14–25.

Hutchison, David, 'Economics, Culture and Playwrighting', in *Scottish Theatre Since the Seventies*, ed. by Randall Stevenson and Gavin Wallace (Edinburgh: Edinburgh University Press, 1996), pp. 206–214.

Iggers, Georg G. and James M. Powell, *Leopold von Ranke and the Shaping of the Historical Discipline* (Syracuse, NY: Syracuse University Press, 1990).

Irving, David, *Accident: The Death of General Sikorski* (London: William Kimber, 1967).

Jameson, Fredric, *The Political Unconscious: Narrative as a Socially Symbolic Act* (London: Methuen, 1981).

——, *Signatures of the Visible* (London and New York: Routledge, 1992).

Jansen, Sue Curry, *Censorship: The Knot That Binds Power and Knowledge* (New York and Oxford: Oxford University Press, 1991).

Jay, Martin, *Downcast Eyes: The Denigration of Vision in Twentieth Century French Thought* (Berkeley: University of California Press, 1993).

Johnson, Kathryn, 'Apart from Look Back in Anger, What Else Was Worrying the Lord Chamberlain's Office in 1956?', in *British Theatre in the 1950s*, ed. by Dominic Shellard (Sheffield: Sheffield Academic Press, 2000), pp. 116–135.

Johnston, John, *The Lord Chamberlain's Blue Pencil* (London and Sydney: Hodder & Stoughton, 1990).

Katyal, Anjum, 'Summer of Discontent: Religion, Censorship and the Politics of Offence', *Index on Censorship*, 35.4 (2006), 157–161.

Kermode, Mark, 'Horror: On the Edge of Taste', *Index on Censorship*, 24.6 (1995), 59–68.

Kershaw, Baz, 'Discouraging Democracy: British Theatre and Economics, 1979–1999', *Theatre Journal*, 51.3 (1999), 267–283.

Knowles, Dorothy, *The Censor, The Drama and the Film* (London: George Allen & Unwin Ltd, 1934).

Krakovitch, Odile, 'Avant le Grand-Guignol', *Europe-Revue Litteraire Mensuelle*, 836 (1998), 123–137.

Kristeva, Julia, *Powers of Horror: An Essay on Abjection*, trans. by Leon S. Roudiez (New York: Columbia University Press, 1982).

Kuhn, Annette, *Cinema, Censorship and Sexuality, 1909–1925* (London and New York: Routledge, 1988).

Lacan, Jacques, *Four Fundamental Concepts of Psychoanalysis*, ed. by Jacques-Alain Miller, trans. by Alan Sheridan (New York: W.W. Norton, 1981).

——, *The Seminar of Jacques Lacan. Book 1: Freud's Papers on Technique, 1953–1954*, ed. by Jacques-Alain Miller, trans. by John Forrester (Cambridge: Cambridge University Press, 1988).

Langton, Rae, 'Subordination, Silence, and Pornography's Authority', in *Censorship and Silencing: Practices of Cultural Regulation*, ed. by Robert C. Post (Los Angeles: Getty Research Institute for the History of Art and the Humanities, 1998), pp. 261–284.

Lechte, John, *Julia Kristeva* (New York and London: Routledge, 1990).

Levine, Michael, *Writing Through Repression* (Baltimore: Johns Hopkins University Press, 1995).

Lewis, Reina, 'The Death of the Author and the Resurrection of the Dyke', in *New Lesbian Criticism: Literary and Cultural Readings*, ed. by Sally Munt (New York and London: Harvester Wheatsheaf, 1992), pp. 17–32.

Lucas, Ian, *Impertinent Decorum* (London: Cassell, 1994).

——, *Outrage! An Oral History* (London: Cassell, 1998).

Marx, Karl, Preface to *Contribution to the Critique of Political Economy* (New York: International, 1970).

McConachie, Bruce A., 'Historicizing the Relations of Theatrical Production', in *Critical Theory and Performance*, ed. by Janelle Reinelt and Joseph Roach (Ann Arbor: University of Michigan Press, 1992), pp. 168–178.

McGrath, John, *The Bone Won't Break: On Theatre and Hope in Hard Times* (London: Methuen Drama, 1990).

McKenzie, Jon, *Perform or Else* (London and New York: Routledge, 2002).

McPherson, Mervyn, ed., *Grand Guignol Annual Review* (London: The Little Theatre, 1921).

Métayer, Léon, 'Le Grand-Guignol? Une Bonne Affaire!', *Europe-Revue Litteraire Mensuelle*, 836 (1998), 184–193.

Mills, Sara, *Michel Foucault* (London and New York: Routledge, 2003).

Murray, Timothy, *Drama Trauma: Specters of Race and Sexuality in Performance, Video and Art* (London and New York: Routledge, 1997).

Newton, Esther, 'The Mythic Mannish Lesbian: Radclyffe Hall and the New Woman', in *The Lesbian Issue: Essays from Signs*, ed. by Estelle Freedman et al. (Chicago and London: University of Chicago Press, 1985), pp. 7–26.

Nicholson, Steve, 'Censoring Revolution: The Lord Chamberlain and the Soviet Union', *New Theatre Quarterly*, 8.32 (1992), 305–312.

——, 'Unnecessary Play: European Drama and the British Censor in the 1920s', *Theatre Research International*, 20.1 (1995), 30–36.

——, 'Foreign Drama and the Lord Chamberlain in the 1950s', in *British Theatre in the 1950s*, ed. by Dominic Shellard (Sheffield: Sheffield Academic Press, 2000), pp. 41–52.

——, *The Censorship of British Drama 1900–1968: 1900–1932*, Vol. 1 (Exeter: University of Exeter Press, 2003).

——, *The Censorship of British Drama 1900–1968: 1933–1952*, Vol. 2 (Exeter: University of Exeter Press, 2005).

O'Higgins, Paul, *Censorship in Britain* (London: Nelson, 1972).

Osment, Philip, ed., *Gay Sweatshop: Four Plays and a Company* (London: Methuen Drama, 1989).

Patton, Cindy, *Inventing AIDS* (London and New York: Routledge, 1991).

——, 'Performativity and Spatial Distinction: The End of AIDS Epidemiology', in *Performance and Performativity*, ed. by Eve Kosofsky Sedgwick and Andrew Parker (London and New York: Routledge, 1995), pp. 173–196.

Pauvert, Jean-Jacques, *Nouveaux (et Moins Nouveaux) Visages de la Censure* (Paris: Les Belles Lettres, 1994).

Peacock, Keith D., *Thatcher's Theatre: British Theatre and Drama in the Eighties* (London and Westport: Greenwood Press, 1999).

Pearson, Mike and Michael Shanks, *Theatre/Archaeology* (London and New York: Routledge, 2001).

Phelan, Peggy, *Unmarked: The Politics of Performance* (London and New York: Routledge, 1993).

Pierron, Agnès, ed., *Le Grand Guignol: Le Theatre des Peurs de la Belle Epoque* (Paris: Robert Laffont, 1995).

——, 'Avorter, Vomir ou S'évanouir', *Europe-Revue Litteraire Mensuelle*, 836 (1998), 101–107.

Plato, *The Republic*, ed. by G.R.F. Ferrari, trans. by Tom Griffith (Cambridge: Cambridge University Press, 2000).

Post, Robert C., ed., *Censorship and Silencing: Practices of Cultural Regulation* (Los Angeles: Getty Research Institute for the History of Art and the Humanities, 1998).

Pradier, Jean-Marie, 'Bon Sang!', *Europe-Revue Litteraire Mensuelle*, 836 (1998), 98–100.

——, 'La Science ou la Passion D'éventrer', *Europe-Revue Litteraire Mensuelle*, 836 (1998), 108–122.

Price, Janet and Margrit Shildrick, eds., *Feminist Theory and the Body: A Reader* (Edinburgh: Edinburgh University Press, 1999).

Puchner, Martin, *Stage Fright: Modernism, Anti-Theatricality and Drama* (Baltimore and London: Johns Hopkins University Press, 2002).

Puchner, Martin and Alan Ackerman, *Against Theatre: Creative Destructions on the Modernist Stage* (Basingstoke and New York: Palgrave Macmillan, 2006).

Quinet, Antonio, 'The Gaze as an Object', in *Reading Seminar XI: Lacan's Four Fundamental Concepts of Psychoanalysis*, ed. by Richard Feldstein, Bruce Fink and Maire Jaanus (Albany: State University of New York Press, 1995), pp. 139–148.

Rapi, Nina, 'Hide and Seek: The Search for a Lesbian Theatre Aesthetic', *New Theatre Quarterly*, 9.34 (1993), 147–158.

Redmond, James, ed., *Violence in Drama* (Cambridge and New York: Cambridge University Press, 1991).

Reinelt, Janelle, 'Towards a Poetics of Theatre and Public Events', *TDR*, 50.3 (Fall 2006), 69–87.

——, 'The Limits of Censorship', *Theatre Research International*, 32.1 (2007), 3–15.

Report from the Joint Select Committee of the House of Lords and the House of Commons on the Stage Plays (Censorship) together with the Proceedings of the Committee, Minutes and Appendices (London: Government Publications, 1909).

Rich, Adrienne, 'Compulsory Heterosexuality and Lesbian Existence', in *Blood, Bread and Poetry: Selected Prose 1979–1985* (London: Virago, 1986), pp. 23–75.

Riviere, Francois, Gabrielle Wittkop and Henri Veyrier, *Grand Guignol* (Nancy: Bernard Pere, 1979).

Roberts, Philip, 'The Trials of The Romans in Britain', in *Howard Brenton: A Casebook*, ed. by Ann Wilson (London and New York: Garland Publishing Inc, 1992), pp. 59–70.

Robertson, Geoffrey, *The Justice Game* (London: Chatto & Windus, 1998).

Roman, David, *Acts of Intervention: Performance, Gay Culture, and AIDS* (Bloomington and Indianapolis: University of Indiana Press, 1998).

Rose, June, *Marie Stopes and the Sexual Revolution* (London: Faber & Faber, 1992).

Salih, Sara, *Judith Butler* (London and New York: Routledge, 2004).

Saunders, Graham, *Love me or kill me: Sarah Kane and the Theatre of Extremes* (Manchester: Manchester University Press, 2002).

Schauer, Frederick, 'The Ontology of Censorship', in *Censorship and Silencing: Practices of Cultural Regulation*, ed. by Robert C. Post (Los Angeles: Getty Research Institute for the History of Art and the Humanities, 1998), pp. 147–168.

Sedgwick, Eve Kosofsky, *The Epistemology of the Closet* (New York and London: Harvester Wheatsheaf, 1991).

Sedgwick, Eve Kosofsky and Alan Parker, eds., *Performativity and Performance* (London and New York: Routledge, 1995).

Shaviro, Stephen, *Passion and Excess: Blanchot, Bataille, and Literary Theory* (Tallahassee: Florida State University Press, 1990).

Shaw, Roy, ed., *The Spread of Sponsorship in the Arts, Sports, Education, the Health Service and Broadcasting* (Newcastle: Bloodaxe Books, 1993).

Shellard, Dominic, *Kenneth Tynan: A Life* (London and New Haven: Yale University Press, 2003).

Shellard, Dominic and Steve Nicholson with Miriam Handley, *The Lord Chamberlain Regrets . . . a History of British Theatre Censorship* (London: The British Library, 2004).

Shepherd, Simon and Peter Womack, *English Drama: A Cultural History* (Oxford: Blackwell, 1996).

Sierz, Aleks, ' "Art Flourishes in Times of Struggle": Creativity, Funding and New Writing', *Contemporary Theatre Review*, 13.1 (2003), 33–45.

Sinclair, Andrew, *Arts and Cultures: The History of Fifty Years of the Arts Council of Great Britain* (London: Sinclair-Stevenson, 1995).

Sinfield, Alan, 'Private Lives/Public Theater: Noël Coward and the Politics of Homosexual Representation', *Representations*, 36 (1991), 43–63.

——, *Out on Stage* (London and New York: Routledge, 1999).

Smith, Bonnie, *The Gender of History. Men, Women and Historical Practice* (Cambridge, MA: Harvard University Press, 1998).

Smith, Patricia Juliana, *Lesbian Panic: Homoeroticism in Modern British Women's Fiction* (New York: Columbia University Press, 1997).

Soloway, Richard, *Birth Control and the Population Question in England 1877–1930* (Chapel Hill, London: University of North Carolina Press, 1982).

Sontag, Susan, *Illness as Metaphor and AIDS and its Metaphors* (London: Penguin, 1991).

Sprigge, Elizabeth, *Sybil Thorndike Casson* (London: Victor Gollancz Ltd, 1971).

Steiner, George, *After Babel: Aspects of Language and Translation*, 3rd edn (Oxford: Oxford University Press, 1998).

Stewart, Susan, *Crimes of Writing: Problems in the Containment of Representation* (Oxford: Oxford University Press, 1991).

Still, Judith, 'Horror in Kristeva and Bataille: Sex and Violence', *Paragraph*, 20.3 (1997), 221–239.

Stopes, Marie, *A Banned Play and a Preface on Censorship* (London: John Bale, Sons and Danielsson, Ltd, 1926).

——, *Wise Parenthood*, 23rd edn (London: Putnam and Co. Ltd, 1940).

——, *Married Love* (London: Victor Gollancz, 1995).

Stowell, Sheila, *A Stage of Their Own: Female Playwrights of the Suffrage Era* (Manchester: Manchester University Press, 1992).

Thompson, Carlos, *The Assassination of Winston Churchill* (Gerards Cross: Colin Smythe, 1969).

Thomson, Rachel, 'Moral Rhetoric and Public Health Pragmatism – the Recent Politics of Sex Education', *Feminist Review*, 48 (1994), 40–60.

Thorndike, Russell, *Sybil Thorndike* (London: Thornton Butterworth Ltd, 1929).

Titus, Mary, 'Murdering the Lesbian: Lillian Hellman's The Children's Hour', *Tulsa Studies in Women's Literature*, 10.2 (1991), 215–232.

Travis, Alan, *Bound and Gagged: A Secret History of Obscenity in Britain* (London: Profile Books, 2000).

Trewin, J.C., *Sybil Thorndike* (London: Rockcliff Publishing, 1955).

Tribe, David, *Questions of Censorship* (London: George Allen & Unwin Ltd, 1973).

Tynan, Kathleen, *The Life of Kenneth Tynan* (London: Phoenix, 1995).

Tynan, Kenneth, *A View of the English Stage 1944–1965* (London: Methuen, 1975).

Vicinus, Martha, 'Distance and Desire: English Boarding School Friendships', in *The Lesbian Issue: Essays from Signs*, ed. by Estelle Freedman et al. (Chicago and London: University of Chicago Press, 1985), pp. 43–66.

von Krafft-Ebing, Richard, *Psychopathia Sexualis*, trans. by Franklin S. Klaf (New York: Bell Publishing Co., 1965).

Weeks, Jeffrey, *Sex, Politics and Society: The Regulation of Sexuality Since 1800* (London: Longman, 1981).

——, *Coming Out: Homosexual Politics in Britain from the Nineteenth Century to the Present*, rev. edn (London and New York: Quartet Books, 1990).

——, *Making Sexual History* (Cambridge: Polity Press, 2000).
White, Hayden, *Tropics of Discourse: Essays in Cultural Criticism* (Baltimore: Johns Hopkins University Press, 1978).
——, *The Content of the Form: Narrative Discourse and Historical Representation* (Baltimore: Johns Hopkins University Press, 1987).
White, Michael, *Empty Seats* (London: Hamish Hamilton, 1984).
Whitehouse, Mary, *A Most Dangerous Woman?* (Tring: Lion Publishing, 1982).
Williams, Raymond, 'Base and Superstructure in Marxist Cultural Theory', in *Problems in Materialism and Culture: Selected Essays* (London: NLB, 1980).
Wilson, Elizabeth, 'Is Transgression Transgressive?', in *Activating Theory: Lesbian, Gay, Bisexual Politics*, ed. by Joseph Bristow and Angelia R. Wilson (London: Lawrence and Wishart, 1993), pp. 107–117.
Witney, Frederick, *Grand Guignol* (London: Constable & Co., Ltd, 1947).
Yorke, Liz, 'Constructing a Lesbian Poetic for Survival: Broumas, Rukeyser, H.D., Rich, Lorde', in *Sexual Sameness: Textual Differences in Lesbian and Gay Writing*, ed. by Joseph Bristow (London and New York: Routledge, 1992), pp. 187–209.

Unpublished material

British Library Manuscript Collections Reference Guide 3, The Play Collections (unpublished leaflet, ref no: GRS/JC1225, July 1996).
Burbank, Carol, 'The Fine Art of Giving Offence: The Uses and Abuses of Irreverence in Comic Action', paper given at the Performance Studies International Conference in Aberystwyth, April 1999.
Florance, John A., 'Theatrical Censorship in Britain 1901–1968', unpublished thesis (Cardiff: University of Wales, 1980).
Fox, Christine, 'Conduct Unbecoming: Noel Coward, Censorship and the Fallacy of Inconsequence', unpublished thesis (Brighton: University of Sussex, 1996).

Selected websites

www.AandB.org (Arts and Business Sponsorship).
www.artscouncil.org.uk.
www.asiansinmedia.org.
www.fortnight.org/current/CULTURE.HTM (Fortnight magazine).
www.ireland.com/newspaper/ireland/1999/0723/north6.htm (*Irish Times*).
www.outrage.org.uk.
www.publications.parliament.uk.
www.stonewall.org.uk.

Television

Clive Barker's A-Z of Horror, BBC A&E Network Productions, broadcast 25 October 1997.

Radio

Mark Lawson, *The Third Soldier Holds His Thighs*, BBC Radio 4, 18 February 2005.
The Birmingham Rep Riot: Behind the Scenes, BBC Radio 4, 23 August 2004.

Index